W9-ADO-140

THE DRAGON AND THE WILD GOOSE

Recent Titles in
Contributions to the Study of World History

The Myth of the Revolution: Hero Cults and the Institutionalizaton of the Mexican State, 1920–1940
Ilene V. O'Malley

Accommodation and Resistance: The French Left, Indochina and the Cold War, 1944–1954
Edward Rice-Maximin

Genocide and the Modern Age: Etiology and Case Studies of Mass Death
Isidor Wallimann and Michael N. Dobkowski, editors

Because They Were Jews: A History of Antisemitism
Meyer Weinberg

Societies in Upheaval: Insurrections in France, Hungary, and Spain in the Early Eighteenth Century
Linda Frey and Marsha Frey

The Practical Revolutionaries: A New Interpretation of the French Anarchosyndicalists
Barbara Mitchell

THE DRAGON AND THE WILD GOOSE

China and India

Jay Taylor

CONTRIBUTIONS TO THE STUDY OF
WORLD HISTORY, NUMBER 8

GREENWOOD PRESS

NEW YORK
WESTPORT, CONNECTICUT
LONDON

Library of Congress Cataloging-in-Publication Data

Taylor, Jay, 1931–
The dragon and the wild goose.
(Contributions to the study of world history,
ISSN 0885-9159 ; no. 8)
Bibliography: p.
Includes index.
1. China. 2. India. I. Title. II. Series.
DS706.T39 1987 951 87-7563
ISBN 0-313-25899-6 (lib. bdg. : alk. paper)

British Library Cataloguing in Publication Data is available.

Library of Congress Catalog Card Number: 87-7563
ISBN: 0-313-25899-6
ISSN: 0885-9159

First published in 1987

Greenwood Press, Inc.
88 Post Road West, Westport, Connecticut 06881

Printed in the United States of America

The paper used in this book complies with the Permanent Paper Standard issued by the National Information Standards Organization (Z39.48-1984).

10 9 8 7 6 5 4 3 2 1

For Betsy

There must be recollections
Of things not seen on earth,
Deep nature's predilections,
    Love earlier than birth.

—Kalidasa
c. AD 400–500

THE DRAGON

The dragon is the Chinese emblem of royalty and the symbol of great ability, wealth, or daring. Hidden in the caverns of inaccessible mountains or coiled in the unfathomable depths of the sea, it awaits the hour when it shall slowly put itself in motion. It spreads out its coils in the clouds of the tempest, and washes its mane in foam-crested pools. It is the image of that organic electricity which makes vibrant the inert mass of worn-out matter. Coiled upon its strength it mixes its wrinkled skin in the battle of the elements, and for an instant is seen half-revealed by the brilliant shimmer of its scales.[1]

THE WILD GOOSE

The wild goose, mount of Hinduism's creative universal force, Brahma, exhibits the twofold nature of all beings. It swims on the surface of the water, but is not bound to it. Withdrawing from the watery realm, it wings into the pure and stainless air, where it is as much at home as in the world below . . . it is the homeless free wanderer, between the upper celestial and the lower earthly spheres, at ease in both, not bound to either. It symbolizes the divine essence which, though embodied in and abiding with the individual, remains forever free from and unconcerned with the events of individual life.[2]

Contents

Acknowledgments

This study was made possible by a grant from the Una Chapman Cox Foundation. I would like to thank those who read and commented on the manuscript, including Ram Thapar, Leo Rose, Peter Tomsen, Doak Barnett, Hondah Chiu, Charlie Martin, Harry Barnes, John Taylor, Peter Burleigh, Grant Smith, Mary Dean, Charles Freeman, and Herb Levin. Special thanks to Cornelia Levin for editorial assistance and to Betsy who accompanied me on my travels and provided support, patience, and love. The views expressed and the conclusions drawn are my own and they do not necessarily reflect those of the Department of State.

A Note on Romanization

Chinese proper names are, with limited exceptions, given in the "pinyin" romanization employed by the People's Republic. On first use, the Wade-Giles romanization is given in parentheses. The exceptions are the most prominent place names in China, which for historical and literary continuity as well as sentimental attachment need not be changed (e.g., China, Peking, Canton, Tibet, etc.). Quite sensibly, the Chinese continue to call San Francisco "Old Gold Mountain."

PROLOGUE

A Tale of Two Countries

"Would you rather be the poorest man in China or in India?" my companion asked as our river steamer, *The East Is Red, No. 49*, swept into the second of the three gorges of the Yangtse. On the left bank a troop of fifteen men and women were struggling along the rocky shore, pulling a fishing junk upstream. It was a scene repeated on the river for millennia.

The sense of timelessness evoked the memory of an Indian barge unloading sand at Banaras near a burning ghat. As a woman's body went up in flames, more than a hundred men, women, and children filed past using headbaskets to carry sand up the steep bank of the Ganges. In both India and China life often gives illusions of immutability.

My friend and I discussed the Hobson's choice which he had proposed. The important condition was that one's personality with its baggage of memories and emotions would be transmitted into the body of either the poorest Chinese or the poorest Indian. To eliminate the problem of locating the absolutely worst-off individuals in these countries, we agreed to talk in terms simply of those *among* the very poorest. After ruminating over this question, we concluded that in addition to knowing about material conditions—which of the two people had the most to eat, which the best health—we also needed to understand the social, political, and cultural milieu in which they lived. Do the masses of India and China live by bread alone? What horizons are open to them? What dreams might they and their children have?

We did not reach a conclusion that day, and as we sailed on our thoughts turned to other subjects. The Yangtze swirled by. Later in the afternoon we passed out of the high gorges and, as the sun was setting, steamed past the construction site of the great Da Zhouba project. The channel was almost traversed. In a few months the water in the gorges would, for the first time in history, be calmed and regulated by giant sluice gates. The Yangtze would be partially tamed. Da Zhouba would be a modern engineering wonder in any country. Again, I thought of Indian parallels—the Hirakud Dam across the Mahandi and the Bhakta Nangal that spans the Sutluj.

This 1980 journey and the thoughts it stimulated led to this comparative study. Having lived and worked in Chinese cities for eleven years, I had some understanding of China but at that time little experience of India. In 1982, I began a year's sabbatical from the State Department, supported by the Una Chapman Cox Foundation. I spent this sabbatical reading in the library at Harvard University and traveling in India collecting material and impressions. I set out to find my own answer to the philosophical choice posed by the two most populous states in the world, India and China.

The reader may be happy to discover that the book that has emerged does not focus on economic performance. Over the years there has been a great deal of comparative analysis of the economies of these two countries and there is little we can add to the storehouse of knowledge on this question. But we can try to examine the dynamics behind the comparative performance of the two economies and, perhaps, learn something about the common prospects and problems of large, low-income countries, whatever their political economy.

Several famous scholars have compared Asian and Western development. Some, like Max Weber, emphasized the differences in Eastern and Western values; others stressed contrasting social and economic conditions. The most famous of the latter was Karl Marx, who propounded the "Asiatic mode of production." Building on Marx, but with an anti-Marxist slant, Karl Wittfogel expounded the theory of "oriental despotism," evolving from "hydraulic" irrigation societies that required the organization of large-scale bureaucracies. After Marx, Lenin insisted it was capitalist imperialism which had stunted the growth of science and modern industry in Asia.[3]

Western observers often lumped India and China together as oriental civilizations; but some have made clear distinctions between the two—Gunnar Myrdal, for example, emphasizing the different cultures of the two countries, and Barrington Moore stressing their distinctive social and economic institutions. There has, however, been no in-depth exploration of the cultural and historical differences that have shaped the responses of India and China to the challenges of the modern world, nor a broad comparative look at their performances today in culture and politics, as well as in economic and social development. This book is an effort to fill that gap. It is not a technical work, but a broad-brush survey of the two societies in both their traditional and their contemporary lives.

But is it possible to compare such different societies as India and China? "Piffle!" one Indian journalist snorted, inspiring a title. "It's like comparing a dragon and a wild goose. One is strong and determined. The other wings hither and yon."

That, however, seems to be the point. It is far more interesting to compare the unlike than the like. The purpose of any comparative analysis, after all, is not simply to record differences and similarities, but in the process to gain a new understanding of the dynamics of each society and why it has developed in its unique way.

A survey of sweeping histories and rich cultures like those of India and China will be highly selective and tend toward either profundity or absurdity. I leave it to my betters, on whose scholarship I have had to depend, to judge. Generalizing about national character is an even more hazardous game. Yet it is irresistible. Indians themselves are particularly fond of dissecting their own collective personality and, while they can be irritatingly proud, such introspections are most often highly critical. This helps our task immensely. The Chinese are more inscrutable on the subject of their own Id, and when they do write about themselves it is usually in praise. Already we have learned something.

With each generalization, however, a hundred exceptions can be made. This is particularly true of India, which is rich in regional and social variety. Occasionally I have noted regional differences and exceptions; but the reader should be aware that all assertions about cultural values and how things work or do not work in India and China should be tempered with an understanding of the complexity of these two enormous societies.

It should also be noted that in speaking of Indian society as well as the Indian character, I am referring primarily to Hindus. Moslems, who comprise about 12 percent of India's population, have of course made enormous contributions to Indian culture, but for the purpose of this work we may reasonably limit ourselves to Hindu tradition. In China, it is even more excusable to direct our discussion to the Han, who constitute 93 percent of the population. On the subject of Indian culture we are also often referring to the "high Hindu" in contrast to the lower castes. In China, traditions of the elite are less distinct from those of the common man.

Statistics and reports on national economic performance, social conditions, and political developments, as well as conflicting analyses of what these mean, flow like a torrent out of India. If nothing else, the Indians are madly studying their problems and debating them with vigor and candor. In virtually every major Indian city there is at least one institute of social and economic development where large numbers of Ph.D.s are busy collecting data and writing endless monographs. The staff members of such institutes, like all Indian intellectuals, are not only willing, but anxious, to share their views. Hundreds of journals and digests are published in India covering every conceivable area of social concern. In India, the problem is selecting from a surfeit of information and conflicting views.

In China today, data are abundant compared to the ciphers and falsehoods that were the daily fare of China-watchers during the Cultural Revolution and the Great Leap Forward. The Chinese have learned that the trouble with telling lies to foreigners is that then one also has to tell them to oneself.

Still, it is hard to know what the full truth is in China. Peking itself is still not sure of the accuracy of all the figures that come up from below, and the center remains selective regarding what it releases. The Chinese no longer knowingly give false figures, but in most things they do not tell all. Moreover, internal debates and differences of interpretation of data are closely held.

Since the death of Mao, the Chinese, realizing the value of fostering some measure of intellectual autonomy separate from party and bureaucratic structures, have revived numerous academic institutes, many under the Academy of Social Sciences. Most of the intellectuals in these centers were victims of the Cultural Revolution, and some were purged as far back as the 1957 anti-Rightist campaign. Despite their age and traumatic experiences, many are still capable of producing insightful and relatively objective work. Some of the most prominent are easily accessible, but other staff members are still often reluctant or unable to talk with foreigners. Chinese intellectuals are now free with criticism of the past, but much more guarded with comments about the present or the future. Good intellectual rapport, and indeed real friendship, is possible with many Chinese; but, except for the rare maverick, there is a wall of political inhibition that surrounds most discussions in China of social, political, or economic conditions, a wall that does not exist in India.

Like the *Rig Veda* and Mao's thoughts, statistics can be used to prove anything. Thus any comparison of national development will be selective and elements of subjectivity will inevitably creep in. Marxist writers as well as those who believe in the primacy of liberal democracy can both write objectively about the development of nations, while making clear the values and normative assumptions which lie behind their interpretations. I believe democracy must be paramount, but I accept that in exceptional circumstances, the common good may require that it be limited. In this connection, two of the questions which we will seek to explore in this book are: (1) is democracy workable in India? and (2) to what extent are China's successes—and its failures—due to its non-democratic and highly centralized political and economic systems?

Happily, I find no ethnic favoritism tilting my views one way or the other. American specialists on the Soviet Union—diplomats and reporters, anyway—generally do not like most Soviet *apparatchiks* whom they know. Average Russians are another thing. Most Western China watchers, whatever they think of the political system in Peking, are charmed by Chinese in general, including most of the officials with whom they deal. There are of course exceptions: the very likable Soviet bureaucrat and the freeze-dried Qing (Ch'ing) dynasty PRC (People's Republic of China) cadre. I have had the pleasure of knowing both types in each country.

People who know the sub-continent, on the other hand, come either to love Indians or to despair of them entirely. Long ago I fell under the spell of the Chinese, but I have also come to greatly admire the Indians.

I hope my friends in both countries will be tolerant of my effort at a critical and sweeping review of their past, their present, and their future. I have tried to show them both with all their moles and infirmities as well as virtues. Perhaps some of the judgements will seem harsh, but my admiration and respect for these two magnificent civilizations should also be apparent.

THE DRAGON AND THE WILD GOOSE

CHAPTER 1

Convergence and Divergence

The Big Sisters

India and China are the only modern states for which a comparative analysis logically can begin 3,000 years ago. But age and civilization are not the only characteristics that they share. Both are continental nations with vast resources and enormous and talented populations. For good or evil, much of the planet's future lies with these two countries, between them nurturing almost 40 percent of the world's population. India has more people than Africa and Latin America combined, and China more than all of North America, Europe, and the Soviet Union. In these two countries together more people are born in five years than constitute the total population of Japan.

They are the most powerful and important states in the Third World and the only members of the nuclear explosion club outside of the industrial powers; yet in per capita terms they rank among the lowest third of developing countries. Although poor, Peking and New Delhi are not backward, for they have the aggregate economies and scientific and intellectual talents to play in the high-stakes games of space and nuclear technology. Sixty million of China's peasant population in 1986 had a per-capita income in cash and kind of less than $40 a year. China, however, produces nuclear ballistic submarines, intercontinental missiles, jet airplanes, and computers with technology ten or fifteen years behind the West. India likewise reflects the contrast of extreme poverty and impressive achievement, including the development of space satellites and nuclear power reactors.

Indian and Chinese cultures both have produced a breed of men and women suited to the pursuit of science and competition in the modern world. Indians and Chinese appear especially unbeatable when they operate outside of their own societies. There are less than a million Americans of Chinese descent and about 312,000 Indian Americans. Together, they comprise less than 1 percent of the total U.S. population. But the percentage of prominent American scientists and academics with a Chinese or Indian heritage is far greater.

Despite different national personalities there is something about Chinese and Indian family life and culture that, given the right conditions, makes them good students and good workers. Both countries have a long tradition of an educated, highly cultured elite, but when given the chance, the common people also show themselves to be achievers. In the nineteenth century, European planters introduced Chinese laborers to places like Singapore and Indonesia, and Indians to South Africa and the Caribbean, because they were disciplined workers. The descendants of these immigrants quickly moved into commerce and the professions and in countries such as Malaysia where there are both Indian and Chinese communities, they soon dominated the local business economy.

The cultural vigor of India and China hardly needs stating. Almost all of Asia has been shaped in part by Chinese or Indian ideas. Japanese, Koreans, and Vietnamese first learned to read in Chinese characters; and Confucianism, Chinese-style Buddhism, and art forms from both China and India influenced all the countries that comprise what is called Sinic-civilization. In much the same way the Himalayan states, Ceylon, and most of non-Vietnamese Southeast Asia developed in the orbit of Indian culture.

Indian and Chinese societies present striking contrasts in their way of life and their way of thinking. Yet there are remarkable historic parallels, including separate failures to meet the Western imperialist challenge. Once superior to Europe in learning, Indians in the eighteenth and nineteenth centuries appeared stupefied before a few thousand Englishmen,[4] and the highly civilized Chinese gyrated ineffectively between passive obscurantism and xenophobic frenzy.

The two big sisters of Asia, while striving to recover their ancient glories, are still struggling to escape from the past. India, with its impressive veneer of modernity, remains the most stratified society in the world. Thirty-nine years after independence it has not been able to break through the barriers of stultifying tradition. Yet India has so far confounded the doom-sayers who saw it inevitably sucked into a Malthusian blackhole of misery, collapsing inward, at some point exploding in a big bang of communal strife.

Meanwhile, the new China, having thrown out its ancient way of life, seized on a succession of utopian reforms, all with negative results. According to the Chinese Communist Party's own account, twenty of the first thirty years of its rule were self-destructive. Today, in China, the 1966–1976 Cultural Revolution is termed "the black decade" and Mao's political and economic campaigns beginning in 1957 are admitted to have brought misery and persecution to hundreds of thousands and early death to millions through starvation and malnutrition. But in spite of this self-inflicted turmoil, the new China has held together and made remarkable advances in public health and literacy and in building a large, if inefficient, industrial base.

In different ways, each nation is paying the price of its national hubris and a schizoid outlook on the world. India, the spiritual sister, in seeking a socialist democratic path could end up with the worst of both—an inefficient economy and an ineffectual and corrupt government. China, burdened with a new orthodoxy and a massive new bureaucracy, and still haunted by the old fear of foreign influence, could settle back into the stagnant rigidity of a Stalinist state. Both countries have developed new, unique structures of inertia, but both have inherent advantages for growth.

Change and Culture

As they followed separate courses to freedom, so have India and China gone by different vehicles in search of economic growth and national power. Each has had to carry the heavy baggage of an old civilization. It has been a bumpy road, or a bumpy flight; and, once, along the roof of the world where their continental plates ram together, the two giants collided in war and twenty years of hostility ensued.

Nevertheless, in many ways the courses of India and China are converging. Both countries are pursuing the universal goals of better health, literacy, higher standards of living, and an equitable distribution of income. Both have adopted the modern culture of progress and proclaimed their faith in the new gods of technology and science. The current fascination of Indian and Chinese intellectuals and youth with computers is symptomatic of the new pragmatism that has displaced political and social theory as the hope of tomorrow in both countries.

Technological development is unilinear. Basically there is only one way of building a hydroelectric dam or a tractor factory and their impact tends to be the same everywhere: urbanization and the emergence of a bureaucratic-technocratic elite. Writers like Weber, Heilbroner, and others have seen technology as an independent force reshaping the future of all societies including character traits, behavior, and cultural values.[5] The new elite of managers and technocrats, whose power in capitalist as well as socialist states is based on function rather than ownership, requires an achievement- rather than a family-oriented society, formal laws rather than informal rules of behavior, impersonal rather than personal administration, and the linking of education to occupation rather than social status.[6]

Modernization also requires the creation of a literate, civic culture, the accumulation of capital stock, and the mobilization of resources to improve the quality of life. These basic common objectives have presented New Delhi and Peking with similar dilemmas of choosing between: freedom and control; present or future consumption; agricultural, industrial, or social investment; and centralization or decentralization of management and planning. They have tried different approaches over the years, but each has had to discover that neither the laws of economics nor of human nature can be repealed.

There are only a few routes open to modernization and they lie across the same range of mountains, under the same sky. It is not surprising that India and China today face similar problems of overpopulation, a deteriorating environment, and inefficient use of capital. Even in the political realm, both countries are troubled with the passing of an old guard, the emergence of a new skeptical generation, public ennui, and bureaucratic corruption.

Both countries have been swept up in the new world culture that began with the Industrial Revolution and accelerated after World War II with the explosion of mass communications and technology. As the ultra-powers of the developing world, India and China have also taken on international roles which, like their domestic goals of modernization, reflect the new world order and require intellectual and cultural perspectives far different from those of the past. Like modernization, the advancement of national power and security depend on the rational manipulation of objective realities, realities that do not differ very much in New Delhi or Peking. Acceptance of the new universal goal of progress has narrowed the range of both domestic and external policy choices open to the leaders of India and China and, indeed, to all other Third World countries.

In recent years, both countries, working within their separate political economies, have moved to production- and incentive-oriented development strategies. Likewise, the trend over the past sixteen years has been toward similar pragmatic foreign policies, which stress regional stability and a dynamic balance between the superpowers, and which emphasize the ascendancy of development goals. These policies also reflect the similar break-throughs that each country made in the 1970s in its strategic position.

While material and external limitations restrict the rational possibilities in Indian and Chinese foreign relations and economic policy, domestic politics and culture are much more susceptible to idiosyncratic development. These are the two areas in which India and China continue on the most divergent paths. It is differences in these fields, much more than in economic organization, that account for differences in their economic performance. A study of India and China confirms that cultural values and the system of political governance are more important than economic organization or even material and resource factors in the direction of social and economic development. The fact that Punjab in northwest India has achieved higher growth than any Chinese province and that the Indian state of Kerala, with a lower per capita income than China, has done as well or better in literacy and health confirms this thesis.

Even where tradition and ideology have been drastically changed, as in China, inner cultural values persist in shaping the possibilities. Cultural trappings can be banned or eliminated, but attitudes and inner values cannot be fundamentally altered within a generation or two, even by all-out assault. Nevertheless, they can be changed. Culture both adapts and absorbs, whether in India or in China, and the synthesis which emerges reflects old traditions as well as modern pressures.

In many ways, India and China are growing more alike and coming closer together than they have at any time since the Indus and Yellow River civilizations began. Societies in the first post-industrial age, however, will not emerge exactly alike any more than they did in the post-hunter-gatherer age of settled agriculture. As Daniel Bell suggests, the convergence of modern societies will occur along separate lines of political, social, cultural, and technological development. Societies may converge along one line and diverge along others. The convergence may also be like asymptotic lines in geometry that are always approaching but never actually meet![7]

India and China present an intriguing case-study with which to test the theories of convergence and divergence in national development, for they have been doing both longer than any other two societies. Such a study will highlight not only the commonality of problems that transcend cultural, as well as political and ideological, differences, but also the extent to which everything and nothing seems to have changed in both countries. In sum, it will underscore the persistence of culture and its telling impact on the development of nations.

Questions which we will try to address in this study include the following: Why does India have a chaotic but viable democracy and China command politics of the elite? Why has China been obsessed with uniformity and the doctrinaire, and India tolerant of all heresies? Why are art and literature in India more vital and alive than in China? Why is Chinese agriculture productivity so high and Indian literacy so low? Why is poverty both greater and more apparent in India than in China? Why is industry in China plagued with wasteful production and uneconomic capital construction, while in India the problem is underproduction and inefficiency? Why do Indian scientists excel in hypotheses and theoretical studies while their Chinese colleagues are best at observation and data gathering? Why is China a political society and India more a religious one? Why is nationalism more potentially threatening in China than in India? And finally why is the world's largest democracy linked closely to the Soviet Union, while the most populist Leninist state finds the United States the most compatible of the superpowers?

To find answers to these and other paradoxes we must first look at brief cameos of the contrasting histories and cultures of the two countries. Only then can we see how India has produced a heterogeneous, turbulent, stratified, but free and lively society and China a homogeneous, orderly, controlled, somewhat egalitarian, but regimented and until very recently anyway, a relatively dull society.

Each country's political legacy would shape its modern political culture, which in turn would be the most important element in its social and economic development. The Indian democratic-socialists replaced the limited authoritarianism of the British Raj. Although the British ruled with an iron hand, in their colonies as well as at home they separated power and law. The Chinese communists came to power 38 years after the collapse of the Qing dynasty, but Mao and his followers were the real successors of the old imperial Confucian order. The new absolutism replaced the old. As Hannah Arendt once noted, "nothing, indeed, seems more natural than that a revolution should be predetermined by the type of government it overthrows."

CHAPTER 2

Legacies

The Dawn of Two Civilizations

Indian and Chinese civilizations each began in the dawn of history in the valleys of two rivers flowing from separate headwaters on the Tibetan plateau. Although not the most ancient of civilizations, India and China are the most continuous societies on earth, each linked to a distant past by culture and race. Similarities over the centuries included dynasties and empires which rose and fell in cycles of growth and decay, recurrent invasions and prolonged alien occupation and, finally, humiliation by the West. Still, from the beginning, their different fates were marked.

Whatever its origins, the caste structure of India has been one of the strangest, but most stable, social systems in the world. The triumph of the virile Aryans who conquered the Indus River Valley about 1500 B.C. set a pattern that would continue throughout Indian history, including the British Raj, in which successive invaders would form new layers or castes rather than dissolving into a homogeneous mixture.

In China, the assimilation process from the beginning absorbed all intruding barbarians into the budding Chinese culture. The Yellow River Valley has a semi-arid climate with frigid winters, quite similar to the homeland of the nomads who swarmed around China. As barbarians conquered areas of North China there was no epidemiological, racial, or cultural barrier to the "digestive" process of assimilation.

Conflict and interaction with outside aggressive forces would dominate Indian and Chinese history for 3,000 years. In both cases, periods of high cultural development and political order would be followed by internal decay and weakness, and this in turn would open the way to foreign conquerors. The Chinese were sometimes faced with invaders who were temporarily stronger or more determined in war, but always culturally inferior—a distinction recognized by both parties. The conquerors of China were, without exception, relatively unsophisticated tribesmen who eventually became Chinese—or else went home.

India, however, was not isolated from the hotbeds of civilization in the Middle East and the Mediterranean. While India would have her share of wild, uncouth invaders who would eventually be Hinduized and established as new castes, unlike China she was also set upon regularly by advanced civilizations. Just as the new Hindu society emerged from its long silent gestation in the sixth century B.C., it was attacked by a succession of civilized invaders, including Persians and Greeks. Later, Moghuls and then Englishmen would rule for almost 800 years.

Thus differences in the nature and timing of the barbarian onslaughts against the Indus and Yellow River civilizations determined the fates of both societies. India was a conquest society, in which each wave of conquerors added another strata to Indian culture. India became a great geological bed of caste and cultures layered one upon the other; while China—the siege society—developed an amazing monochrome heritage.

Texts and Hymns

The Chinese and most of the Indian classics were composed in a span of centuries prior to the creation of the first Indian and Chinese empires in the fourth and third centuries B.C. respectively. Classic literature is still read and honored by the educated in both countries, although the Vedic literature remains a much more essential part of Indian life than is the case with the classics in China today, even in conservative Chinese societies outside the mainland. The strikingly different nature of the two sets of classics—Chinese texts and Indian hymns and epics—tells us much about the two cultures.

Most Hindus still believe that the Vedic literature is inspired and holy. The Chinese, however, even in ancient days professed only that Confucius had edited or annotated the five famous classics. The ancient Chinese texts are marked with order and balance and contain nothing like the rich epics of the *Ramayana* or the *Mahabharata*. The Indian classics are panoramas of titanic wars, of struggles of good against evil, of capricious fate, of venal Gods and indulgent heroes. In the end, the final victory of good paradoxically turns inside out, revealing the futility of all that had gone before and leaving the reader with a post-coital feeling of melancholic exhaustion.

In the *Mahabharata*, Arjuna's invincible arms fail him, the heroic Pandavas clan struggles across the snow-swept Himalayas, falling dead one by one, and in a final moving passage Krishna is killed and "the sapphite towers are drowned beneath the flowing cliffs of the sea." The narrator concludes: "Cherished King, time is the root and the seed, it gives and it takes away. I bow to God, who lives in this world with us; whoever calls Him by any name, by that name does he come."[8] In the *Ramayana*, Rama at last rescues his beautiful and faithful wife Sita from the Demon God Ravana but, because of untrue rumors about her chastity while under the control of the Demon, Rama himself banishes her.

The *Book of Odes* (*Shi Jing*) is the closest the Chinese Classics come to such literature. Many of the odes have a sweet romantic quality, but none of the lusty vigor of the Indian epics. In a typically Confucian fashion, most are folk songs in praise of good officials or criticism of bad ones. Even the romantic odes were usually interpreted as carrying a social or political message. For example, the following ode (in abridged form) is about a woman who has been seduced and cast aside, but Chinese commentators interpreted it as a rebuke to a dissolute duke who was an infamous womanizer:

> Before the Mulberry Tree
> Has shed its leaves
> How rich and glossy they seem.
> Ah thou dove,
> Eat not its fruit,
> Seek no licentious pleasures
> For when a gentleman indulges,
> Something may still be said for him,
> When a lady does so,
> Nothing can be said of her.
> When the mulberry sheds it leaves
> They fall yellow on the ground.

Rituals are a prominent feature of both Chinese and Vedic classics. The *Book of Rites* (*Li Ji*) was a Chinese handbook of etiquette reflecting social relationships and setting out the rituals of ancestor worship. The rituals of the *Rig Veda*, however, are infinitely more exotic, not to say erotic. Among the most bizarre was the Royal Asvemedha, or horse sacrifice which ensured fertility and the power of a king or chieftain over other dominions. To begin the ceremony, a stallion was set free for a year and wherever it roamed the ruler of that land would have to submit or fight. At the end of the year the horse was returned to the sacrificial enclosure where it was worshipped by the King's wives and then suffocated. The still-warm stallion was stretched out on a sacrificial altar and, before the eyes of the King and the priests, the senior Queen lay down and simulated coitus with the stallion. The chief sacrificer called for the steed to lay its seed in the channel of the one who had opened her thighs and set in motion the nourisher of life, darting "into the sheath, their hidden lover, darkly buffeting, back and forth."[9]

The Chinese classics reveal belief in a supreme deity, Xiang Di (Hsiang Ti), who was an anthropomorphic god keenly interested in wordly doings. Brahma, Xiang Di's Indian counterpart, was a much more amorphous force, the reality underlying the superficial material world and the essence of each individual human personality or "atman." The Chinese believed that their departed ancestors resided in heaven, where they continued to look after the affairs of their descendants on earth. Consequently, ancestor worship became the central element in Chinese religious belief and ritual.

While the Chinese classics were stressing ancestor worship, the Upanishads marked the transcendental course that Indian philosophy would follow throughout the centuries. In Vedic rituals, "the religious quest is closely linked to the vitality of the physical world." One of the early Upanishads, for example, equated various parts of the sacrificial horse in the Royal Asvamedha with corresponding elements of the cosmos. The later Upanishads are the first Hindu scriptures to describe the religious quest for release (*moksha*) from the world and the endless cycle of rebirth (*samsara*) which is perpetuated and determined by one's deeds (*karma*).[10]

The Chinese emerge from their ancient classics as sober and down-to-earth, the Indians as mystical and sensual. In the Chinese classics we see the continuity of a settled agricultural population which itself was the product of thousands of years of evolution in neolithic times.[11] Ancestor worship and a sequential view of history were natural choices for those who had lived by the agricultural clock for several thousand years. In the Indian classics, on the other hand, we sense the vigor of the campfire and a thousand generations wandering under the stars.

Historic and Ahistoric Views

The strong Chinese sense of biological continuity and their lineal view of life are also reflected in their attention to history. Two of the Chinese classics were chronicles—the *Book of History* and the *Spring and Autumn Annals*. History, for the Chinese, was either a vindication or a negative lesson. It did not, however, reflect abstract thinking which could produce synthesis or generalization. Chinese history served a political, rather than an intellectual, purpose. In contrast, as Hegel noted, despite India's achievements in geometry, astronomy, algebra, and philosophy, history in India before the Moghuls was "rather nonexistent." Marx categorically asserted that India had no history.

There is a "white ant" theory that holds that because records in India were inscribed on leaves or other digestible materials, termites literally ate up Indian history. But even the stone inscriptions of the Mauryan empire tell us little about the history of the court or the life of the people. A Greek envoy to the Mauryan empire and Roman historians, like Chinese pilgrims in the Gupta period, are the only sources on Indian events of those times.

While Hindu writers in the first Christian millennium were producing a great body of drama and epics, and works on the arts and sciences, they produced no history at all. Meanwhile, ever since the Zhou Dynasty, the

Chinese had been meticulously recording minute details of their history; and in the second century B.C., China produced Si-ma Qian (Ssu-ma Ch'ien), an historian of equal rank with Herodotus and Plutarch.

Hegel suggested that Hindus were not interested in history because of their cyclical view of life, their sensual preoccupations, and their belief in the transience of the physical world. The old philosopher was carried away in his view of Hindu rationality as a "state of dreaming and mental transiency."[12] Nevertheless, a pessimistic view of life and a non-lineal thought process does presumably encourage an ahistorical mentality. The Hindu's perception of a recycling future and of the unreality of time could not but affect the importance which he attached to the past.

The Hindu saw life as a revolving wheel, from which one sought escape, whereas the Chinese saw cycles of growth and decay, but a process that traveled along a straight line extending indefinitely into the future. Thus, in the Chinese view, keeping meticulous chronicles was an important and rewarding task. The cult of the dead connected the present for all Chinese to both the past and the future.

The different nature of early Indian and Chinese history also shaped their respective disregard for and fascination with chronicles. From the beginning, the continuity of Chinese history provided the sanction for successive dynasties which felt compelled to rewrite the chronicles of their immediate predecessors. But early India was a conquest society in which the Aryan conquerors did not have any interest in preserving or even rewriting the history of those that had come before. Thus, ironically, the Hindu upper castes had no memory of their Aryan origin or of the long *volkewanderung* of the past. Indian political history over the centuries was strikingly discontinuous, that of China remarkably unbroken.

Paradoxically, Indian history was interwoven with world history, while China was much more cut off from historic developments in the West. Yet Chinese records of contacts with ancient civilizations, such as the Romans, are relatively extensive—while in India there are no such records. Hindu India had little interest in either its own past or that of others. One Indian academic explained that ancient India interacted with China and other states but "was not really aware of China," for it was not aware of itself. India was a self-sufficient, unself-conscious society.

Robin Hood and the Thugs

The Chinese peasant was taught by Confucian tradition that the most important moral and social value was acceptance of the authority of father, elder brother, magistrate, and emperor. Over the next 2,500 years, Chinese country people, like peasants everywhere, were usually stoic in the face of oppression and exploitation. Nevertheless, from ancient times, the theory of a just rebellion was established as part of the common lore, and cyclical peasant uprisings erupted in China, resulting in great upheavals and the fall of dynasties.

The most famous of all Chinese novels, *Water Margin*, is the story of 108 men in the thirteenth century A.D. who were persecuted by various unjust officials and who took refuge on a great mountain surrounded by a reed marsh. The plot is based on the true story of a group of popular bandits in the late Song (Sung) Dynasty who fought unjust rulers and robbed the rich.

This sort of Robin Hood theme is missing in classical Indian literature. The Aryans had swept away the old order and there was no thought of justifying their actions in terms of the right of rebellion. Indian peasants who in desperation turned to banditry simply became part of another caste—the "thugs." Such acts of desperation in India did not grow into social and political movements, as often occurred in China. Indian history contains few examples of revolution from below.

In contrast, through the centuries, secret societies, such as the Yellow Turbans and the White Lotus, were a feature of Chinese life. Such groups sporadically spread throughout the country as mystical, military organizations that plotted and fought against local authorities, exploitation, decadent dynasties, or barbarian rulers.

Ideas of State and Authority

Along with their engineering skill at building walls, the Chinese, at least in the first millennium and a half of their history, enjoyed more success in the martial arts than their Indian counterparts. One reason for this was China's relative cohesion and political consciousness. The Chinese were unified by their sense of history, Confucianism, and the Chinese written language. The use of ideographs meant that Chinese throughout the Empire, who spoke mutually unintelligible languages, could understand each other through the written word. Even more important, China had long had a sense of racial as well as cultural unity; in other words, a national consciousness.

As far back as the Zhou Dynasty in the seventh and eighth centuries B.C., the Chinese were referring to themselves and their land by the same political term they use today—"Zhonggua" ("Chungkuo") (pronounced Jung-gua)—which means "middle country." Originally the Chinese used "Tien Xia" ("T'ien Hsia") ("under Heaven") and "Sz Fang" ("Szu Fang") ("the four sides") to refer to those states practicing the same civilized (Chinese) life-style and arts, while "Zhonggua" referred to each ruler's domain. Surrounding the "middle lands" were the various barbarians. In the Han Dynasty, "Zhonggua" gradually replaced "Tien Xia" as the Chinese name for their country (the Western term "China" apparently was taken from the name of the Qing (Ch'ing) Dynasty. The word "zhong" or "middle" expressed a supposed geographic fact, but it also came to reflect the Chinese image of themselves as the central and only civilized culture in the world.

Confucius stressed the importance of loyalty to the ruler, and a highly patriarchal and centralized form of government evolved in China. While feudalism persisted in India until modern times, the destruction of feudalism in China by the first Emperor Qin Shi Huang (Ch'in Shih Huang) in the third century B.C. removed objects of political loyalty intervening between the individual and the emperor. Despite the importance of clans and sometimes of secret societies, there were no independent classes, castes, or religious orders, as there were in India, who had common vested interests and the political power to defend them. Notably, in China the emperor was also chief priest for the nation and only he could communicate with the Lord on High. In India, kings were separate from the priesthood and in most cases, as members of the warrior castes, they also theoretically ranked below the brahmans. Also, there was no supreme national priest in the Hindu order. Indian rulers claimed divine rule, but brahmans, cows, sticks, and stones also had divine powers. The force of Indian religious life, much less than in China or in the Moslem orders, buttressed loyalty to the ruler or encouraged the idea of a political community.

Although Hindu empires had existed, Indians generally lacked a strong sense of commonwealth based on a collective existence that transcended clan, caste, and religion. Indians, differing widely in race and sharing no common language, identified with each other, like Europeans, primarily through religion. The continuity and cohesion of India was spiritual, not historical. Its unity was one of religious values and related social structures. Whereas, for the Chinese, the main elements of community were not only cultural but political, historical, and racial.

Hindus had no body politic nor even a word for India. "India" is a Greek corruption of the Persian word "hind" which comes from the Sanskrit "sindhu" meaning river or specifically the Indus. Persians and then Greeks and Romans called the land across the Indus River, Hind or India, but Indians did not consistently use the term until the coming of the Moslem rulers who called their new domain "Hindustan."

The Indian Constitution is perhaps the only national charter that identifies its country with two distinct names—India and Bharat. Hindu nationalists in the nineteenth century revived the name Bharat, which had been used in Indian literature such as the Puranas to describe the territory that stretched from the Himalayas to the sea. Bharat was an early and probably mythical Aryan king. As used historically, the term Bharatavara (or "land of Bharat") referred to a cultural rather than a political realm. Until the coming of the British, however, few Hindus ever thought of themselves as men or women of India or Bharat, but identified themselves by caste, sect, and locality or language. For example, "a khatik (mason), devotee of Vishnu, from Maharastra."

The idea of a political imperium suggests acceptance of a central authority. The Chinese have traditionally sought authority from their leaders and are frustrated without a strong and effective government. Indians, on the other hand, accept authority but do not trust those who struggle for it.[13] "Power is polluting . . . and (aside from the warrior or ruling caste) must be held with reluctance and never sought or cherished."[14] For Indians, the ideal leaders traditionally have been those who, like Gandhi, renounce power. The political order in India was something to be avoided as much as possible. Life revolved around social and religious authority. But in traditional China, "the political system operated as the only society-wide system, and it could be assumed that all social requirements would be taken care of if the political order were properly maintained . . . authority therefore became a vital matter, not just for power relationships but for all welfare and human concerns."[15]

Qu Fu and Banaras

China's holy places were mostly mountains. The most sacred town was Qu Fu (Ch'u Fu), the birthplace of Confucius. Qu Fu is at least as old as Banaras (Varanasi) having been the capital of the state of Lu when Confucius was born in the sixth century B.C. The town was then already at least 400 years old; after Confucius' death it was declared sacred and a temple was built, then expanded and reconstructed 60 times up to the eighteenth century when it acquired its present form. Portions, however, are 900 years old. Since at least the Han dynasty, Confucius' family, the Kungs, have lived in Qu Fu, and direct male descendants have served continuously as guardians and administrators of the temple for more than 2,200 years.

The Kungs are perhaps the only family in the world that can convincingly trace their family to such ancient roots. Certainly they are the only one to have a family graveyard containing 76 generations of bone and dust. What more haunting testimony could there be to the Chinese passion for the continuity of family and veneration of the past?

Qu Fu is botanical as well as biographical history. On the road to Confucius' tomb and the family graveyard are rows of 800 year old evergreens that replaced other 800 year old specimens that had supplanted the originals sometime in the first centuries of the Christian era. In the garden of the Great Temple there is also a Juniper tree that, according to legend, springs from the root of the original planted by Confucius. For the Chinese there is something satisfying about an old tree, the more gnarled by wind and age the better, for it reminds them of the venerable scholar, bent with years and outrageous fortune, still standing noble, at peace with himself, in harmony with his surroundings.

Qu Fu is a memorial to statesmanship and sociology; above all it is a nation's memorial to itself. It is a visit to Monticello or better still to the marble temple that houses the famous words and the great brooding statue of the wise and kind Lincoln. There was also once an enormous statue of

Confucius in the Qu Fu temple, but during the Cultural Revolution, Red Guards broke it into so many pieces it could not be restored. The old sage would be sad but not surprised. Confucius, probably sitting on the nearby "apricot platform," once said, "I will not be afflicted at men's not knowing me; I will be afflicted that I do not know men."

Today, bus loads of Chinese students, teachers, soldiers, and cadre come to wander casually through the grounds of the temple and graveyard, taking snapshots of each other. They appear as irreverent as the few foreigners who find this out-of-the-way place. A loudspeaker warns visitors not to write on the walls or spit.

One Westerner caught in a summer storm takes refuge under the portico of a small temple facing the grave of Confucius. He strikes up a conversation with a municipal official from Shanghai. What does the old Master mean to modern Chinese? The cadre wipes his glasses and ponders the question. "He was very wise for his time," comes the reply, "but he is important because he was Chinese and part of history." The sage would surely know his countrymen today.

Banaras is one of the most unusual spectacles in the world. They say it was the first-born metropolis of creation, the city of Shiva and a million of his libidinous linga that sprout up everywhere in this Forest of Bliss. But, unlike Qu Fu for the Chinese, it is not age or history that makes Banaras the most holy of places to the Hindu, or for the foreign traveler the most extraordinary. It is the *samsara* of Banaras, the drama of worship, life, and death, and its *moksha*, the vision of transcendence and liberation that captivates Indian and foreigner alike. It is a life and ethos little changed in 2,600 years.[16]

While Qu Fu reflects the veneration of a sage and a nation, Banaras displays the vitality of an ancient faith and the Hindu's eternal quest for release. It is said that to die in Banaras is to escape rebirth, to cross the Ganges directly, and to become one with the universe. The benefit applies even to beggars, who, after death, are not burned but weighted with rocks and sunk in the middle of the river. And so the Hindu come to Banaras, holy men, thieves, rug merchants, and the sick and demented. Simple pilgrims who fail to die in the sacred city return to their villages with the next best thing—a small brass urn of Ganges water.

The Ganges here is more than a quarter-mile broad in the dry season and much more during a good monsoon. The eastern shore is flat and seems to flow into the farmland that extends to the horizon. The western, sacred bank of the river is protected by tall cliffs and here lies the holy city cascading down to the bathing and burning ghats in a torrent of Hindu steeples, palaces, Shiva shrines, ashrams, and linga; and on top of it all, Aurangzeb's insult, the Jnāna Vāpī mosque built over the ruins of a grand Hindu temple.

Banaras is part renaissance—the maharajahs' decaying palaces; in part medieval—abandoned widows begging for alms; in part inferno—bodies burning over fires stoked with long poles by untouchables, whose life mission is thus fulfilled; and part primitive—the worship of the rising sun, immersion in the all forgiving river. It is bizarre, romantic, base, and spiritual. Like most wonders of the East, it is rather bedraggled. Bovine wanderers, goats, and monkeys mix with deformed supplicants, saffron robed pilgrims, and insistent hawkers. And near the umbrellaed rows of brahman priests and pious bathers, a man bares his bum and offers an odorous salutation to the sun.

Buddha and Confucius

India is the mother of four religions—Buddhism, Jainism, Hinduism, and Sikhism. China gave birth only to Taoism, which was more philosophy than religion. Significantly, of all the Indian religions only Buddhism took strong root outside of the sub-continent, including China, and yet Buddhism is the only one to have virtually vanished in the country of its birth. Hinduism spread with Indian immigrants and merchants to Southeast Asia, but survives only in Bali. Hinduism has become the basis of numerous cults in the West, but essentially Hinduism, Jainism, and Sikhism have not been missionary religions. Because of its unique social quality, real Hinduism can only live in India or in a society of Indians.

Hinduism is a non-doctrinaire, non-institutional, and usually tolerant religion. Hindus can believe virtually anything. Thus, as N.C. Chaudhuri maintains, Hindus could hate the person of non-believers but not their dogma.[17] Hindus did not in fact have a word for "Hindu" or "Hinduism," thus there was no such thing as a "non-Hindu." Benighted souls might flaunt the laws of dharma and thus become fallen castes, but they would be punished for this in the next life. What held Hindus together was a broad acceptance of the sacredness of the Vedic literature—not any particular interpretation of that literature—and caste. Caste is the life-support system of Hinduism.

Buddhism may well have disappeared from India because it made a universal appeal and tried to adapt itself to foreigners. Jainism, the other reform sect that was contemporaneous with Buddhism, maintained much closer links with Hinduism and did not pursue missionary work abroad. Jainism still survives today as a small but very prosperous sect. The word of Buddha, however, was submerged back into the fire of Hinduism.

The best known Chinese in all of history and his Indian counterpart were born within a few years of each other in the sixth century B.C. Confucius' life is an undramatic one, adorned with relatively little myth and no supernatural aspects. Living in a time of civil chaos in China, Confucius was preoccupied with the political and social questions of how to bring about order in the state and harmony in human relations. His thoughts were not divinely revealed, but were reflections on the past and a reaffirmation of old values. He emphasized respect for the hierarchical structure of society but he believed in rationalism and humanism. After Confucius, the life of a scholar or statesman—not saint or holy man—became the Chinese ideal.

In contrast to the mundane story of Confucius, the life of Buddha was surrounded by a thousand legends, and endless fables were required to recount all the miraculous deeds performed during his previous reincarnations. While Confucius was an unemployed scholar who sought with little success to advise the rulers of the day on the affairs of state, Buddha at the age of 29 gave up family life—itself a very un-Confucian thing to do—and in the Hindu tradition became a wandering ascetic. Although the ethics of Buddha and Confucius are strikingly similar to each other as well as to the Christian creed, Buddha did not seek to improve human society, much less perfect it. With Hindu pessimism, he saw all life as ineffably sorrowful. The way to erase the endless wheel of pain was through meditation and renunciation, but also through moral conduct.

The emphasis on moral conduct set Buddha apart from the Hinduism of his day and led to his rejection of caste, the hereditary priesthood, and animal sacrifice. The purpose of Buddhist moral conduct, however, was not a better human society, but rather escape into Nirvana, the "blowing out" of the self, like extinguishing a lamp.

Annihilation of the personality did not appeal to the Chinese. When Buddhism came to China it was in the more popularized cloak of the Mahayana School, which offered salvation to all and not just to monks who could pursue the rigorous life of meditation and renunciation. Nirvana evolved from a state of annihilation to a land of bliss—"the Western Paradise" where all good Chinese would dwell happy and prosperous forever.

Thus Buddhism in China evolved into a popular religion that served human needs, spiritual and social. Chinese believers were concerned with assuring good fortune not with transmigration of the soul. Although Buddhism dominated Chinese religious thought for close to a thousand years, it eventually merged into an eclectic belief system that incorporated Confucianism and Taoism.

Despite the patronage of the great Mauryan Emperor Asoka in the third century B.C., Buddhism failed completely in India. Buddhism apparently was never the dominant religion in the subcontinent and following Asoka's death, there was a brahmanical backlash. Buddhism, however, did spur reforms in Hinduism, which adopted the concept of *ahimsa* and ended animal sacrifice. As a result of Buddhist influence there arose popular sects of Hinduism concentrating worship on one specific Hindu diety as a fatherly God or a Mother Goddess.

There are several possible explanations as to why the Indian masses stuck with Hinduism. The ruling classes in India had a strong interest in seeing that the system which best protected the status quo was not abandoned. The triumph of Hinduism, however, probably did not come about through coercion, but must have had the acquiescence and support of the populace. The reason for this may again in part be related to the foreign onslaughts on Indian civilization. Faced with a succession of invaders, primitive barbarians, the sword of Islam, and culturally advanced imperialists, Hinduism provided the best safeguard against disintegration, the only assurance of cultural continuity.

But there were other reasons relating to the Indian psyche. Buddhism required a critical examination of the ways of the world and of human conduct which was foreign to the Indian mind.[18] Buddhism proved to be too organized, intellectual, and non-sensuous for the Indian and the later version adopted by the Chinese too tame. Only the erotic rituals and beliefs of their ancestors—not Buddha's path to enlightenment—could satisfy the thirsting of the Hindu for the fusion of sexuality and religion.[19]

The yogi's ability to erase human self-consciousness, as well as Hinduism's celebration of fertility, reflects the antediluvian nature of Indian religion. Freud recounts the suggestion that the sensation of coenaesthesias created by a yogi's inward withdrawal and concentration on his bodily functions is a regression to states of mind which have long ago been overlaid.[20] In other words, the yogi slips back into a mental state that pre-dates the emergence of *homo sapiens* and his and her unique self-awareness. Of all the major religions practiced today, Hinduism is the only direct survivor of the primeval fertility cults that were among humankind's first religious experiences. It is as if Europeans still worshipped the Greek gods, who so resembled those of the Hindu pantheon.

Taoism and Hinduism

In Chinese thought, Taoism comes closest to the transcendental and erotic view of Hinduism. The sacred Taoist texts, however, were written in the third or fourth century B.C., long before the first known contacts between the ancient civilizations of India and China.

Despite the similarities, there are fundamental differences in spirit and objective between Hinduism and Taoism. The Taoists pooh-poohed dull Confucian morality and ritual and talked of the Dao (Tao), or The Way, as the essence that underlay all reality and the ultimate unity in which physical and moral contradictions were dissolved. This primeval unity of good and evil, black and white, up and down, was similar to the cosmology of Hinduism. Tao was the order of the universe, the law of all nature. But, as Holmes Welch observes, Lao Ci (Lao Tzu), the presumed founder of Taoism, was tentative and obscure in his claims about the Dao.

> They (the references to Dao) lack the fire, lyricism, and definition which generally characterizes mystical writings. There is no sentence like that in the Upanishads

which cries out: "Listen, O ye children of the immortal, I have found the one great Absolute Being resplendent in high glory beyond a mass of darkness." Instead Lao Tzu mutters in Chapter I about "the Mystery or rather the Darker than Mystery, the Doorway whence issued all secret essences." In Chapter 6 he amplifies this by telling us that the Doorway is attached to the Mysterious Female who appears to be identified with the Valley Spirit. It is not even clear if he is talking about the Dao at all.[21]

The Taoist sage was the man who understood the Dao, freed his life of desire and strife, and followed the doctrine of "wu wei" (literally, "not doing"). This sounds very similar to the withdrawal, non-violence, and passivity of the wandering Hindu ascetic. But as Welch points out, a Taoist practices "wu wei" and requites hatred with virtue because that is the most effective technique of getting people to do what he wants.[22]

As water can destroy stone, so the weak can overcome the strong. "Humility and compassion together, if they come from our original nature, make it possible to act upon others passively, to obtain ends without the use of means." The Taoist objecive, in other words, was a practical one. Like Confucius, Lao Ci lived in the violent and prolonged Warring States period, and in his writings he gave instructions on how a wise ruler should conduct his government without the use of force. Such a ruling sage would return his people to a life of simplicity and peace in tune with nature, a life stripped of materialistic civilization and the vanities and hypocricies of invented morality.[23]

Not surprisingly, Taoism did not get very far in politics. Instead, as C. P. Fitzgerald remarked, it became the personal philosophy of Chinese agnostics who wished to leave the madding crowd and seek a life in communion with nature. More important, it added zest to the dull fare of Confucianism and enlivened Chinese art and literature. The self-benefitting goals of Taoism, however, were continued in its early transformation into a magical search for eternal life or, failing that, long life to be achieved by control of one's breath and sexual essence. Some Taoists taught that man strengthened his spiritual being and prolonged his life by bringing as many young females to orgasm as possible without losing his own essence through ejaculation.

Moral relativity and transcendentalism also led the "left-handed" schools of Tantric Hinduism and Buddhism in India to practice outlandish acts such as eating feces and sexual orgies. These rituals, it was said, would shock the initiate into realizing the unity of all life and would dissolve his or her moral prejudices; some modern gurus ("dispellers of darkness") have found an audience in the West for the thesis that since all things are illusions of the mind, sexual promiscuity should have no effect on those who have reached the heights of spirituality and are thus ready to escape the circle of tears.

The Taoists would have agreed with the amoral philosophy of the Tantric schools, but the eroticism of Taoism was not intended to demonstrate spirituality and detachment from the physical and moral worlds. On the con trary, the Taoists believed that by returning to nature they could best enjoy themselves. Taoists, like all Chinese, were looking for the good life and a way to prolong it, not to escape from it.

Chinese morality was thus essentially utilitarian. Goodness and truth were judged by whatever was appropriate in the social and political context. Enlightened self-interest shaped the ethics of Chinese society. Morals were a means to a civilized and tranquil community.

In India, the moral law (*dharma*) stood above even the gods, and the absolute itself was not a god but a force that defied human imagination. Ethical behavior was overshadowed by the transcendental and the mystical.

As people pursue the good life, so they pursue truth. The Chinese had no concept of truth, for it was revealed through practice. Westerners discovered truth through observation. Indians felt it intuitively.

Cows and Pigs

As well as establishing patterns of worship, the earliest nomadic invaders had a permanent impact on the Indian diet. The Aryans were cattle-breeders, and most Indians of today, like other Indo-European descendants, are great eaters of dairy products. The Chinese, however, traditionally have not liked milk at all, although as any recent summer visitor to Peking can attest, they have fallen in love with ice-cream. The strong Chinese dislike of milk and cheese possibly is in part a social prejudice based on milk's key role in the diets of China's backward minorities—that is, the barbarians of old.

Dairy-oriented invaders were able to occupy only limited parts of China in the first millennium of its history. By the time of the extended barbarian dynasties beginning in the ninth century A.D., Chinese civilization, including its eating habits, were too solidly established to be much affected. The barbarians were already very much influenced by Chinese culture by the time they established control over parts of the empire. And the milk-consuming invaders were soon relishing sweet-and-sour pork and turning their noses up at yogurt.

Why did a strong religious taboo develop in India against eating beef, the other major dish in the cattle-herders' diet? Marvin Harris has suggested that rising population and intense pressure on resources in India made meat-eating unsupportable.[24] The intensification of population pressure in India also came at the time of the emergence of two reformist religions—Buddhism and Jainism—which rejected animal sacrifice and held all life to be sacred. Harris suggests that those farmers who accepted this belief and did not slaughter their cows or oxen, which were essential for plowing and providing milk, were more likely to survive the recurrent famines of India.

The Chinese claim to have domesticated the pig about 2900 B.C. Today, China has 45 percent of the world's pig population. India has at least 20 percent of the world's cows—and probably as many dogs—but the pig was not a notable feature of Indian village life. Harris argues that because of the more intense land pressure, India had to use the same animal—the cow—as village scavenger as well as for ploughing and haulage. The Chinese villagers, with more hilly and other non-cultivatable land around for pasture of their draft animals, could afford to employ pigs as the village scavengers.

Harris is wrong, however, in believing that there was greater land pressures in India than in China. Well over half of China consists of the remote and inhospitable Tibetan and Quinghai plateau, Xinjiang, and Inner Mongolia. Man/land pressure was much higher in China. The great majority of Chinese peasants in the past, as today, very likely had less pastureland available nearby than did Indian farmers. Indians also used dogs as scavengers but unlike the Chinese did not relish dogmeat. It seems likely that Indians did not eat dogs nor much develop pig husbandry because of the religious sanction for vegetarianism and because dogs and pigs were thought to be rather polluted animals. Economic factors probably had little to do with it.

Whatever the case with pigs, there was a marked difference in the Indian and Chinese attitude toward the draft animals which were vital to both for survival. The Chinese peasant had and still does have a certain affection for his work animals—horses and oxen in the north, and water buffalo in the south—but when these creatures wore out, they were, and are, taken off to a slaughter-house.

Not being pastoralists, however, the early Chinese never worshipped cows, as did the ancient Aryans. During the Vedic period in India, the cow was considered sacred and therefore to be eaten to obtain purity; subsequently in the Buddhist era the cow continued to be worshipped, but abstinence from eating its flesh became the way to purification.[25] Such veneration did not have its roots in economics, but in the peculiar spirituality of the nomadic Indo-European and his erotic linking of eating, sexuality, and religion. The cow became the symbol of the milk-giving mother, the image of non-erotic fertility, of goodness and love.

CHAPTER 3

Historic Contacts

The Cultural Flow

Historically, Indians and Chinese have been distinctly ethnocentric. Hindus traditionally considered foreigners to be outcastes, while Chinese lumped together non-Chinese of all sorts as barbarians or "foreign devils." Westerners to the Chinese were "big noses," and Dutchmen, "red bearded devils." The famous condescending letters of the Qian Long (Ch'ien Lung) Emperor to George III and of Commissioner Lin to Queen Victoria seem humorously pretentious, but they simply reflected a great ignorance and unreality about the world. It was not always so. By the beginning of the Tang Dynasty in the seventh century A.D., China had had centuries of tentative communication with other civilizations, first along the "Silk Road" and the borders of Chinese Turkestan, and then with foreign traders sailing to southern China.

China had much less direct contact with other civilizations than did ancient India, but it did enjoy a long and fruitful contact with India itself. About 128 B.C., a Chinese envoy, seeking an alliance for China with a powerful tribe living in the Oxus River Valley, learned of the large country of India, or "Shentu," to the south. Shortly afterwards the Han Dynasty began to assert its suzerainty over large areas of central Asia and the "Silk Road" started to funnel traders and eventually Indian missionaries into the Middle Kingdom.

In 65 A.D., the first Indian Buddhist missionaries arrived in China and established the famous "White Horse" monastery. In 399 A.D., Chinese pilgrims led by the monk Fa Xian (Fa Hsien) began the long trek to India. The pilgrims returned laden with Sanskrit manuscripts which were translated into Chinese. By the fifth century most Chinese were Buddhist in one fashion or another. Chinese society became fascinated with India and its culture.

Chinese historians recorded the names of many of the Indian missionaries and astronomers who came to China, and Chinese emperors dispatched envoys to the capitals of the Indian rulers.

India had a powerful influence on Chinese art, as well as religion, and Hellenic styles and motifs also passed to China through the influence of Indo-Greek sculptors in Gandhara and Mathura. In the seventh century A.D., Chinese bibliographical catalogues included the titles of numerous Indian books on astronomy, mathematics, medicine, and other subjects.[26]

Typically, Chinese chronicles reported the "submission" of Indian princes and the dispatch of "tribute." No doubt, these assertions represented exaggerations by Chinese envoys eager to maintain the myth of Chinese centrality and to win good marks at home.

Indian food also spread through China, and in the Tang Dynasty one could find good Indian restaurants in the major Chinese cities. Perhaps one could also hear a raga while dining, for Chinese texts describe Indian music as practiced in central Asia and report the presence of Indian performers in the cosmopolitan Chinese capital of Changan (Ch'ang An).

India, on the other hand, took little notice of China—intellectually, politically, or culturally. Trade was carried on; silk, vermillion, and bamboo were known to come from "Cina," and some Chinese inventions were very likely carried back to India. With all the comings and goings of pilgrims, traders, and missionaries, presumably there was some curiosity in India about China but evidently not enough to be recorded. In the seventh century, the Indian King Harsha sent a mission to China, apparently at the urging of the Chinese pilgrim Yuan Zhuang (Yuan Chuang).[27] So far as we know, however, this gesture was not repeated.

Chinese Taoism and the Tantric cults in India must have enjoyed some cross-fertilization around this period, but documentation on the subject is scanty. In the seventh century A.D., two Chinese envoys reported the interest of a certain Hindu king in Taoism, and the Chinese emperor ordered the dispatch of Taoist texts. Nothing more, however, was recorded of the episode. [28] There are only a few references in Indian literature to "Cina"; one refers to "Maha-Cina" or "Great China" as the seat of the mystic cult called "Cinacara" or "the practice of China," whatever that might have been.[29]

Meeting the West

During a short period in the Ming Dynasty, Chinese fleets under the eunuch Zheng He (Cheng Ho) sailed as far as south India, the Persian Gulf, and Africa. The purpose of these impressive voyages, Fitzgerald tells us, was less commercial than political—to show the flag and collect curiosities, such as zebras, for the amusement of the Chinese palace. Zheng He sailed into the Indian Ocean only about sixty years before Vasco de Gama made his way around the Cape of Good Hope and reached India. From there, the Portuguese would soon find the route to China. In both countries the Iberians behaved like conquistadors; but the reactions of India and China to the interlopers were quite different. The Ming Court, after several unpleasant experiences with the Portuguese, successfully expelled them from several trading ports in China and in 1557 restricted them to Macao.

At the same time, India was in another state of turmoil and fragmentation. The Portuguese seized Goa from the Sultan of Bijapur in 1510, only sixteen years before Babur won the battle of Panipat which opened the door to the Moghul conquest. There was no official reaction from the Indian government in Delhi to the Portuguese, who must have seemed a minor element in the chaos of the times.

In China, despite the voyages of Zheng He, the Ming Dynasty was generally a time of increased isolationism and xenophobia. Several factors contributed to this mood, including a reaction to Mongol rule, neo-Confucianist rejection of foreign influence, and the continued threat from nomads and pirates, including the Portuguese. This trend was continued in the Qing or Manchu Dynasty. The rulers of the Ming and the Qing, fearing cultural contamination, restricted travel abroad and forbade private dealings with foreigners by Chinese. By this time, the Hindus considered travel abroad as polluting, although such travel was never officially banned.

The Manchus from the beginning of their reign were concerned about the subversive potential of foreigners backing Chinese rebels. Thus, following the Ming restriction of the Portuguese to Macao, the Qing court limited all foreign trading ships to nearby Canton. This restriction lasted until the nineteenth century when the Chinese were compelled by force to lift it. During the same period in India, which included the zenith of Moghul power, the British, Dutch, Danes, and French opened numerous "factories" and forts along the east and west coasts of the country, including Calcutta, Bombay, Madras, and Pondicherry.

In some cases the Westerners obtained rights to open facilities from the Moghul court; in other instances such rights were simply provided by local nawobs and princes. Conflict between the Europeans and local Indian authorities sometimes occurred, but generally the spread of Western commercial facilities, including forts to protect them, was taken as a matter of course. Indeed, the Indians welcomed the trade, which primarily took the form of purchasing Indian spices, cloth, and other goods, for silver. Western trade was also favorable to China, until the introduction of opium in the nineteenth century, but the Chinese originally kept tight control over this commerce, allowing it, they said, out of benevolent recognition that constipated Occidentals could not live without the purgatives of Chinese tea and rhubarb.

The Moghuls entered a period of rapid disintegration in the early 1700s, while the Manchus began a similar period of decline in the 1800s. The Moghul decline had little or nothing to do with the Western presence in

India, but the time of troubles for the Manchus was directly related to their military defeats and subsequent humiliation at the hands of the Western imperialists. Following her traditional pattern, India quickly fragmented as soon as Moghul power began to wane. But after the Opium War, Manchu rule over China still continued for sixty years as virtually a hollow shell. China was rent by the Taiping Rebellion in the 1860s, but nevertheless somehow remained united under alien rule until the overthrow of the Qing Dynasty in 1911.

The British began picking up the pieces in India in the early eighteenth century and before they knew it, they were ruling the entire subcontinent. Whereas the Qing had controlled China with, at the end, perhaps 3 million Manchus, the English did the same in India with 40,000 British. The Hindu elite readily acquiesced or collaborated with British rule while the mass of the Indian people remained apathetic. A number of factors accounted for this reaction. First of all, extension of the British Raj brought peace and order to a chaotic situation. The Hindu saw British rule as no worse than that of the Moslem, just as later, with the rise of Indian nationalism, many Moslems would see continued British suzerainty as preferable to the hegemony of a Hindu majority.

In homogeneous China, there was no such communal barrier to unity against the foreigner. In addition, in the eighteenth century the great majority of Hindus entertained no loyalty to any Indian imperium, Hindu or Moslem. Indians had long learned to separate the political order from their cultural identity and from their communal loyalties. But in China, for 2,000 years under either barbarian or Chinese rulers, the political order had been a central part of Chinese culture.

The fact that there was a 100-year lag in the coming of the Western imperialist threat to China also made the situation different from that in India. By the second half of the nineteenth century, rivalries among the Western powers gave the Chinese more of a chance to play the barbarians off against each other; thus, a full-scale colonial takeover, as in India, was not possible, although the Japanese would later attempt the impossible. The Chinese tried confrontation, conciliation, and internal reform to try to meet the Western challenge, but nothing seemed to work. The root cause of this failure was the strength of Chinese orthodoxy and the resistance of the landlord-scholar class to social changes that would have threatened their position.[30] Privilege and power remained based on land ownership. A class of Chinese industrialists did spring up in Shanghai and other treaty ports, but the scope and the dynamism of this movement was small.

Protective Reaction

The 2,000-year-old Chinese social and political order would at last be overcome, not by foreigners, but by foreign ideas. The gentry and scholars were correct in fearing that the Confucian system and China's ancient way of life would be destroyed by Western contamination. China's materialistic society and the humanist philosophy of the elite were subject to corrosion by a materialist and humanist Western culture that was, for the moment, technologically superior. Spiritual and non-rational Indian ideology, on the other hand, proved relatively immune to the West.

India's succession of cultural infusions, its long history of subjugation to the Moslems, and the isolation of the Hindu way of life gave Indians a more tolerant and less anxious view of Western influence. If Hindu culture could persist in the face of 600 years of Moslem rule, there was no need to be alarmed about administration by a tiny European elite or proselytizing by a few thousand Christians who, while persistent, were not directly threatening to Hindu culture. Thus, it was easy for Indians to become dedicated servants of the British Raj, without feeling one bit disloyal. Indian troops and police kept the peace and Indian civil servants staffed the lower and middle-ranking positions throughout the British administration.

Chinese reaction to the West was at first xenophobic and nationalistic, then cunning and pusillanimous, and then half-hearted adaptation, but when all these approaches failed, the Chinese proved much more open to drastic and foreign-oriented change than was the case in India. As we have seen, the Chinese over the centuries could also passively accept foreign hegemony. The Manchus, with a smaller ruling minority than the Moghuls, enjoyed a longer period of peaceful obedience by its subject people than did the Indian Moslems. The difference, of course, was that the Manchus accepted and worked within the ancient Chinese social and political culture. The intrusion of foreign hegemonists from a civilization as culturally advanced as that of China and technologically superior was traumatic for the Chinese. It was not for the Indians.

Sepoys and Taipings

The greater Chinese susceptibility to Western culture and ideology is apparent in a comparison of the most important social upheavals in India and China in the nineteenth century. The Sepoy mutiny in India (1857–1858) was sparked by Hindu and Moslem fears that the English were moving to undermine their religion and caste. In particular, there were rumors among the Sepoys (native troops) that they were to be converted to Christianity. In addition, those with traditional land-rights in north India were angry because the British had taken away their powers and taxed the peasants directly. The Moslem rulers were of course eager to oust the British. The uprising itself was sparked by the well-known story of cartridges supposedly greased in the fat of either sacred cows or impure pigs. In short, the Sepoy mutiny was nativistic, anti-Western, and in defense of traditional values. It was brutally put down by Sikhs and Gurkhas in a year and a half.[31]

In comparison to China's Taiping Rebellion (1851–1864), the Sepoy mutiny was a brief protest. The Taiping uprising was one of the great social upheavals of modern times. As many as 20 million Chinese may have died during the course of this rebellion and its bloody suppression.[32]

While the Sepoy mutiny was spurred by traditional values, the Taiping Rebellion was a Chinese-Christian movement inspired by the Bible and Western reformist concepts. The Taipings sought an equal distribution of land to the peasants, simplification of the Chinese language, monogamy, and prohibition of foot-binding, opium-smoking, and other evils of the day. The Taipings, under their leader Hong Xiuzhuan (Hung Hsiu-chuan), captured Nanking and most of China below the Yangtze. Millions of Chinese were swept up in the movement. The Taipings won support because they were a Chinese sect and not Methodist or Catholic, but their ideology, whatever its peculiarities, was decidedly Christian, and their social and political reforms were heavily Western influenced. The Taipings were eventually crushed by the Manchus, but only with the assistance of the Western imperialists—most Christian missionaries having short-sightedly viewed the movement as heretical. Almost a century later, the Chinese people were to flock to the banner of another messianic leader espousing a nationalist version of another Western ideology—Marxism.

In the 1830s in Calcutta there was a small group of intellectuals who argued that India should accept the West *in toto*.The movement and its leader, the Anglo-Indian Derozio, died an early death. Other Indian movements, such as the Society of God, formed by Rammohun Roy in the early 1800s, incorporated Christian ethics into Hinduism; but nothing faintly similar to the Christian-inspired Taiping movement ever occurred in India.

Untouchable and Rice-Bowl Christians

Western missionaries did not have sweeping success in making conversions in either India or China. One could argue that this was because both countries possessed a sophisticated culture. But a good case can be made that, like Buddhism, Christianity as an historical, intellectual, and ethical religion appealed more to Chinese than Indians. When Sinicized and led by Chinese, as was the Taiping Movement, Christianity could generate mass support. When China was secure and prosperous, as during the Tang Dynasty, new religions including Buddhism and Christianity were relatively successful, although they always faced the possibility of suppression by the forces of established orthodoxy.

In addition to the Taiping phenomenon, the flourishing of the Nestorian Christians in the seventh and eighth centuries A.D. in China suggests that, with a different throw of the dice, Christianity might have developed as an indigenous church in China.

When the famous Nestorian Tablet was erected in Chang An (Ch'ang An) in A.D. 781, the Nestorian Church was flourishing and enjoyed the patronage of such notables as the Grand General of the Tang Army. When the church was suppressed in A.D. 845 by the ardent Taoist emperor Wu Cong (Wu Tsung), two thousand Nestorian Christian monks and nuns reportedly were forced to renounce their religion.

The only parallel in India was the Syrian Christian church, established in Kerala, as local tradition has it by the disciple Saint Thomas himself. The Syrian Christians, along with a tiny Jewish community in Kerala, persisted even through an inquisition carried out by the Portuguese in the sixteenth century. They did not, however, spread significantly outside of their original area in the south. The different fates of the Nestorian and Syrian Christians reflected Hinduism's greater imperviousness toward and, paradoxically, its greater tolerance of foreign religions.

The Jesuits also fared somewhat better in China than in the Moghul court. Beginning in 1850, Jesuits in Goa were summoned several times by Akbar, who wished to hear them explain their doctrine. Despite early optimism, the Jesuits never made any important converts among the Moghuls and Akbar went on to declare his own eclectic and short-lived religion. Akbar's son and successor, Jahangir, likewise summoned Jesuits to court, but it was suspected that he was more interested in obtaining Portuguese cannon than in the scriptures.

In the late sixteenth century, the first Jesuits, led by Matteo Ricci, reached China and won respect and permanent residence in Peking, through their knowledge of astronomy, mathematics, and—as in India—the casting of cannon. The Ming court was also more intrigued with the technical than the theological feats of the good fathers, but a number of important converts were made among Chinese scholars such as Xu Guang-ji (Hsu Kuang-chi) and Li Zhi-zao (Li Chih-tsao) as well as among members of the royal family. The last Ming empress was a Christian and her son was baptized under the name Constantine. The Ming court, however, was already in flight from the Manchus, and Constantine did not live to reign. The Manchus retained the Jesuits, who headed the Peking astronomical observatory for 200 years. During that time, small Catholic congregations spread throughout China, but neo-Confucianist conservatives eventually triumphed and Christianity was banned in the Yong-zheng (Yung-Cheng) period (1723–1735).

In 1813, the British East India Company finally admitted Christian missionaries to India and, after the Opium Wars of the 1840s, the Manchus were forced to open the door to European and American evangelists. By 1949 there were an estimated 4 million Chinese Christians and some 10,000 missionaries.

A large number of Chinese converts were "rice-bowl" Christians who had joined for worldly benefits; but they also included a large number of intellectual, urban, and Westernized Chinese who were sincere believers. In Republican China, the two most prominent Chinese were Christian: Sun

Yat-sen and Chiang Kai-shek. Madame Chiang and her influential brothers and brothers-in-law were converts as was the warlord Feng Youxiang (Feng Yu-hsiang), who gained theological fame by baptizing his troops with a fire hose.

In India, besides descendants of the Syrian Christians, the great majority of Christian converts were tribals and to a lesser extent untouchables who had converted in "mass movements." Most outcastes surprisingly were not attracted to the egalitarian tenets of either Christianity or Islam. Upper caste converts in India, however, were even more rare.

Despite important converts among the Chinese elite, most Chinese intellectuals in the twentieth century rejected Christianity as they had rejected Confucianism—because it was neither modern nor scientific.[33] Indian intellectuals at the same time shunned Christianity much more solidly because it was untraditional, not because it seemed inconsistent with modern ideas.

Breaking with the Past

The Manchu-encouraged Boxer Uprising of 1900 was the anti-foreign Chinese parallel to the Sepoy mutiny. The Boxer movement was the culmination of a long period of struggle between Chinese reformers and reactionaries, who advocated different ways of meeting the Western challenge. The ineffective Self-Strengthening Movement and the abortive "one-hundred days of reform" in 1898 reflected the views of those who believed China could selectively adapt Western techniques and reforms and, in the process, revive Confucianism.

The Chinese political scene, however, was soon dominated by modernizers like Sun Yat-sen and Hu Shi (Hu Shih), who were educated in the West and who derived their inspiration primarily from Western thought. The New Culture Movement expounded Western ideas of democracy, progress, and pragmatism, and denounced traditional Confucian values—setting the stage intellectually for the advent of the Chinese Communist Party. In the late 1960s, denigration of China's past would be carried to its extremes by the Cultural Revolution which condemned as reactionary such traditional pursuits as Peking Opera and raising goldfish. But no significant wing of Indian nationalism would ever include open rejection of Hindu culture. Nationalists like Rammohun Roy and Rabindranath Tagore sought to promote a more humanistic and ethical Hinduism, but they always thought that while India had a great deal to learn from the West, its spiritual and cultural superiority was beyond doubt.

Chinese reformers, however, around the turn of the century became more and more extremist in their rejection of Chinese traditional values and society. The extremists in the Indian national movement were more nativistic than the moderates, not less. Chatterjee, Tilak, and Ghose attempted to stir the masses to Western-style patriotism with appeals to Hindu parochialism.

Nothing more symbolized the dual aspect of the Indian national movement than Gandhi at his spinning wheel.

China's initial xenophobic and obscurantist reaction to the West was to be expected. But, in retrospect, we can see that the Chinese were probably destined eventually to break with the past in a revolutionary manner, building a new culture on the basis of Western ideology—whether communist, Christian, liberal, or capitalist. Because intellectually China is a political, not a religious, animal, it was eventually bound wholeheartedly to embrace modernization and to discard its old culture to the extent it believed necessary to achieve success. The pragmatic outlook of the Chinese, and their focus on happiness in this world, as well as their historical sense linking the present with both the past and the future, made a break with tradition the logical response to an encounter with a civilization that had clearly moved ahead of China in producing stronger nations and a better material life.

Thus, today it is India that, for good or evil, has retained its religion and traditions in the face of Westernization. The revolution in China, however, has swept away the entire superstructure of traditional society. China under the Communists remains a China for the Chinese, as it would have been had the Taipings succeeded. Yet both the Taipings and the Communists represented a triumph of Western thought over ancient Confucian values. Both movements also represented a victory of Chinese pragmatism and eclecticism; when old ways no longer seemed to work, the Chinese were prepared to pitch them overboard. In any event, neither the Taipings nor the Communists represented the sort of Western triumph that the missionaries or treaty port merchants had envisioned.

CHAPTER 4

The Balance of Cultural and Physical Factors

An Overview

As they began their modern era of national development, India and China enjoyed sophisticated cultures with organizational skills and educated elites which gave them great advantages in human resources over most other Third World countries. But each was more receptive to certain kinds of change than the other.

Between the two, China's pragmatic and homogeneous culture—with higher standards of literacy and health—seemed much more likely to evolve a successful development strategy. China was unified in race—93 percent Han Chinese—and in language—70 percent native speakers of Mandarin, with virtually all literate Chinese reading the same ideographic text.

Culturally, China was a monochrome from Harbin in the northeast to Canton in the south; important regional differences, of course, existed, but a foreign traveler today, as in the 1940s, is still struck by the relative sameness of the lives of the Han everywhere in that immense land. The Chinese sense of a political order also promised to make them responsive to the appeals of modern nationalism, and thus more easily mobilized. Although compliance was often superficial, the Chinese peasantry had for centuries been accustomed to directives from a central government, and even more important, the Chinese had traditionally honored prosperity and perceived education as a ladder to success. The idea of social progress was not a primary value in Chinese culture, but it was not foreign to it. Chinese cultural values in 1950 thus held the promise of a relatively dynamic and disciplined response to the challenges of modern economic development.

India, by comparison, was a hodge-podge of races, ranging from snow-white north Indians to the ebony Tamils. In addition to fourteen major languages, India possessed over 200 dialects. Although Indian nationalism had developed to a relatively high state by the end of World War II, it was fractured by linguistic, regional, communal, and caste loyalties. Indian villages were much more self-contained and isolated than Chinese villages and, while a strong central government could carry out certain national programs, such as an extensive reorganization of the tax system, there had been relatively little government involvement in other aspects of village life in India.

India seemed more afflicted with atavistic attitudes and other-worldly concerns. Despite the National Congress Movement and the rise of the idea of Indian nationalism, India appeared to be a politically atomized society of hundreds of thousands of villages, thousands of castes, hundreds of linguistic groups, and dozens of princely states—all existing as separate organisms held together by religious beliefs and the system of caste, but incapable of concerted action.

Vital statistics for the period reflect the cultural and social advantages for modernization that China enjoyed. The birthrates for India in 1950 and for China in 1952 were approximately the same (38 and 37 per 1,000) but, despite the long period of chaos that China had suffered, the death rate was much lower in China (12:1,000 versus 24:1,000 in India), reflecting traditionally higher nutritional and literacy rates in the middle kingdom. The Chinese had for centuries enjoyed a higher grain consumption per person than the Indians, who, despite eating more milk products, consumed fewer calories on the average in 1950 than did the Chinese. Life expectancy in devastated China in 1950 was only 36 years; in India after 200 years of peace and British administration it was even lower, about 32 years. In 1950, the literacy rate in India was 17 percent, about a third less than that in China.

Farming and the Ownership of Land

Chinese agriculture for centuries had been much more intensive than Indian farming. In the seventeenth century, the Chinese were producing on the average of 2.3 tons of paddy rice per hectare compared with the 1970 yield in India of 1.7 to 1.9. With far greater population pressure on the land, the Chinese traditionally employed much more terracing and irrigation than did their Indian counterparts. But the most important factor was the extensive use of organic fertilizer in China. Indians did not in an organized way recycle human waste back into the fields because there was more arable land per person in India than in China, but also because the pollution phobia of the Hindus discouraged the use of human manure on food crops, while animal dung was largely used as fuel.

Indian farms thus did not enjoy the mass recycling of nutrients that occurred on Chinese farms. In ancient times as today, Chinese soils probably had many times the nutrient value of Indian land. Human feces, however, were not entirely wasted in India. Farm land immediately adjacent to Indian villages was and still is the most fertile because of the primitive toilet habits of rural (and even poor urban) Indians who simply deposit their excrement on the nearest open space. One of Gandhi's many futile campaigns was to convince Indian peasants to carry a spade to the fields when they did their morning bowel movement. As an example to the masses, Gandhi saw to it that a portable toilet accompanied him on all his treks.

By 1952, Chinese paddy yield was 2.5 tons per hectare, compared to 1.3 in the same year in India. Chinese wheat yields, at 1.1 tons per hectare in 1952, were also higher than India's similar figure of 0.7 tons.[34] In 1950 an acre of cultivated land in India supported 0.6 persons; the comparable figure in China was more than triple—1.9. Moreover, Chinese farm production had diminished because of prolonged conflict and internal disorder. According to official figures, agricultural production in China in 1949 was about 70 percent of previous peak levels. Thus an initial burst of rural productivity in China was inevitable once peace returned. The relative efficiency of Chinese farming was also due in large part to social factors—the longstanding tradition of private land ownership in China and the existence of caste in India.

China and India historically were archetypes of Karl Wittfogel's hydraulic societies—that is, extensive agricultural civilizations that became increasingly dependent upon complex irrigation works and flood control and which, consequently, developed despotic governments to carry out the collective labor necessary to maintain the system. As Wittfogel notes, in India throughout most of its recorded history, the bulk of cultivated land was not owned privately but was controlled by the princely rulers who regulated its division and use.[35] At times, Indian peasants could transfer or bequeath use of the land they tilled to relatives and certain others, but they could not freely alienate it. This system, together with high apportionment of the crop by the state, acted as a major disincentive to production. Hindu tradition awarded one-sixth of a peasant's produce to the rulers, but the Moghuls expropriated one-third of the value and assigned local *zamidaras* to collect it.

Neither tenancy nor landlordship as such existed in India. Although a large percentage of lower castes and untouchables were laborers working lands traditionally controlled by the families of dominant castes, the right of occupancy, whether by upper or lower caste agriculturalists, was never protected in law or practice before the British.

China was the exception in Wittfogel's model; private, including peasant, ownership of land became the established pattern far back in the third century B.C. Most Chinese, including soldiers and officials, sought to own at least a small piece of land. Landholdings naturally tended to accummulate and tenancy and absentee landlordism waxed and waned but were always major features of the Chinese scene. The barbarian dynasties of China awarded land to tribal leaders and to Chinese supporters but, according to

Wittfogel, in the last days of the Manchu Dynasty 93 percent of the land in China was privately owned. The percentage of tenancy and the proportion taken in taxes or rent varied greatly from area to area and from time to time. When the situation became oppressive, peasant rebellions would break out. In the 1930s, for example, landlords and rich peasants constituted 12 percent of the population and owned 50 percent of the land.

British land reforms of the nineteenth century in India made matters worse for most Indian peasants. Although many tillers were given land, the British reforms lacked backup in terms of providing the new landed peasants credit and cooperative marketing arrangements. The Indian peasant had always borrowed money, but the moneylenders had no lien on his land, which the peasant did not own, and by Hindu custom, interest payments could not exceed the sum of the principal. Thus there had always been a strict limit to a peasant's debt and in any event he could never lose the use of the land because of debt. But under the British reforms, peasants could mortgage their land, and they did; by 1950 about 80 percent of all farmland in India was tilled by tenants.

Weather and Climate

In terms of climate, China again seemed to have been dealt a relatively better hand than India. China was the only ancient civilization to develop in an area of extreme variation in temperature, including a severe winter. Indeed, China is one of the few developing countries that is not largely in the tropics or subtropics. Because of its higher latitude, China enjoys more daylight in summer than does India, but India has a greater proportion of land suitable for double cropping.

The Himalayas and the Hindu Kush protect north and northwest India from the cold winds of the Tibetan Plateau and, except for Kashmir and other mountain regions, the average temperature of the whole of India is about 80 degrees. While the Indus and Yellow River valleys are both semi-arid, only the latter suffers from bitter cold winters. Northern India can become chilly but not nearly so frigid as large parts of China. Rattling through China's Gansu Province in wintertime in an unheated train is one of the coldest experiences available. We can only speculate about the social effect of this sharp contrast in Chinese seasons, but very likely thousands of years of preparing for hard winters encouraged the ancient Chinese to industry and accumulation.

Personality may also have been affected. It is an old saw that people from cold climates are relatively dour; even today, southern Chinese are more exuberant and generally more gregarious with foreigners than are their northern cousins.

Both the Indus and Yellow River Valleys look exceedingly inhospitable, but presumably civilizations first appeared in these areas because of the relative absence of disease and parasites which were to be found in abundance further south and east in both countries. As William MacNeill has suggested, disease probably slowed the movement of the Aryans into the Gangetic Plain, and even more so into tropical south India. Nevertheless, it was in the steaming Gangetic Valley that Aryan civilization crystallized. MacNeill believes that one of the reasons for the instability of Indian political structures was the heavy microbe parasitism characteristic of the Gangetic Valley and the rest of India's best agricultural lands. Today, the Ganges region still sustains cholera, malaria, dengue fever, and a variety of parasites. Infestation and infection, MacNeill argues, also reduced individual vigor and the capacity for physical labor.

An Indian, however, can best describe the climate of the Gangetic Plain:

> There is perhaps not one other (region in the world) which so irresistibly draws civilizations to it and strangles them as irresistibly as does the Indo-Gangetic Plain. It is the vampire of geography which sucks out all creative energy and leaves its victims as listless shadows. The high mean temperature, together with its immense daily range of rise and fall, hardly allows the human body to attend to anything more fruitful than the daily adaptation to the weather. The unbroken flatness of the Plain finds its counterpart in dullness of the mind, monotony of experience and narrowness of interest. With this climate and physiography is combined a diet which is so highly adapted to the environment that it is as fatal to creative energy as the other two. Starch, seasoned with spices, is the typical food of the Indo-Gangetic Plain, and it is capable of nurturing no other forms of human activity or outlook on life than that which possesses its own insipidity.[36]

The Chinese expanded first into the North China Plain, an area with almost equally harsh winters as those of the earliest Chinese societies in what are now Shaanxi and Gansu provinces. They moved only slowly into the humid Yangtze Valley, an area which the historian Si-ma Qian described as decidedly unhealthy. Most of China south of the Shandong Peninsula and east of the Tibetan Plateau is in the same category of a sub-tropical monsoon climate as most of India. The Yangtze Valley also blisters from intense summer heat, although its winters are cooler than those of the Gangetic Plain. Average rainfall is higher in most of India, but also more erratic. For a variety of reasons, higher humidity and temperatures in India result in generally poorer soil than in China.[37]

Poorer soils in turn resulted in less nutrients for the population and, thus, reduced working capacity and weakened resistance to disease. Together with disincentives in the political and social systems, India suffered a cycle of poor nutrition and inefficient labor.

Management and Commerce

Chinese and Indians have both had historic experience in management of complex and large organizations, including gigantic armies, centrally controlled bureaucracies, tax systems, and large cities. The Chinese experience in management on a national level, however, in many sectors was far more continuous and effective than in India where chronic disorder made large-scale undertakings more difficult. In China, centrally managed engineering projects of immense scale included the Grand Canal, the Great Wall, and extensive irrigation and flood-control works. The Moghuls and local satraps squeezed Indian villages to the maximum to finance their military establishments and palaces, but, unlike China, there was little investment by the central government in public projects or infrastructure unless it was related to these two purposes.

China was also a more commercialized society than India. Merchants ranked in the upper castes in India, while in the Confucian order they theoretically came below both farmers and artisans. But because the Chinese put a high value on the accumulation of wealth, and commerce was a much quicker path to riches than farming, successful merchants were fairly high in the Chinese pecking order. Only with money could one send one's children to school so they could become scholars and eventually elevate the family into the highest ranks. Family connections between merchants and the social elite of gentry and scholar-officials were numerous, with the former providing wealth and the latter prestige to a marital union.[38]

In India there was also a sophisticated class of merchants. Guilds, letters of credit, and other aspects of a banking system existed in the eighteenth century. But unlike China, wealth was not an avenue to social status or to political power and, because of caste rules, there were few if any family connections between merchants and the two higher castes above them—the brahmans and the kshatriyas. The predatory Indian state could and did confiscate the wealth of merchants whenever it felt like it. Indian merchants lacked the same sort of understood symbiotic connection with the state and the status system through membership in the gentry group which most Chinese merchants enjoyed.[39]

Rhoades Murphey has shown that in the period of Western domination the great bulk of Chinese commerce remained in the hands of Chinese merchants and that traditional Chinese trade guilds and Chinese native banks expanded during this time. The weak point in China was industrialization, which continued overwhelmingly to be concentrated in the treaty ports and in Japanese-dominated Manchuria. The bulk of China's capital surplus was naturally in agriculture and it was the failure of the landed gentry and scholar-official class to invest their capital in industry which resulted in China's failure to "take off" economically as did Meiji Japan.[40] Nevertheless, the Chinese merchant class, despite its relative shortage of native capital, responded energetically to the Western challenge. Later, in 1949, many Chinese merchants fled to Taiwan and Hong Kong, but the tradition of commerce left an important legacy to the Communist regime.

British investment in infrastructure in India, however, surpassed what the imperialists left behind and war had spared in China. By 1932, for example, imperialists left behind and war had spared in China. By 1932, for example, India, including what is now Pakistan and Bangladesh, contained 44,832 miles of railroad track while China in 1950, excluding Manchuria and Taiwan, could claim only 6,032 miles.[41]

Total U.K. investments in Indian industry, on the other hand, were surprisingly small and concentrated in food and fiber processing. At independence these investments totaled only $423 million and this figure itself had been fairly constant for the preceding thirty years.[42] The British had actively discouraged local industries that would compete with their own manufacturers for the Indian market. The Chinese Communists were no better off. They inherited large but mostly outdated industrial complexes in Shanghai and other treaty ports, and the Soviets carted off most of the capital equipment in Japanese-built plants in Manchuria. Consequently, in 1950, both India and China had nineteenth-, not twentieth-century industrial economies.

Nevertheless, India was ahead in industrial output in important fields in terms of volume as well as per capita output. In 1949, China's industrial output was 30 percent of its previous peak, but by 1952, when initial recovery had been largely completed, the comparative figures were:[43]

Output Per Capita	India, 1950	China, 1952
Coal (kg)	97	96
Pig Iron (kg)	5	2.8
Crude Steel (kg)	4	2
Electric Power (kw)	0.01	0.005
Cotton Spindles (units)	0.03	0.01
Cement (kg)	9	4

Aggregate industrial production figures in both cases were extremely low and agriculture overwhelmed industry, accounting for over 80 percent of population and GNP in the two countries. Overall, the two economies were rather comparable:[44]

	India, 1950	China, 1952
Gross National Product (GNP) (million 1952 dollars)	22,000	30,000
GNP per capita	60	50
Population (millions)	358	575

In sum, the Union of India began with a lead over the new China in industrial production, although in both countries the industrial base was small and outdated. More important was India's lead in infrastructure, including railroads and electric power, which reflected the previous 150 years of relative peace and stability. India and China both enjoyed excellent hydroelectric potential and a wide range of mineral deposits, including coal and iron ore. Oil, however, was to prove to be much more abundant in China—through the 1980s in any event—and beginning in the early 1970s this was to play an important role in China's ecnomic development.

The Capacity to Change

India and China shared many attitudes that posed serious obstacles to modernization. Some cultural traits that work against rational economic development, however, existed to a greater extent in China than in India. The Confucian fixation on orthodoxy and its fear of foreign influence had resulted in China's technological stagnation for 600 years before the Western intrusions. Eventually, China proved it could make radical change, but its penchant for dogma and orthodoxy would persist.

It was apparent in 1950 that, unlike China, radical reforms in India could unleash powerful forces and fragment the new state. The bloody trauma of partition in 1947, in which hundreds of thousands were killed, underscored the violent impulses that lay beneath the surface of ahimsa. Consequently, while Indian reforms would prove to be painfully slow, they would for the most part eschew utopian schemes or the imposition of a single-minded dogma.

Modern China united and at peace under any rational political and economic system appeared likely to succeed and, in the near- or mid-term, to outstrip India's performance. Whether China's economic performance would have been better or worse under a non-communist regime, authoritarian or democratic, is a moot question. The Chinese communists did, in fact, begin their drive to modernization after 1949 with revolutionary institutions that provided real potential advantages in carrying out dynamic reforms. But they also carried potential disadvantages.

The new regimes in both Peking and New Delhi were committed to removing social and cultural obstacles to growth, but the Chinese government possessed a much greater ability to mobilize the population for national goals and to carry out sweeping innovations in social engineering. Exercised with prudence and rationality, these powers appeared to provide the new China with distinct advantages over independent India where modernizing reforms seemed to face the insurmountable opposition of tradition and an entrenched establishment. But total party control, the liquidation of autonomous institutions and social sectors, and the lack of political checks and balances in the new China could, and did, result in the multiplication of its errors. While in India, old traditions proved adaptable and often more efficient than the mores of social revolution.

CHAPTER 5

Gandhi and Mao

At one point, hopes were high that with independence in India and liberation in China these two nations could move rapidly toward achievement of the ideals of their great leaders—Mahatma Gandhi and Mao Zedong (Mao Tse-tung). Gandhi and Mao were products of distinctly different conditions existing in India and China in the first half of the twentieth century. But there were similarities. Both men were nationalists, idealists, and egalitarians and, until the last stages of their careers, both were pragmatic politicians who achieved success by rallying peasant masses to their cause.

Although intellectuals themselves, Gandhi and Mao distrusted the intelligentsia and urban life. Like Gandhi, Mao, out of fear of creating an intellectual elite, came to advocate a reduction of the period of schooling. Gandhi was opposed to most science and technology, although at times he allowed that some industry might be necessary. His ideal was a self-reliant agrarian economy based on subsistence rather than surplus. Mao, on the other hand, wanted to create a modern technological society that somehow would not be ruled by bureaucrats, technocrats, and experts. Both were inspired by Western thought: Gandhi by the non-conformist radical thinkers of nineteenth-century England and Russia, and Mao by Marx, Engels, and Lenin. Western-influenced reformers in India and China had come and gone before, but the genius of Gandhi and Mao was their success in adapting respectively the radical humanist and revolutionary thought of the West to social conditions in their own countries.

While Mao did not travel or study abroad until after liberation in 1949, and only then to Moscow, Western thought deeply influenced him during his years at Changsha University (1913–1918). Mao characterized his mind at the time as a curious mixture of liberalism, democratic reformism, and utopian socialism.[45] Mao later fell under the influence of the two founders of the Chinese Communist Party (CCP), Chen Duxu (Ch'en Tu-hsu) and Li Dajiao (Li Ta-chiao) and he became a solid Marxist rooted in Chinese nationalism.

Gandhi also originally came to grips with his Indian heritage through Western eyes, first reading the Indian classics in English translation.[46] As a liberal reformer, Gandhi fought for the abolition of untouchability, but he remained mesmerized by the Hindu past. Once untouchability went, he believed, the caste system would be purified. While Mao had visions of a new social order—a truly classless society—Gandhi looked backward to an idealized past.

One of the greatest successes of both Gandhi and Mao was their development of revolutionary tactics of political mobilization. Gandhi's visionary work, *Hind Swaraj*, embarrassed Jawaharlal Nehru and most other Congress leaders for its espousal of an India returned to its villages, its cities abandoned. He left the world the concept of non-violent civil disobedience, while Mao contributed the theories of people's war, protracted struggle, and the continuing revolution. Gandhi espoused a spiritual, gradual, back-to-nature approach to improving the quality of life and it is certain that, if he had lived, he would have adhered to the philosophy of gradualism despite its failure to make dramatic progress in independent democratic India.

Indian and some Western writers are prone to emphasize the similarities in the agrarian, anti-bureaucratic, and egalitarian ideals of Gandhi and Mao.[47] Gandhi's objective was a society marked by peace of mind, acceptance of life, and a return to the primeval, more natural existence of man. Mao, however, sought not only an egalitarian society, but one that was productive and powerful. Since he, too, abhored consumerism, the use of the national power he sought centered not only on basic welfare for the population, but also on achieving the ability to influence the behavior of others and the course of history.

There is a recurrent debate in India: was Gandhi essentially a lawyer who became a saint because that was necessary to lead the movement, or was he actually a saint who acted by instinct rather than design? Whatever the answer, it is clear that he would not have succeeded had he remained a lawyer in his English clothes. It was in keeping with the image of the holy man that Gandhi, quite unlike Mao, spurned the perquisites of power. The totally Indian image he cast won the hearts of millions who never saw him or heard his voice. Gandhi combined ahimsa (nonviolence) and Christian pacifism to appeal to the Indian peasants' susceptibility to spiritual claims and their reluctance to risk all-out attack on those in power.

At the same time in China, Mao was playing his own role to a different audience. While always maneuvering to strengthen his authority within the CCP, Mao maintained an image of being withdrawn and above the political fray. As a young revolutionary leader in the 1930s, he projected an aloof and scholarly mien. After liberation, he assumed an even more imperial cast, withdrawing from day-to-day affairs, disappearing for months at a time and then reappearing to issue some Delphic message or to perform some symbolic act such as swimming the Yangtze or accepting a gift of mangoes. It was the very picture of a sage emperor.

The upper-caste ascetic and the rebel-peasant-become-wise-ruler were images which fit the traditions of India and China, respectively. Gandhi, however, was a unique sort of holy man, for he had a political and social mission rather than a religious one. It is said that traditional India was the most religious of all countries but also the most immoral, lacking any sense of social justice. The holy men and gurus of India, even less than kings, were not concerned with the suffering of human beings. True, people were exhorted to perform good deeds, but in addition to gestures such as feeding beggars and ants, this meant carrying out the duties, obligations, and rituals of one's caste. Hindu religion taught that suffering as well as pleasure were transitory illusions and that man's ultimate purpose was to escape from the wheel of existence, not to improve upon it.

Before Gandhi and since, there has never been an Indian holy man whose goals were more humanistic than spiritual.[41] A profound humanism overrode Gandhi's political goals as well as his religious nature. He understood the enormous latent communal violence that lurked beneath the surface of Indian society. Terrorism against the British would inevitably lead to terrorism among the Indians themselves. Thus, Gandhi gave overriding priority to avoiding violence and to fostering the unity of Hindu and Moslem. Richard Attenboro's 1982 film dramatically portrays this theme in Gandhi's life. Gandhi's wisdom and humanism make him a saint among the political leaders of history; no one has ever commanded the allegiance of such millions in a national struggle while stressing means more than ends.

For Mao, however, achievement of the ideal political order warranted employment of any means, most desirably violence, because the greater the violence the more likely that the old order would be destroyed.

In both cases, ends and means were closely related. Mao's communes and Gandhi's self-sufficient village communities were only superficially alike in terms of certain professed ideals; but the fundamental characteristic of each shaped its entire nature—one was compulsory, the other voluntary.

Gandhi's immortal contribution to India was not independence, which would have come in any event. In the end, he failed in his goal of avoiding a holocaust of violence and retaining the unity of India. It was as if Abraham Lincoln had lost the Civil War, having neither avoided a blood-bath nor preserved the Union. Gandhi's real achievement was to cajole and shame India into accepting humanist ideals. Indian society may continue to suffer injustice for generations; but after Gandhi, a just social order would forever be the Indian ideal, however much violated in practice.

Mao's achievements were more concrete. He did not rally the peasants of China with the tenets of Marxism-Leninism; rather, he mustered their usually latent but powerful tradition of rebellion against foreign invaders and decadent regimes. Mao, of course, had to deal with the Japanese and the Kuomintang (KMT), much stronger and more ruthless foes than the British in India. Even before Gandhi appeared on the scene, it was clear the British did not have the stomach to suppress the national movement indefinitely. Informed Englishmen knew that Indian independence was a matter of time, although Kipling and most colonial administrators assumed this would be a process of another hundred years or more.

China, in the first decades of the twentieth century, had endured civil war, economic collapse, and piecemeal imperialist exploitation, culminating in the Japanese effort to dominate all of China. The banner of Chinese nationalism went to the strongest military movement and the leader who seemed most likely to rid China of its enemies and to unite the country. Chinese patriotism seems to come sporadically in great waves, and the 1930s and 1940s were such a time.[49] China cried out for a strong leader like Mao. The revolution might have succeeded without him, but perhaps not. In any event, he left behind not only a new dynasty, but a new orthodoxy.

In the end, at the peak of their fame, both Gandhi and Mao were consumed by their images. Gandhi had acted so long as a saint that he came to believe he was one. Alas, the fate of holy men. Mao, likewise, came to believe his idolators and to see himself as a colossus bestriding the world, while in reality, like many emperors of old, he had simply fallen into the hands of a palace faction led by his wife.

Gandhi only briefly outlived his legend. The new Indian government under Nehru inherited the responsibility of governing, and ahimsa could no longer be a guiding principle. Nehru immediately used troops to put down the communal riots and to assure the accession of Hyderabad, and he dispatched units to defend Kashmir from Pakistan. Official sources claimed Gandhi had approved these moves, but he never confirmed it. Gandhi himself realized he had become useful only as a legend, not as a leader of a great cause. Shortly after the Mahatma was killed in January 1948, General Smuts wrote to Churchill, "the saint has left us; for good, let's hope."

Mao's anachronistic period was much longer. According to Chinese leaders today it was twenty years too long. There was a saying in Peking that if Mao had died in 1946, he would have been China's Marx; if he had died in 1956, he would have been China's Lenin; or if he had passed on in 1966, China's Stalin; but instead he died in 1976 as China's Mao.

Both men understood that the organizations they had built would eventually destroy their respective ideals. Mao anticipated the bureaucratization of the Communist regime and he moved drastically to resist it by sanctioning mob action, kangaroo courts, and stints at farm labor. His objectives were to instill terror in party and government officials and to eradicate any sense of institutional loyalty and protection beyond allegiance to himself and his thoughts. To paraphrase Hannah Arendt, Mao's goal was simply to make every official, bureaucrat, and intellectual recognize that he or she would be safe only by repeating in the afternoon whatever Mao or *People's Daily* said in the morning.

Gandhi was also fearful of the corruption of power and suggested the Congress organization disband after Independence. Mao-like, he even advocated that officials and bureaucrats should spend time working in the villages. But unlike Mao, Gandhi was neither willing nor able to take concrete steps, much less violent ones, to purge the Congress or prevent the ossification of the bureaucracy. Gandhi, however, departed the scene before the cancer of corruption had infected the old party of Indian nationalism.

CHAPTER 6

New Societies and Old Attitudes

Revolution and Tradition

The over-turning of the old system in China beginning in 1949 was as complete as it was in the Soviet Union after 1917. The new social, economic, and political structures created by the Communist Party were even more foreign and revolutionary in China than they had been in European Russia. Suppression of political dissent, insistence on orthodoxy in every realm and deification of a leader were hardly new to China; but the physical liquidation of hundreds of thousands, if not over a million landlords, and assignment of the remainder to a new, inverted, hereditary class order was as sweeping in its effect as Qin Shi Huang's elimination of the feudal system in the third century B.C. The abolition of private landownership, which had existed for over 2,000 years, and the collectivization of agriculture and division of harvest and income within a village on the basis of hours worked were reforms unprecedented in scope and nature. The mass purging of intellectuals, and the creation of a whole new value system had also not been attempted for over 2,000 years.

The relative speed with which these and other sweeping reforms were carried out attest to China's readiness in the middle of the twentieth century to accept revolutionary change, the organizational skill of the Chinese, and a tradition among the masses and intellectuals to bend with the wind. The Chinese were also not so attracted to tradition as had been generally thought. In a novel, but insightful, observation, Lucien Pye has noted that the Chinese sense of greatness has been rooted in a profound awareness of their biological ties to their ancestors and of their enduring history; but there are few specific features of their civilization that they self-consciously value or feel they must fight to preserve. The Chinese do not have to work at being

Chinese, Pye suggested, and, thus, no specific traditions are seen as essential to maintain their identity. Consequently, they have been able to accept wholesale abandonment of old customs without any sense of being less Chinese because of it.

Nevertheless, much of traditional Chinese social life and most of the cultural attitudes that surrounded it still persist. The new Chinese society that Mao introduced represented a combination of Confucian and Leninist structures; but underneath, the old values and the old outlook on life remained little changed. In some ways the Chinese revolution, while dramatically altering social, political and economic institutions, at the same time intensified traditional attitudes toward authority and social relations.

Race and history are much less important factors in the Indian identity than the Chinese. Among Hindus, the trappings of culture and tradition provide the cement of collective feeling and a sense of belonging, and are, therefore, much more difficult to surrender. In India, therefore, old institutions, even many now widely considered undesirable, remain.

Almost every Indian politician and intellectual nowadays denounces caste; the Gandhian ideals of equality have been accepted in theory, but the Frankenstein of caste refuses to die, no matter how many legal stakes are driven into its heart. Instead, as in the past, the system adjusts and absorbs and, like a coral reef, is forever building, forever changing. Yet, when we examine closer, we are struck by the extent to which old social structures and traditional attitudes in India are eroding and new ones evolving.

Looking at modern China, the primary impression is of revolutionary change and the secondary one, the persistence of culture. In the case of India, we are struck first by the continuity of tradition, and secondly by the change that is taking place underneath the surface. Indian and Chinese societies traditionally were highly status-conscious, and group solidarity and the extended family played key roles in social relations. From these common roots have sprouted today's "feudal" modes of behavior, including the relative lack of a work-ethic or of a sense of public spirit or civic responsibility. Chinese and Indians alike can sit around on the job all day doing nothing and never feel a twinge of conscience. Both Indian and Chinese leaders frequently complain that feudal attitudes are the cause of persistent paternalism, corruption, nepotism, and resistance to initiative, reform, and acceptance of responsibility.

Typically, the Indians have been the most loquacious, discursive, self-flagellating, and pessimistic in their self-analysis. A leading Indian intellectual journal, *Seminar*, in 1982 devoted a whole issue to a discussion of the national character in the context of modernization.

The conclusions were almost unanimously dismal. The Indian was described as being: unable to see any linkage between his or her efforts and the goals he or she cherished, uncaring of the public good (or anything outside his own family and caste), unwilling to make decisions or take responsibility, guilty of hypocrisy and exaggerated self-importance, dependent and slavish toward his superiors, and so on.

Social critics in China are not given to psychoanalysis of the national psyche, but there has been a great deal of fulmination led by Deng Xiaoping himself about the tenacious hold of "feudal" ideas in China and the infuriating features of bureaucratism. These self-criticisms, while cast in Marxist and historical, rather than psychological, terms, are similar to the dissections made by Indian intellectuals.

The Chinese are among the world's top conformists, but Indians conform to much more differentiated roles than do the Chinese. Because of the unlimited number of these roles in India, and the great variety of caste, religious, racial, and other differences, Indians are more individualist than Chinese and less subject to discipline by political norms. While the Indian is a slavish conformist to the mores of caste and family and, like the Chinese, is usually servile toward his village or work-place superiors, he or she is even less concerned than the Chinese with conforming to community or national patterns that transcend these basic social units. While the leaders in Peking are frustrated by the continuation of "feudal" ideas in China and the threat to modernization that these entail, their problem is less than that faced by Indian modernizers. On the other hand, the centralized Chinese political economy, the one-party system, and the fixation on orthodoxy tend to perpetuate a modern version of the old patriarchal and patronage-ridden society of hierarchical relationships.

Family and the Work Unit

The new regime in Peking, with its activist approach to social engineering, has been attacking the problem of "feudal" ideas and social relations for more than three decades. In the cities, these efforts have had a considerable impact. Although there is a serious job shortage in China and, as is evident in any Peking shop or factory, much under-employment, almost all urban women below 55 years of age, including young mothers, have since the early 1950s been assigned full-time jobs. Babies and pre-schoolers are cared for in an extensive and impressive system of nurseries, most of which keep their charges six days and nights a week. The social purpose of this system has been to reduce the "feudal" centrality of the family and to encourage more loyalty and sense of responsibility to the party, the state, and "the people."

This approach was carried to an extreme during the Cultural Revolution, during which time the government went out of its way to assign couples to work in different cities. Even today it is not unusual to find men and women in China who have been married for 20 years or more, but who have never lived in the same city as their spouse. The Cultural Revolution witnessed other types of forced separation of families, as youth were sent off to the countryside and officials were dispatched to long stints in cadre schools in rural areas.

Such extremes have been ended, but concerted efforts to produce a civic rather than a family-oriented culture in China continue. The most striking result is the emergence of the work unit or *danwei* as the surrogate family or clan. Until 1986, when the revolutionary "contract labor" system was introduced, urban school leavers and almost all college graduates were assigned to an office, factory, shop, or institution. In the majority of cases this was a life-time assignment. The danwei still determines one's income, assigns living quarters, provides basic medical care, issues ration coupons for items ranging from rice to bicycles, allots scarce tickets to cultural events, arranges weekend outings, awards vacations (which are not automatic), approves marriages, and even allots quotas for births—one to each couple.

The familial nature of the work unit was exemplified in the practice of hiring children of employees. When a worker retired, a son or daughter would automatically be given a job, although a senior worker would, of course, move up into the position actually vacated. Whether the contract system will change this practice is unknown, but probably it will not.

It is uncertain how much the danwei has actually succeeded in inculcating loyalty to the work unit and in improving productivity. Combined with economic management reforms which allow enterprises more leeway in retention and use of profits, it is very likely continuing to have some effect in this regard. Still, official exhortations against poor labor discipline and the abuse and theft of unit property suggest that such a socialization process is a very long-term one. Continuation in practice although not in principle of the "iron rice bowl," or permanent guaranteed employment for workers taken on by a unit, has encouraged sloppy work-habits and low industrial productivity. The new directives authorizing the firing of incompetent workers has so far had limited effect on managers, who do not wish to make waves by dismissing employees.

Hindu philosophy's stress on relativity and unreality justifies the absence of an ethical concern among Indians to do a fair day's work for the money one receives, and also reinforces acceptance of corruption and the stealing of public or company property. India has no parallel to the danwei, except in tea and other plantations where cradle-to-grave care is provided and generations of employees succeed each other. Even on the plantations, however, companies would not dare interfere in personal decisions such as marriage or births. Some big companies, like those in the Tata group, have excellent labor relations and relatively good productivity records. But generally, work-place loyalty has hardly been a significant motivating factor in India; certainly it has had no effect in reducing the strength of family loyalties.

India does have its own "iron rice bowl" system in the modern "organized" sectors, private and public, mandated by law, union contracts, and long practice. Large private firms, as well as public-sector companies, in effect cannot retrench a regular worker either for economic reasons or for incompetence. Many companies consequently hire temporary workers, a tactic that is also used by life-time employment Japanese firms. But, unlike the case in Japan, neither the Chinese nor the Indian "iron rice bowl" has been very effective in spurring life-time employees to harder work.

The nuclear family, in terms of residence, has become the social pattern in both Indian and Chinese cities, and increasingly in the countryside as well. In India, separate lodging for various units of the extended urban family seems to have had limited effect so far on the actual strength of family ties, which remain paramount. This explains the conservatism of Indian society and the Indian reluctance to embrace radical changes which might endanger the social order and threaten the family. The Indian family system softens the effect of unemployment and poverty, the raw numbers of which are appalling. There are tens of thousands of unemployed college graduates in India, for example, but virtually all of them are supported by their families—if necessary, for life.

Chinese in the cities as well as the countryside also remain family-oriented; but significant changes are taking place in urban areas. Universal nursery-school boarding and the danwei system have had some limited but still important impact on watering down the centrality of the family in Chinese cities. More significant in the long term, however, will be the effect of the "one child" family policy. If this policy continues to be implemented with success in the cities, it will sharply reduce kinship possibilities by eliminating Chinese uncles, aunts, cousins, etc. The next generation of urban Chinese could constitute the most exclusive nuclear family structure the world has seen. It is hard to say what this may mean in social and psychological terms, but among other things, it could encourage development of the desired "civic culture" in urban China.

Another less talked about "feudal" legacy in both countries is the arbitrariness and high-handedness of authority and the individual's obsequious reaction to it. Over the past three decades the Chinese public has responded either enthusiastically or passively to whatever campaign, outlandish or not, the Peking government has promoted. There was no popular resistance, for example, to the squashing of the democracy wall movement in China in 1979, not only because China lacks a traditional democratic culture, but also because it has a culture of survival. On a less dramatic level, this means that subordinates, much more than in the West, tend to be "yes" men. The Chinese remain highly rank conscious; they pay great attention to the ordering of names and of positions in photos and motor convoys. At receptions and other functions, Chinese guests wait until the senior among them leaves, then they all decamp.

A survival strategy also dominates Indian society. Indians are notoriously deferential and sychophantic toward superiors who, in turn, are habitually autocratic. Because of the political system, however, Indians can—and freely do—lambast, denounce, and harass those in authority on whom they are not directly dependent. It is not unusual for city officials or university deans to be held prisoner in their offices by protesting citizens or students. No one in India is spared the righteous fury of the press; but when the iron fist is shown, as for example during the 1975–1977 emergency, Indians are also quick to crumble before power and authority.

The High and the Humble

Visitors are struck by the disparity in India between the very wealthy and the very poor, while the attire of Chinese still gives an egalitarian impression, particularly in the countryside. Numerous beggars in India and their relative scarceness in China are among the most vivid images that travelers carry away from the two countries.

Only about 2 percent of Indians ever beg (13 million, according to the 1971 census), but their numbers seem inflated by their persistence and their concentration in favorite localities. Indian culture is tolerant and indifferent toward beggars, who are seen as living out their destiny. The ritual of the ascetic, begging his meals, and the custom of giving alms before a temple or holy place also has provided the profession a certain tradition, if not respectability.

Today, the government has shelters for lepers and other incapacitated persons; but life in such places is austere by Indian standards, and grim by western ones, and many handicapped Indians prefer a life of begging. Occasionally, the Indian government tries to clear beggars off the street. Fifteen states and two union territories have anti-begging laws, but these are only sporadically enforced. Sanjay Gandhi sometimes ordered beggars in the capital rounded up and trucked out of town. Members of Parliament, however, complained that every Indian, including beggars, had the right to live where he or she chose, and, sure enough, the beggars always returned.

During the Asian games in 1982, some $600,000 was spent to keep all the Delhi beggars in homes during the length of the events, and while the 1983 Non-Aligned Meeting was in progress in the city, local beggars were given government employment in out-of-the-way locations.

If full freedom of movement existed in China as in India, many of the 100–200 million Chinese peasants living on bare subsistence would pour into the big cities, as they did before the Revolution. In 1979, during the Democracy Wall period of political relaxation, thousands of dirt-poor farmers did come into Peking to petition for government relief. They were soon persuaded to leave.

With the new rural reforms and relaxation of controls in the mid–1980s, many more mendicants are making their way into Chinese cities. In November 1986, the *Shanghai Liberation Daily* reported that in 1985 more than 9,000 vagrants and beggars had been rounded up in the city and shipped back to their home villages. In the people's restaurants of Shanghai and China's other big cities one can occasionally spot a bedraggled adult or child begging food from the tables. The Chinese police, however, usually keep such specimens away from tourist-frequented spots. The appearance of abject poverty is still suppressed in China, while in India it is allowed to flaunt itself.

Under Mao, China also reduced to a minimum conspicuous consumption as well as conspicuous poverty. Even under the Dengist reforms, no one in China has wealth comparable to that of the very rich in India. You can see the latter at the polo fields in Calcutta with the Victoria Memorial looming in the mist; you will find them at the stuffy old Bengal Club; and in the huge new cricket stadium in Bangalore, which can seat thousands of curiously avid fans; or else in the air-conditioned, deluxe booths at the Bombay Turf Club. You can see their handsome, English-speaking children arriving at the Taj Coromandel in Madras for swimming lessons, and their beautiful wives in vivid silk sarees at the Delhi International Center, attending a conference on some serious subject. They ride on Indian airlines, in the new executive class when that is available; they usually have relatives in America or in England, and certainly they have been abroad. They live in seas of green lawn, in large houses that can be seen from the road. They fly to Srinagar for skiing; they keep their sailboats in Bombay; and they entertain each other with lavish banquets of fiery food. They are the new Maharajas.

In China, the high and mighty, by comparison, lead austere lives; but juxtaposed to the lifestyle of the average Chinese, it is quite another world. Except for the emperor and his family, Chinese officials of old did not usually reveal their status in public displays; today, except when meeting foreigners, high cadre usually wear the same style as everyone else, although made from better material. But they travel in the back of curtained limousines, they attend banquets at the Great Hall or at fancy hotels, they have private showings of movies, and they live in houses whose addresses are unknown. They have telephones and servants; but most important of all, they have power and influence, which until recently were the only coin of the realm. They are the new Mandarins.

Disparities

Poverty is divided differently in India and China. According to World Bank estimates, the distribution of rural income in China in 1980 was about the same as in India. That is, the richest 10 percent in the Indian countryside received 28 percent of rural income, and in China the same top percentile received 23 percent. The poorest 40 percent in both rural India and rural China at the end of each year took home approximately the same percentage of total income—20 percent.[50] The difference is that in China poverty tended to be divided geographically, whereas in India it was socially determined.

In individual Chinese villages in the PRC, the range of income distribution tended to be narrow. The great majority of households in any one village was either relatively well-off, very poor, or fell into a middle category. Exceptions to the average household income in a village were primarily among those households that had either above-average or below-average numbers of able-bodied workers. In other words, Chinese villages and their respective occupants as a group could be classified as poor, middle-class, or well-off.

The incentive systems introduced in China in the 1980s have added new elements of income disparity within each village—different levels of initiatives and industriousness. Generally speaking, however, the income level of most Chinese peasants is still determined in large part by the conditions of the village in which she or he happens to be born. Today, those peasants lucky enough to live near cities are specializing in vegetables and dairy products for the urban market and many are joining the ranks of the "10,000 yuan households."

Thus, as a Chinese journal stated in 1982, it is still true today that "rich" peasants in poor areas in China often have lower incomes than "poor" peasants in rich areas.[51] In essence, the place where one is born in China, rather than one's parents (as in India), has determined the individual's economic status. Those peasants who live in the old revolutionary base areas of the Red Army, for example, remain among the poorest of the poor. According to the *Shanxi Peasant News* of September 20, 1984, over 3 million peasants in the province's historic revolutionary areas still earned less than US $50 annual income per capita. The reforms in agricultural policy in China have, however, also benefitted the poorer farmers who live on less productive land, by allowing them free reign to raise pigs, engage in other private production, or shift to jobs in service or local industry.

The income per person of the top 4 percent of landowners in India is only about three times that of the landless households. This is not an extremely high differential, and if comparable figures were available on the per capita income of the top 4 percent and the bottom 28 percent of Chinese rural households, the difference would very likely be as high or higher. The figures on Chinese and Indian per capita income, however, do not reflect differences in property wealth, which in India are extremely unbalanced. In Indian villages, economic power, based on land ownership, translates into both social and political power. In China there is no private land ownership as such. But those households which, under the new incentive system, have greatly increased their income compared to that of their neighbors are evolving into a political as well as an economic elite. Many of the newly prosperous farmers are former rural cadre who know how to work the system.

There is a much greater difference between the two countries in urban income inequality. As the World Bank notes, in China there is an extraordinarily low degree of urban inequality. The share of the poorest 40 percent in

Chinese cities is almost double that in India (30 percent versus about 17 percent). Similarly, the richest 10 percent in India enjoy more than twice the share of total income as the similar group in Chinese cities. This results from the absence of control in India either on how many rural poor can flock into the cities or, with some exceptions, on the accumulation of wealth at the other end of the scale.

The new "rich" class in China's cities consists of the small businessmen who run noodle shops, garment stores, or provide repair and other services. These private households or "getihu" may earn from three to ten times the average per capita urban income. But the amount is still relatively small, the equivalent of several hundred to several thousand U.S. dollars.

The Rural Poor

Large areas of absolute poverty continue to exist in both India and China. The number of Chinese peasants who live on subsistence levels is uncertain. The World Bank's *World Development Report for 1982* estimated that there were at least 150 million Chinese "with living standards little better than those of the absolutely poor in other countries." Elsewhere, the same report estimated that 20 percent of the 1 billion people in the world living in absolute poverty were in China. A Chinese economist in a 1982 *Peking Review* article said that one-third of the peasantry, which would be about 260 million people, were still living in poverty. According to a Chinese media report, about 100 million peasants in 1980 were earning only US $10 a year in cash income, and received less than 150 kilograms in food grains from their production teams, the equivalent of 1,400 calories per day. Ten percent of production teams distributed between 150–180 kilograms. Another report stated that by 1981 the percentage of the rural population with total per capita income in cash and kind below US $75 fell from 65 percent in 1978 to 20 percent in 1981.

On August 12, 1985, *People's Daily*, in an article on income distribution in Heilongjiang Province, stated that "well-off" households—those with a per capita income of more than 500 yuan (about US $132 at the 1986 exchange rate, or about US $250 at the 1980 rate) constituted 18 percent of those surveyed, and those who "earn just enough to cover food and clothing," i.e., with incomes between 200 and 500 yuan, accounted for 60 percent of rural households. One-fifth of the rural population surveyed in the province had a per capita annual income of under 200 yuan. The *China Daily* on September 28, 1985, reported that 11 percent of rural households nationwide had per capita annual incomes below 200 yuan. According to China's first National Symposium on the Economic and Cultural Development of Impoverished Areas, held in 1986, sixty million people in China were living below the poverty line, defined as per capita income of about US $40 plus 200 kilograms of grain.

At least 300 million Indians are estimated to live below the poverty line. Together, the Indian and Chinese rural poor thus constitute about one-half of the one billion people on earth who live on bare subsistence or not far above. In India, the very poor, especially the untouchables, who make up one-half or more of those in the poverty category, are culturally as well as economically deprived, and for many the rise from poverty and backwardness will be a task of generations. Untouchables continue to live as outcastes in segregated hamlets. They are probably still 80–90 percent illiterate and overwhelmingly landless. In some areas of the north, the local establishment simply does not allow untouchables to own land.

A typical upper-caste conservative attitude was expressed by a landowner from Bihar who claimed that when untouchables were given land, they did not know what to do with it—"they'll let it lie," he asserted, "and instead, work another man's fields for wages." The statement reflects a deep prejudice, but there is in fact a pervasive attitude of dependency among untouchables which springs from thousands of years of servitude and ignorance. It also reflects the continuation in many areas of India of an oppressive traditional system of village life in which the dominant land-owning castes combine with marginal land-owners and other poorer "backward" castes to keep down the 20 to 30 percent in the village who are the outcastes. The situation is akin to that which existed in the American rural South as late as the 1960s, in which poor whites with the encouragement of the local establishment and connivance of local authorities intimidated and sometimes terrorized blacks into passive acceptance of their degraded and subservient status.

In China, there were traditionally few, if any, social barriers to the poor improving themselves if they could. Some did, but most, of course, did not because of harsh conditions, high population density, low technology, and also the cultural effect of generations of poverty. From 1957 until 1978, working collectively, most of the lowest income villages in China also failed to make much progress in productivity, although their health and life-span improved and their literacy rate went up. The imposed disabilities that the very poor face in Communist China have been politically, not socially, sanctioned.

During Mao's life, former landlords, rich peasants, and their descendants formed an "outcaste" group at the bottom rung of each village's economic and social order. At the same time, all Chinese peasants were denied the right to decide how to organize themselves economically and to a large extent what to plant. Chinese economists now admit that requiring all farming areas to give priority to grain, whatever the nature of the soil, and insisting on collective farming in isolated mountainous and low-productivity areas made backward peasants even poorer. These restrictions have now largely ended.

One major political disability, however, remains, although it is now being significantly modified. Under Mao, the Chinese peasant was denied the last resort of the poor—to pick up and move. Until recently, there were only three ways in which a Chinese peasant could permanently leave the village or the locality in which he or she was born: (1) through marriage, in which case the woman usually moved to the village of her husband; (2) by passing the university entrance exam, at which only 3 percent of the college-age group nationwide and probably about 1 percent in rural areas succeeded; or (3) by joining the People's Liberation Army or volunteering to work in the mines.

Today peasants are in fact encouraged to leave field work and move to provincial towns, middle sized cities, market communities, and satellites of large cities to find jobs. An immense migration—one of the largest in human history—has taken place in the last five years, as underemployed labor in the countryside has been permitted to flow into old country towns and new urban areas.

Peasants are still forbidden the right to emigrate to the biggest cities, but thousands are finding it possible to avoid the restrictions and to live in the large metropolises as temporary workers or outside the system entirely. According to the *China Law Journal* in 1986, 3.21 million temporary residents were living in China's top ten cities that year.

China's Elite

China invented bureaucracy along with its raw material—paper. The first emperor, Qin Shi Huang, insisted on going through 100 pounds of documents each day before retiring, and this quantitative approach has continued. The party bureaucratic establishment, which today numbers about 20 million officials, has become as entrenched as the Confucian imperial class of old China.

Before the recent dismantling of the communes, the 20 million figure included the 10–20 state cadre assigned to each of the 50,000 communes in China and the 4 or 5 assigned to each of the 50,000 brigades, but not to other staff members of the commune or the local leaders and administrative staff of the 5 million production teams. Since the reforms, the number of rural cadre has diminished. The total cadre figures do not include the approximately 8 million teachers in the country. The Chinese Communist Party membership stands at about 44 million; the 18 million party members who are not cadre would include many of the teachers, but mostly rank-and-file workers, peasants, and soldiers. While enjoying a certain local status, party members who are not also cadre have very limited influence and do not belong in the elite category.

The governing of China—the management of its agriculture and industry, the development of its arts and sciences, the direction of education, control of the media, trade unions and mass organizations, and direction of the police and armed forces—is in the hands of 20 million people (about 2 percent of the population). Its members range from the most junior cadre to the Party Chairman and its structures extend from district committees to the Politburo.

This elite is an enormous pyramid, tied together by lines of bureaucratic and party authority; but the size of the pyramid, larger than most countries in the United Nations, makes it difficult to monitor compliance with central directives, and its components thus tend to become independent kingdoms. There are few positions in China outside of this elite that have prestige, and thus membership in it, as earlier in the scholar-official ranks, is the most valued social goal of young aspiring Chinese. This elite constitutes China's urban middle class in terms of its standard of living and cultural level. A mid-ranking cadre with 15 years service may make three times what a worker earns. This is not a high differential, but in China, cash remuneration is less important than authority, influence, and "perks." The initial core of this elite were party and People's Liberation Army veterans. Political swings during the years allowed in new aspirants, often without technical or administrative qualifications, and counter-swings readmitted those previously purged. Deng Xaioping rehabilitated almost 3 million cadre who had been purged between 1952–1976, but he fired few of the upstarts who had taken their place.

The gerontocracy of the Chinese Politburo and a similar aging problem at other leadership levels underscores the self-perpetuating nature of the elite in China. Cadre have fought retirement tooth-and-nail, for to leave office is to abandon all influence and status.

For 33 years virtually no one retired from the biggest bureaucracy in history unless for urgent health reasons. Even when purged, they continued on the rolls. Over-staffing and inefficiency became endemic. In the summer of 1981 half of the 600,000 central government officials in Peking reportedly went on vacation at the same time, without affecting operations in the least.[52] The number of ministerial-rank officials grew to 98 and the number of vice-ministers to over 900.

Deng Xiaoping saw the inertia, conservatism, and ineffectiveness of the bureaucracy as the greatest obstacle to implementation of his reforms. In August, 1981, Deng scathingly denounced Chinese officialdom:

> The bureaucratic phenomena are the most serious problem for our nation and party. The major manifestations of bureaucratism are: looking down on the people, abusing political power, departing from reality, being separated from the masses, speaking empty words, having ossified ideology, blindly observing absurd regulations, creating redundant organizations, having more people than needed, avoiding decision-making, indifference to efficiency, irresponsibility, betraying trust, multiplying red tape, blocking each other, retaliating against others, suppressing democracy, cheating superiors as well as subordinates, taking bribes, and accummulating personal wealth.[53]

Not surprisingly, Deng gave high priority to overhauling the bureaucracy.

In 1982 he ordered a one-third reduction of the 600,000 cadre at central government headquarters in Peking. He consolidated the number of ministries and commissions to 52 and reduced vice-ministerial level officials to less than 300. New appointments also reduced the average age of ministers and vice-ministers from 64 to 58, and increased the percentage with college education from 37 to 52 percent.[54] To ease out the overaged, the incompetent, and the superfluous, Deng in 1982 came up with an attractive retirement package that not only allowed continuation of full salary, with an additional amount added for each year of service, but retention of quarters, telephones, use of cars, continued access to internal documents, and appointment of some senior elders as councillors or advisors. Re-training and eventual reassignment was promised to the one-third of those below retirement age deemed redundant.

By the summer of 1983 Deng had finally persuaded 470,000 veteran officials, who had held posts before the communist takeover 34 years before, to retire. Within two years, another 700,000 were drawing pensions. Deng was rapidly moving a new generation into office. By the end of 1985, only 13 of the 42 ministers in the State Council had held their posts before the Twelfth Party Congress in September 1982, and only one of 29 provincial party secretaries was a hold-over. At the party delegate conference in 1985, most of the newcomers were elected into the Central Committee, a move which reflected the preeminence of the reformist and technocratic new generation.

The resumption in 1977 of strict academic standards for entry into universities had signalled the return of an achievement-oriented society ruled by a virtuous elite chosen on the basis of merit. Although only about half of today's 20 million officials finished high school, education once more has become the source of power and status in China. Formal acceptance of the official orthodoxy, as in the past, will be required of the elite and the would-be elite, but it is clear that the Chinese meritocracy has been revived.

The rural elite in China until very recently has been primarily bureaucratic: local government officials, schoolteachers, and to a lesser extent party committee leaders in the villages. Those members of this elite who are part of the state cadre system generally earn higher incomes than the average peasant household. Before the Dengist reforms that transformed agriculture, the main advantages of the cadre elite were their perquisites and the more interesting and less taxing nature of the work they did. In the 1980s, however, rural cadre took the lead in exploiting the sudden opportunities that opened to begin private specialized pursuits such as growing chickens commercially or leasing out transportation or farm machines.

The new members of the upper class in the Chinese countryside consist of these former cadre-turned entrepreneurs and other peasant households which have taken off under the household-farming system. A few families in a village may earn enough to become "10,000 yuan households," that is about US $2,600 in total income. Surveys by the State Statistical Bureau, however, indicate that only 1.4 percent of peasant families are so well-off. According to one Chinese report, 43 percent of rich peasants are in fact local cadre or former cadre, and 42 percent are "rural intellectuals" (mostly former city students sent to the countryside during the 1960s and early 1970s) or retired servicemen. While this new rural economic elite constitutes only a small fraction of the peasant population, they already number more than two million. Given their ties to the local bureaucracies these well-off peasants and rural entrepreneurs are probably evolving as a major element in the new social order.

New Elites and Old Castes

India in many ways is still a brahmanical society, but in important aspects this tradition has drastically changed. Only two or three percent of the population are brahmans, but a good percentage of these are not in the modern elite at all. Many remain in their traditional religious roles. It is still mostly brahmans who act as priests in the tens of thousands of Hindu temples across the country, or squat on the banks of the Ganges and other holy places to perform the required rituals for pilgrims, or who come to America as gurus. Some brahmans have fallen on hard times and one finds brahman taxi-drivers and clerks.

But most brahmans have left the villages and abandoned their priestly duties to assume roles in the new, modern, urban elite. This process has been going on for more than a century. The great majority of India's English-educated establishment, its doctors and other professionals, its senior government officials, and the nawobs of Indian academe, are the "twice-born." All of India's prime ministers and the leaders of its major political parties have been brahmans. In old India, for a brahman to advocate egalitarianism was a contradiction in terms, but today those intellectuals and leftists who are calling for liberal reforms or radical change are usually brahmans or other upper castes. Sixty percent of the Politburo of the two major communist parties are upper caste, and their leaders are brahmans. Even the Maoist Naxilites, who waged rural and urban terrorism in the late 1960s and early 1970s, were from the top hierarchy of Aryan families.

Caste still permeates Indian social life. Marriages, including those of the educated middle-class and the urban elite, are with rare exception strictly within caste lines. Those intellectuals who marry without regard for caste are, in effect, members of a new caste and their children marry each other. Likewise, those untouchables (since Gandhi's day called Harijans, meaning "children of God") who, through the system of affirmative action or "reservations" have risen to prestigious positions, such as officers in the Indian administrative and foreign services, become themselves another caste—"the new brahmans." Their daughters and sons marry the children of other successful untouchables or sometimes of liberated upper-caste families. So far, this generation of uplifted untouchables has shown little social or political commitment to the cause of their poor and often still oppressed communities.

Village Moslems and Christians continue to conduct their social lives in groups based on the caste of their ancestors. Rural untouchables who have converted to Islam or Christianity find their positions unchanged; they still must live in separate hamlets and bear the same social disabilities as in the past. Even among the Sikhs, who theoretically abandoned caste, untouchables live separately, use separate wells, and in many Sikh villages separate temples. Those Indians who have been urban Christians for generations also cannot abandon caste, and they still usually marry within their traditional caste communities.

But the social structure in India is slowly changing. The growing market economy in India's rural areas and land-reform laws have not altered the landownership picture so much as they have undermined the traditional symbiosis of caste in the village. When a cow died in the old days the untouchables would be called to take it away; they could eat the flesh, tan the hide, and make implements of the bones. But now the carcass is more likely sold to a townsman who specializes in such matters. In the traditional village, the untouchables were obliged to serve the dominant and land-owning families as laborers and artisans, but the land-owners were also required to see after the minimum needs of the workers and their families. To avoid tenancy laws, most Indian landlords have now ended, or nominally ended, share-cropping arrangements and now simply hire laborers for wages. With the increasing switch to cash remuneration, the organic village life of ancient India is dying, although the economic web of paternalism has by no means been destroyed. Landowners, employers, and other members of the dominant castes continue to be the main money-lenders to the poor because, unlike banks and credit cooperatives set up by the government, they will lend money for consumption purposes—the main reason landless villagers borrow money. While economic dependency remains, however, attitudes have been markedly altered, not only by social and economic changes in the countryside but also by urbanization, politics, and mass communications.

Indian society is now divided not only vertically by social caste, but horizontally, by economic class. This, together with the pattern of increasing urban migration, has provided the individual and family a mobility that traditional India never had. It has also changed the nature of the establishment.

Most of the economic upper class in India, and especially the super rich "new maharajas," are not upper caste; brahmans dominated feudal capital in India, but they do not control the industrial capital of today. Many brahmans are found in business, but the new economic elite of India are by and large non-brahman, non-traditional Hindu, minorities, or members of hereditary communities which have risen from lowly caste status since British rule began. The Marwaris, a Jain group from Rajasthan, for example, control most of the trade in all of the north of India. The Mawaries, including the great Birla family dynasty of Calcutta, are said by some to own as much as 60 percent of the capital of India. The Chittiars, once poor toddy-tappers in Tamil Nadu, are now among the most prominent businessmen in the south and are found in trade throughout India. Bombay is under the economic sway of non-Hindu Parsees, such as the mighty Tatas, and of various commercial castes from Gujarat. Meanwhile, Sikhs and other Punjabis of the old Jat cultivator caste have spread throughout India as tradesmen and entrepreneurs, especially in transport.

The rural elite in India consist of about 10 million families, or about 13 percent of the total land-owing households who cultivate 57 percent of the total arable land, rather similar to the land tenure situation in pre-revolutionary China. Medim-sized farmers who operate 2–4 hectares, or about another 20 percent of the cultivated land area, can produce a surplus if the land is irrigated. Thus perhaps a third of these 11.6 million families could be said to belong to the lower level of the rural elite.[55]

While wealthy by local standards, only a few of the "large" rural holdings are of extravagant size. More than half of the 57 percent owned by the highest category is held by farmers who have between 4 and 10 hectares. The cream of the rural elite are the top 3 percent of families who own more than 10 hectares and account for 26 percent of total land-holdings. With increasing population, average holdings have declined, including those among the top 3 percent, from 18 hectares to 17.5 hectares; much larger holdings, however, are possible through the device of assigning ownership to a wide range of family members, some or most of whom are not working on the land. Other big farmers lease land from small and marginal owners who cannot make a living operating their small plots. Thus, in the Punjab and other areas, particularly in the north, some farmers operate farms of 100 hectares or more. The big and medium land-owners generally have a high literacy rate and are receptive to learning and applying the new agricultural technology.

City Life

A striking difference in Indian and Chinese urban areas is in the color and sound of street life. Indian cities are living caravans of humanity. Beggars and rich merchants, the fat and the thin, cult figures and soldiers, the beautiful and the ugly sweep in torrents through the streets. An Indian market assaults one's senses with a dizzying array of spectacles, ranging from the sublime to the depraved. A Chinese market, on the other hand, while not without its variety and certainly its noise, impresses the nerves with a sense of uniformity. The Chinese have taken to department stores, large, gloomy buildings, stocked with an impressive display of clothing, hardware, and other consumables, while Indians prefer their bazaars with thousands of small merchants peddling everything from rich silk to betel nut to television sets.

The busy commercial streets of Peking, like Wang Fujiing and DaJyalar, are packed with Chinese shoppers; but compared to Indian bazaars, the crowds as well as the shops and the range of goods displayed are unexciting. Having stamped out individual enterprise and retail businesses in the 1950s and 1960s, the Chinese are now fostering their growth. There were, for example, over 10,000 restaurants in Peking in 1949; but in 1980 there were only about 600, and most of these were the Chinese version of fast-food places, serving noodles and other sorts of cheap, standard fare. Private stalls and shops are now multiplying in Peking and elsewhere in China, but retail commerce in the cities still has the look of collective rather than free enterprise. In Indian cities, half the population seems to be selling something to the other half, most of whom are hawking some service of their own.

Traditionally, public urban areas in Asia have been neglected, not to say unclean. China, to some extent, has changed this situation. Although new buildings in China soon begin to look shoddy, unlike India they are not immediately stained with urine and betel juice. In China, assigned residents diligently sweep the narrow hutongs and an army of street cleaners, some motorized, pick up after the avidly littering public. Indians of the sweeper caste also strive to tidy up Indian cities, but in a more desultory fashion.

Indian streets, however, are alive with animal life and this complicates the task of the sweepers. Mongrels only somewhat less than cows abound, and monkeys, camels, and other strange beasts are common sights. In Indian parks one hears a cacophony of bird calls, although cawing predominates. Kites, vultures, and other threateningly large fowl circle overhead.

In China, animals which do not serve or feed man are rare indeed. Dogs, running and otherwise, have been liquidated from Chinese city streets. Even the famed Pekinese is no more. In 1983, Peking municipal authorities began a campaign to wipe out the 400,000 dogs living in the rural and suburban areas of the city. Mao's campaign in the 1950s against birds and flies was only too successful. In the parks of Peking and other cities, birds sing only in the morning when old men gather with their cages. When the birds disappeared in China, bugs became a problem and so the authorities pulled up what little grass existed around the cities to deny breeding places for insects; this, in turn, increased the dust storms of Peking. Pigeons and some other species of birds, as well as grass, are making a comeback in China, but song-birds are still rare even in much of the countryside.

More in China's favor is the relative absence of flies in most Chinese cities, even in open-air meat-markets. In Indian markets one rarely sees fresh meat displayed, although there is plenty of it on the hoof. Even without this attraction, Indian flies have enjoyed their own population explosion.

Death, as well as life, is also more in evidence in India. At all times of day and night shrouded bodies wait patiently for cremation at holy places.

Vultures soar above the Towers of Silence in Bombay, funeral boats glide through the waterways of Srinagar, and the goddess of death is worshipped throughout the land. In a modern Chinese city, one can live for years and never see a funeral and few signs of death. The grim reaper, autonomous and unpredictable, is best kept out of sight in a well-ordered society.

Other things nakedly exposed in India are hidden in China. China has no counterpart to the open Indian suburbs, where dwells the motor-scooter middle class; and the residences of Chinese leaders are hidden behind walled hutungs or in once-imperial parks, now closed to the public. The Prime Minister's residence and office compound in New Delhi is on a busy street corner and the President's Palace is one of the major features of the city. In China, no one even knows for sure where the leadership lives, much less has seen these abodes. Zhongnanhai, next to the Forbidden City, where Mao and many of his colleagues lived, remains a cloistered, private preserve. Until recent years, the park to the north of the Forbidden City was also closed to the public because it gave a distant view from its hill down into the exclusive residential area.

In India and China, as elsewhere in the world, social change is taking place rapidly in the large cities. In China, the danwei system, relative economic leveling, the one-child-per-family program, and recent cultural and economic liberalization are building a new modern society around traditional attitudes. It is not quite the society either Mao or Marx envisioned, but despite the reemergence of old values, it has been a revolutionary change in social structure.

In Indian cities, caste is eroding more quickly than in the countryside and new attitudes are emerging within the old structures. In cities, the Indian upper classes can segregate themselves from the poor, but caste can no longer put distance between them. In the old days an untouchable had to sound a clapper to warn others of his approach or, if he saw an upper caste coming down the road, he was obliged to climb a tree or hide himself so that the mere sight of him would not pollute a superior being. But in the cities of India today, brahman and untouchable press against each other in the streets, the buses, and the trains. Sometimes the upper-caste commuter rushes home to bathe, and in cities, as well as in the countryside, food and drink stalls still provide throwaway clay bowls for the fastidious. But ideas of pollution have to be amended if one is to live in an Indian city.

Urbanization

Urbanization has been relatively slow in both countries, but significantly faster in India than in China. According to the 1982 census 20 percent of Chinese resided in cities and towns, up from 18 percent in 1964. India's urban population, according to the 1981 census, was almost 24 percent of the total, about the average of all low-income countries. The number of

Indian cities with more than half a million in population more than tripled between 1960 and 1980, while the number in China only slightly more than doubled. The agricultural reforms in China in the 1980s, however, allowed a massive readjustment to begin. By 1984, tens of millions of Chinese peasants had left the farm for urban residence, mostly in provincial townships. According to the World Bank, urban population rose 10 percent from 1982 to 1984.

From 1971–1981 India's urban population grew by a record 46 percent. According to Indian census figures, 39 percent of urban residents in India in 1971 were rural migrants, of which 26 percent were from outside the host state.[56] Comparable figures on China are not available, but very likely in 1980 a much smaller percentage of Chinese urban residents were born in the countryside. That percentage is now increasing.

In times past, the Chinese government actually shifted urban population out of the cities. Beginning in 1960 there was a decrease in the urban proportion of China's population and a net outflow of city population into the rural areas from 1960–1976.[57] Although this statistical phenomenon was due, in part, to a change in the definition of urban areas, it also reflected an actual movement of residents from Shanghai and other Chinese cities into remote areas. During the Cultural Revolution about 20 million youths were sent to the countryside.

Migration of the rural poor to Indian cities has led to the proliferation of slums, extreme pressure on basic services, including sanitation, and major problems of pollution. Chinese planners are now deliberately encouraging a similar rural exodus as a key part of their development program. The seventh five year plan called for the rapid growth of small and medium-sized cities to absorb the burgeoning rural population, which is 30 to 50 percent underemployed. At least 60 million peasants have already quit the rice and wheat fields of China and taken up jobs in local industry or commerce. U.S. census researchers believe that by the year 2000, 50 percent of China's population will be urban dwellers. Clearly, as the tide rushes on, China is going to face immense problems of urban health, education, jobs, environmental protection, and law and order.

Even with the strict controls of the past on migration, China's major metropolises already suffer from urban sprawl, industrial blight, and overcrowding. In India there is one room for every 2.8 persons.[58] In China, where new housing construction until 1980 was seriously neglected, there were in that year only 4 square meters of urban housing per person. By 1984 this had risen to 4.8 square meters. Thus India and China both fell in the range of the average developing country ratio of three persons per room.[59] Increased spending on housing under Deng's regime and the opening up of privately owned housing have improved the picture in China in recent years; but overcrowding probably remains about on the same scale as in India. In India, 17 percent of urban residents do not have ready access to safe water and 13 percent lack access to excreta disposal. Residences in the older sections of Chinese cities also do not have piped water or toilets, although public facilities are usually fairly nearby.

Urban public transport is overcrowded in both countries. Both, however, succeed somehow in moving millions to and from work each day. The urban system in China is supplemented by tens of millions of bicycles, while in India private transport includes a wide array to suit the pocketbook: rickshaws, pedi-cabs, pony carts, 3- and 4-wheel taxis, and the occasional Mercedes.

The single largest cities in India and China were both creations of the Western imperialist age. Today among the crowded mega-cities of the world, Calcutta and Shanghai reflect the problems and the promise of their nations.

Calcutta

If Banaras excites the senses, then Calcutta deadens them. In no other city on earth can one see tens of thousands sleeping under the stars on the pavements and thousands of barefoot men, young and old, mostly dark, pulling ancient rickshaws along the streets. Carriages and even stage-coaches clump along in the choking fumes of rattletrap taxis, dilapidated trams and double-decker buses bursting with humanity, tilting crazily, scraping their undercarriages on the streets. A constant flow of humanity jams the miles of arcade along Chowringhee Street. They flow in their white-shrouded millions along the wide pedestrian walks along Howrah Bridge, fill the narrow lanes in the busti or slum areas, and sleep in the inferno of the largest railway station in the world.

Calcutta is the center of the greatest concentration of poor anywhere—East India and Bangladesh. There is no other city for 500 miles around except Dacca, from which, not to, the hungry flee. People go to Bombay to make money, Indians say, to New Delhi to get power, to Calcutta to survive.

They have been coming since 1947, the year Bengalis call The Year of Partition, not the Year of Independence. The 1971 war with Pakistan set off another flood of several million Hindu and Moslem Bengali refugees; but as many migrants have come to Calcutta from the poor villages of West Bengal and other Indian states, in particular Bihar and Uttar Pradesh to the west and Orrisa to the south.

Most of the migrants are men who send almost everything they earn, perhaps 80¢ a day, back to their families in the countryside. But families also come and set up hovels in any vacant spot the police will allow, mostly in the bustis which are located on the outskirts of the city, sprawling along the Hooghly River. The misery and the hunger is bad, but it is better in Calcutta than at home. At least one can scavenge.

It is no wonder that standards steadily deteriorate, not only of city services, but some of the human kind as well. One easily becomes inured, then blind to both suffering and ugliness. Privacy, little known in normal times, shrinks to near oblivion. People defecate along with animals and copulate in dark but crowded rooms.

But the miracle of it all is that this huge, teeming city, with 2 million unemployed and several million surplus males, functions. It has not become ungovernable. It somehow transports millions every day to and from work, and water still gurgles out of standing pipes in the slums, electricity goes on and off every day, but still usually more on than off, and most of those desperate men and women who have fled here find some balm, however little. With big industry in the port of Calcutta long stagnant, work is somehow found for most of the migrants, primarily in hundreds of thousands of workshops, small cottage industries, tiny stores and stalls, shoeshine kits, and individual rickshaws. There are many thin, underfed people about, but no one is starving.

Even more remarkable is the fact that human conduct in Calcutta, despite its cracks and the necessary coating of insensitivity, has not degenerated. Calcutta is still the cultural center of India. Bengali poets, dramatists, dancers and film makers are unsurpassed anywhere in the world in their creativity. The countless bookstores, theaters, and studios of the city attest to its intellectual atmosphere. Four Nobel prizes have been won by residents of Calcutta, the last, of course, being Mother Teresa. Crime in Calcutta is less than in other major Indian cities and certainly much less than in New York. There are 1.4 males to every 1 female in the city, but rape and murder are relatively rare. Homicides are in the hundreds not thousands. Many may be unreported, but it is clear that acts of individual violence are not high. The struggle for survival, for space, and the constant press of humanity has not led to a dog-eat-dog environment.

The potential for explosive group violence, as distinct from individual violence, is apparent in Calcutta as elsewhere in India. Probably 50,000 were killed in the 1947 communal riots and several thousand others died in the Maoist-Naxallite guerrilla conflict of the late 1960s and early 1970s. In the spring of 1982 in Calcutta, fourteen members of a controversial religious sect were torn limb from limb by a mob; gang-fights also occur over turf, prostitution, gambling, and smuggling; and a riot may erupt over a one penny raise in tram fares. But these sorts of outbreaks, horrendous as they have been, are sporadic. Despite the rising tide of Moslem refugees who have raised West Bengal's Moslem population to almost 22 percent, there has been no significant communal violence in Calcutta between Hindu and Moslem for almost 20 years.

The degree of social order that continues within the chaos of Calcutta is a tribute to the strength of the Indian family system and to the inherent stability of Indian society. The street sleepers do not cause trouble. They are saving every paisa to send back to their families in the villages. An enormous sense of responsibility guides the lives of these poor and illiterate people, and gives Calcutta a soul that other cities might envy.

Shanghai

Shanghai is a totally different world today than it was 50 years ago; 30,000 prostitutes, as many beggars, and several times more drug addicts have disappeared. The large foreign community, both the fun-lovers and the evangelists who lived, worked, played, and prayed together in the international settlement, have gone like so many other nomadic tribes who latched on to a bit of China for a while.

Yet in some ways Shanghai is still very familiar. Of all the great cities of the world it has probably changed its physical appearance less than any other. Except for the vanishing of the neon signs in the metropolitan section, the old Bund is almost exactly as it was when the Japanese attacked the city in 1937. The best hotels, like almost half the factories and machinery in Shanghai, are also 50 or more years old. But new highrise hotels and office buildings are now rearing up over the Huangpu River. A new band of foreigners—diplomats and representatives of about 50 companies—are returning to the old haunts. Once again, the swing band plays Jimmy Dorsey numbers in the Peace Hotel, and a steak dinner can be had at the old Cercle Sportiff, today called the Jinjiang Club, while a Chinese violinist plays "Ah, Sweet Mystery of Life."

Unlike any other major Third World metropolis, the population of the Shanghai metropolitan district, after a boom in the early 1950s, actually declined between 1957 and 1979 from 6.3 million to 5.9 million.[60] There was a natural increase during this time in new births of 1.3 million, but, while squatters were flooding into Calcutta, Rio, and Lagos, over a million Shanghaiese were compelled to leave the city under official programs—either as migrants to remote areas, or later as Red Guards packed off to the countryside. Most of the latter group have been allowed to return, and have added to the unemployment problem. Although 1.5 million new jobs are said to have been found in Shanghai over the past six years, primarily through opening up individual and cooperative enterprises, there are still about 200,000 unemployed, mostly youth. At the same time, 1.1 million "temporary workers" moved to Shanghai after the economic relaxations of the 1980s to take construction and other menial jobs.

Shanghai is also up-to-date in terms of other urban ills. Belching smokestacks and the stench of the Suzhou Creek are only the most visible scars of Shanghai pollution, while China's highest lung, stomach, and nose cancer rate is its most disquieting result. As in Calcutta, most households in Shanghai cook with cheap, high-sulphur coal, which contributes a large part of the acid haze that envelopes both cities.

Despite a relatively low rate of population growth for two decades, Shanghai is as crowded as Calcutta; Nanjing Road is a flowing river of humanity, and as in India, commuters pack city buses to twice their capacity and go home to an average of about 6 square yards of housing per person. More than half a million live in less than 3.5 square yards each. After dinner, they may walk in city parks, which provide each citizen with only enough open land to cover less than half a desk-top. Less than a third have flush toilets and bathing facilities.

Unlike other cities along China's eastern coast, Shanghai in the 1980s has not taken off. In the first half of 1986, its economic growth rate was below 1 percent and foreign tourism and investment were lagging. The stagnation is laid in part to the bureaucracy that has foiled Peking's efforts to introduce management reforms into China's most important industrial center. It has also been ascribed to the central government's customary appropriation of most of Shanghai's foreign exchange earnings and revenues. In any event, the city's infrastructure is rundown. Traffic snarls, ships back up in the harbor, and garbage collects in the streets, which flood during heavy rains.

Still, no Shanghaiese would willingly move anywhere else in China. The per capita GNP in the city is more than four times that of the national average. Given the low prices of housing, medical care, and food, the standard of living in Shanghai is probably comparable to that of South Korea. A substantial majority of families own a TV set and are now beginning to buy the newly produced refrigerators. Shanghai, in fact, produces over 40 percent of the consumer goods of China, about 15 percent of the entire gross national product, and more or less the same percentage of exports.

In 1985 and 1986 Shanghai under its new technocratic mayor, Jiang Zemin, began to shake off its lethargy, with plans for a subway, satellite towns, rehabilitation of its sewage system, new efforts to attract investors, and an unprecedented decentralization of its banking system. The city also began to throw off its old neo-Maoist blanket on cultural and intellectual life. In 1986, an increasingly lively press carried the scandals of the day; for example: the son of the Shanghai People's Congress chairman is executed for rape; a smuggling ring run by police and customs officials is uncovered; and the private secretary of a former party second secretary is arrested for corruption. Satirical plays, and a female, American rock band, all denied bookings in Peking, perform that year in the city. And finally, in December, 50,000 university students demonstrated down the Bund calling for greater democracy. Shanghai, it seems, was beginning to play its traditional role as a door to Western cultural and intellectual ideas.

CHAPTER 7

Political Streams

Micro and Macro Democracy

For the Indian and the Chinese governments, no less than others, the credibility of their coercive arms is vital to their survival. But each has a basic political structure that makes explicit coercion normally a secondary factor.

In India populist and open politics provide an outlet for grievances, as well as a sense of participation. India, however, enjoys more of a "macro" than a "micro" democracy. Despite the existence of village councils called *panchayats* and other community development efforts to involve local residents in local decisions, in most areas there is not much life in the process. The panchayats have little authority over economic resources or economic decisions. Most such decisions in a village are made by peasant landowners and local officials. Therefore, it is not unusual to find panchayats headed by an untouchable; to the village establishment this is not a seat of power.

At regional or national levels, power in India divides along interest, caste, and class lines to compete for allocation of resources from government structures which control assets. Those who are not well-organized, such as the poorest half of the rural population, have much less influence on government policy than the more affluent; yet their right to vote and their organizational and protest movements have given them significant influence as well as a sense of power.

The Chinese peasant today runs either a small farm or a household enterprise or else he or she works in a local industry and tills a small plot. In effect, the great majority of Chinese rural dwellers are now self-employed, and thus they have real economic decisions to make and a real voice over village matters that affect their daily lives. Compared to the landless half of the Indian peasantry, Chinese peasants under the Dengist reforms enjoy a considerable degree of freedom of choice on the micro level.

Popular power, however, is atomized in China and not allowed to coalesce into movements or pressure groups which extend beyond the village. The Chinese peasant has virtually no influence on decisions or selection of personnel with real authority immediately above the grass-roots in the commune or the township, not to speak of the national level. Although "democratic centralism" is the official term for the representative system, real democracy in China is, in fact, of a "micro" variety—decentralized and concentrated at the village level. That is not to say it is unimportant.

In any society many or most people play a relatively passive role in representative structures and this is true in Chinese villages as well. Local cadre and party committees exercise a strong hand over decisions. Nevertheless, micro-democracy, while strictly controlled, appears relatively vigorous in rural China.

In urban areas, however, Indian democracy is more effective on the grass-roots level. Indian workers, students, slum-dwellers, and other urban groups can and do organize protests and strikes to influence concrete decisions by officials, employers, or administrators, affecting their immediate economic livelihood. While they seldom have their way completely, they do have effect, and the exercise of these rights, as well as the right to vote in hotly contested elections, provide outlet for competing views.

In China such unofficial movements are discouraged and occur only rarely. Urban neighborhood and street committees in China deal with hygiene, social order, and other matters not related to the economic life of the residents. Likewise, Chinese unions, worker congresses, women's organizations, and other "mass" institutions are agents for implementation of government policy and control, not for the expression of vested and competing interests. Chinese workers lack the decision-making powers over their economic lives that Chinese peasants now enjoy.

Shaping National Policy

China, like India, is a society of scarcity.[61] There is limited patronage; only a small fraction of high school graduates can go to university and become part of the cadre elite; there are only so many good jobs; there is only so much capital to be invested, so much grain for relief. Competition for these limited opportunities and scarce resources dominates the politics of both societies, but in China this is essentially either a bureaucratic process or one of personal and factional maneuvering. While market forces are being introduced, individuals, units, localities, and ministries still lobby within party and state bureaucracies for assignment of most capital, input materials, power, and other limited resources. Major decisions come down from the top and cannot be easily challenged.

Above the village level the Chinese citizen still has no effective way to voice his real opinion on how the society is to be organized or resources divided. He or she can write letters to the editors protesting that bureaucrats are not carrying out party policy honestly or fairly, but one cannot protest the policy itself, much less organize to change it.

Individuals and factions in the Chinese leadership see their own futures in part dependent on their success or failure in improving the public welfare and they try to be responsive to public needs. There is no distinct correlation, however, and no specific time or fashion in which the performance of the Chinese leaders is weighed in the balance. Serious failures of policy in China may stimulate factional struggles and possibly lead to new coalitions and a change of leadership; or, as under Mao, the entrenched group may be able to purge its critics and ride over major policy failures, even disasters.

The Party Congress in 1987 is scheduled to address the question of political reform. The problem Deng and his colleagues face is how to make the system politically more responsive, participatory, and open without losing control. For the present, national policy still depends on maneuverings within the Politburo or a slightly larger leadership group. Whether or not there is a leadership shake-up, or whether the government has or does not have popular support, the Chinese Communist Party continues to rule through its organizational control and, if necessary, the government's coercive arms. Thus, while China remains supremely a political culture, as in the past, politics above the village level does not exist in the sense of a dynamic open competition between conflicting claims and interest groups for resources and for justice.

The major feature of modern India, however, is the vigor of its national and state politics. There is much debate whether politics in India is changing the caste system or vice versa. The truth is that both are happening; caste and politics are inter-reacting to form a unique "Hindu democracy" that is corrupt, manipulated, and inefficient, but also populist, free, and dynamic.

The religious and caste-centered Indians, who traditionally had divorced themselves as much as possible from political life, have created a carnival of popular politics. The common man in India, as part of a sub-caste, a village, a class, an institution, an enterprise, a linguistic group, and a religion, is engaged at numerous points in interaction with bureaucrats, policemen, politicians, and the rest of the body politic, competing, agitating, and using his vote to obtain rights and advantages in a competitive system.

Many aspects of Indian politics will seem familiar to Americans: survival-oriented rather than ideological politicians seeking to placate and accommodate all interest groups; a plural and divided polity that is at once cynical and enthusiastic; movie-star politicians; the festival of elections; ethnic politics; popular movements that suddenly well up and as suddenly recede; a circle of corruption and reform; the noise of a press that lives on the meat of incumbents; the cries of despair from intellectual ivory towers;

exhortations from extremes; and the sound of millions of partisans shouting and mostly—but not always—enjoying themselves.

If democratic politics is the free and open interplay of private and group pressures, then Indian democracy on the national and state levels is alive and well. Yet it pays a price, as every democracy does, in terms of order and the continuation of certain social evils with which a less democratic regime might more easily deal.

Aborted Democratization in China

Like the Indian National Congress, the Chinese Communist Party has fallen on hard times. The glory days and the mystique are gone. The majority of living Chinese (as well as Indians) were born after 1950 and neither ruling party can expect support on the basis of its nationalist or revolutionary record of a generation ago. Moreover, both the Congress and the CCP over the past twenty-odd years have badly punctured their own images. Like the Congress, the CCP has also split several times over the years, but in the communist pattern of winner-take-all, losing factions, like those of Peng Dehuai, Liu Shaoqui, Lin Biao, Jiang Qing, Hua Guofeng, and Hu Yaobang do not form new parties but disappear into either prison or limbo.

The dramatic shifts in political line since 1957 have sapped the credibility of the CCP. Liu Shaoqi was China's esteemed president, then he became a hated "capitalist roader" and fifteen years later, after his death, was reborn an honored leader. For several years Lin Biao was Mao's "closest comrade in arms"; then one day the nation awoke to hear that he was a notorious traitor and would-be assassin of the great chairman himself.

Jiang Qing was the cultural czarina of all China and the most intimate interpreter of her husband's thoughts; then abruptly she was jailed as a conspirator and persecutor of thousands. Hua Guofeng, whose portraits after 1976 appeared all over China, was touted as Mao's anointed successor and he was on the verge of entering the state of "beloved leader," then, without explanation, he was stripped of his titles and—because he went quietly—was allowed to fade away.

Hu Yaobang had settled in as party chairman for six years and his possession of power in fact as well as name seemed only to await confirmation of the aging Deng's ephemerality. But without a word of warning to the Chinese people he was unceremoniously dumped. And of course the great chairman, the father figure, the emperor surrogate, who had been glorified as only Stalin and Hitler before him, was criticized posthumously for arrogance and grave errors that led to disasters for the nation, errors that no one in China had mentioned at the time.

Not surprisingly, ideology has gotten a bad name in China. As in India, skepticism and political cynicism are widespread in the PRC today. The most able young people in India no longer go into politics nor do the top achievers among young Chinese choose a party career. In both countries, the best and the brightest are selecting science, engineering or some other technical field.

After Mao's death, the reform group around Deng Xiaoping, seeking to deal with this crisis of confidence and a grossly inefficient economy, not only sought to liberalize the economy but also to enliven the political process as well. Having been purge victims themselves, the reformers and most particularly the intellectuals in Deng's camp, whom we shall call the innovators, sought to institutionalize collective leadership, encourage a more plural society generally, and adopt various other safeguards against the abuse of power.

The reformers on several occasions in the 1980s encountered a sharp backlash from conservative elements in the party and the army. Until 1987, the mainline reformers around Deng largely sided with the more liberal innovators, although at times pulling them back from too liberal measures. Eventually, the most daring of the top reform leaders, Hu Yaobang, fell victim to a coalition of the party-bureaucratic conformists and the Deng middle roaders, including the feisty old *eminence grise* himself.

Innovators and Neo-Maoists

Politics and philosophy have always been intertwined in China. Unity over the centuries was cemented, not only by a cultural affinity, but also by the broad acceptance of a coherent social doctrine that gave moral authority to the order of society and to the power-holders. But the rigidity of the doctrine, whether Confucianism or Marxism-Leninism, has varied over time.

Today's struggle between orthodox and more liberal elements within the Chinese Communist Party parallels the contest between innovators and conservative neo-Confucianists before and during the early Song Dynasty. The innovators, typified by Wang Anshi (Wang An-shih), minister to the fourth Sung emperor, were reformist and pragmatic and, unlike the neo-Confucianists, they saw no need to turn the social doctrine of Confucius into a universalist ethical system. The neo-Confucianists preferred a strict orthodoxy and sought to diminish foreign influences such as Buddhism. The neo-Confucianists eventually prevailed, directing imperial China into an intellectual rigidity and obscurantism which afflicted China down to the modern era.

In the modern version of this struggle, Deng and the reform group, emphasizing pragmatic slogans such as "seek truth from facts" and "liberate the mind," have sought to provide more scope to the industriousness of the Chinese peasant and worker and to the creativity of Chinese intellectuals. They have also tried to assure that China did not again close its doors to the outside world.

Since 1978, the reform leadership has envisioned an enlightened but authoritarian regime led by an elite meritocracy dedicated to the welfare of the people and to the restoration of China's greatness. In other words, the Dengist embraced an historical Chinese concept of authority shaped for modern times.

On the philosophical plane they have sought to construct a new eclectic social doctrine based on Marxism, the pre–1957 concepts of the CCP and of Mao, selected borrowings from East European socialism, and last but not least, Chinese tradition and nationalism. The doctrinal underpinning of Deng's "bean curd communism" first emerged during the 1979 party debate on the purpose of socialist production and the triumph of the view that the goal of production was improvement of the lives of the people. That is, the purpose of socialism is not some universal or utopian objective, but meeting common needs. This was quite consistent with the traditional Chinese view that human happiness is essentially measured in material terms.

The most liberal of the CCP thinkers, however, went further. They envisioned a plural and politically relaxed socialist society. One of the innovators, a leading theoretician of "Marxism-Leninism-Mao Tsedong Thought," explained privately in 1984 that only with "genuine democratic reforms" could China prevent the abuse of concentrated power, free the creativity of the Chinese people, achieve rapid modernization, and prevent hegemonic foreign policies such as those pursued in the Soviet Union.

Hu Yaobang became the leader of these remarkable modern-day innovators, presumably in part because he was philosophically in tune with them. But expediency also drove him to make common cause with the intellectuals. Unpopular with the conservatives and the military, Hu developed a constituency where he could find it—among the liberals, the academics, and the students. Deng and his supporters had exploited such groups in the past; for example, at the anniversary of Zhou Enlai's death in the spring of 1975 and during the "democracy wall" period of 1978–1979.

Deng, however, believed that freeing the peasants from collectivization, introducing major reforms in industrial management, encouraging a more mixed economy, and keeping the door open to the rest of the world for trade, investment, education, and technology was quite sufficient reform for the rest of the century. As the consummate pragmatist, Deng carefully drew the boundaries of pluralism with his "four principles," which made clear that no one in China could challenge socialism, the dictatorship of the proletariat, leadership by the Communist Party, and "Marxism-Leninism-Mao Tsedong Thought." Like Hu, Deng's position on reform very likely reflected a philosophical proclivity but also a hardheaded political calculation of what was possible.

The conservative neo-Maoists were agitated enough with the economic reforms and the consequences of China's opening to the world. This group did not constitute a cohesive faction but was composed of diverse elements who shared a common discomfort with the erosion of old dogmas and the dangers of foreign influence and of a "commodity economy."

While the neo-Maoists favor pragmatic policies up to a point, like the neo-Confucianists of the Song period they long for the security of a more rigid doctrine whose authority is enhanced by universal claims and a transcendental cause. They reject the fanaticism and radicalism of Mao's last two decades and, indeed in one respect, they have less in common with Mao than the innovators. Although the innovators have a totally different approach to the problem than that of the departed Chairman, they are also concerned with the ossification of a bureaucratic state and the gap between the rulers and the ruled in a Marxist society. The neo-Maoists, on the other hand, wish to return to a more tightly organized state with a high degree of central planning and, while they accept the necessity for various reforms including material incentives, they are disturbed by the loss of political and social discipline inherent in a consumer-oriented society. They see the answer to social ferment and dissent in tighter controls and revival of a more vigorous spiritual and political effort to motivate the population.

In the early 1980s, the innovators, seemingly with Deng's support, sought to achieve a system of checks and balances by several reforms:

- Separating party and state functions;
- Re-orienting the party role to that of watch-dog, broad leadership, and moral upliftment;
- Re-invigorating local representative bodies, the People's Congresses, by having competitive elections;
- Giving the National People's Congress some credibility, by permitting negative votes, reducing its unwieldy numbers, and having permanent NPC committees oversee government work;
- Reviving Worker Congresses and shaping them into real institutions of participatory work-place democracy on the Yugoslav model, separate from party committees and government-controlled unions; and, finally,
- Allowing investigative media reporting and more scope for press criticism of government and party actions.

The NPC which met in the summer of 1980 was the most vigorous in history. A handful of individual delegates for the first time voted "no" on certain motions. A few delegates were quoted in the press calling for longer sessions and permanent watchdog committees. Meanwhile *People's Daily* led the way in investigative reporting, unveiling the suppressed story of the accidental sinking of a Chinese oil rig, which went down with great loss of life. Other papers followed suit and one even attacked the Minister of Commerce for taking free meals in a restaurant. Local elections to the People's Congresses that year and in 1981 were dutifully carried out with alternate candidates among whom the 400 million voters could choose. Thirty percent of the candidates chosen by local nominating committees under the auspices of the CCP were not members of the Communist Party.

The Backlashes

While these reforms were generally implemented smoothly, some trouble did occur. In a very few constituencies, mostly college campuses, some people took the electoral reforms seriously and campaigned as open critics of the Communist government. Efforts by local authorities in some instances to negate the election victories of such opposition candidates led to protests at several universities. Meanwhile, a few scattered factory strikes occurred, apparently led by those who had been carried away by talk of giving real power to the workers.

These events, as isolated as they were, alarmed many CCP leaders. Neo-Maoists, including conservative military leaders, became concerned about the threat to party control and the loss of ideological commitment. Moreover, by the end of 1980, Deng was accelerating his efforts to ease out Hua Guofeng and he needed to broaden his consensus to win support for his personal choice of successors—Zhao Zeyang and Hu Yaobang—for his various economic and bureaucratic reforms and for the official party condemnation of Mao which he was then orchestrating. Pushing liberal political and cultural reforms had been useful when Hua was ascendant, but once having won out in the struggle with Hua, Deng was prepared to pull back on the non-economic reforms. Again Deng probably had mixed feelings on the subject, personally appreciating the need for effective checks on the concentration of power within the CCP but also concerned that reforms in this direction not undermine stability, the party's control, and the economic reforms.

The much heralded democratic reforms of 1980 were watered down, newspapers were instructed to notify officials before criticizing them, and various reprisals were taken against those who ran as true independents in the local People's Congress elections. The idea of strengthening the NPC was not mentioned in the new constitution adopted in December 1982. Worker Congresses were instituted but firmly under the authority of the party committee and union in each enterprise and thus with no real authority.

In 1981, Deng acquiesced in the return of certain Maoist practices including an adulterated ideological program and a new emphasis on political study sessions. Criticism of "bourgeois liberalism" sputtered into a quasi-movement in 1981–1982 and was followed by a more inflammatory but brief campaign in late 1983 against "spiritual pollution" allegedly brought into China by Western influence.

By the end of 1984, however, the innovators were again on the offensive. Intellectuals close to Hu Yaobang and silenced during the "spiritual pollution" campaign reemerged, a discussion of humanism revived, and in an October speech to the Central Advisory Council (published on January 1, 1985) Deng made explicit his goal to return China to the type of openness that China has not known since the Tang Dynasty.

Deng said that great suffering had befallen China as a result of the decision to close the door to the world during the Ming Dynasty. Efforts to open up were made after the Opium War with the British in the 1840s and again after the Communist takeover in 1949, he said, but the contacts then were limited to the Soviet Union and its allies in Eastern Europe. In 1966 the Cultural Revolution had again closed the door and, "not much progress was made after that," he said. Deng warned that no country could develop by closing its door. "We suffered from this," he declared, "isolation landed China in poverty, backwardness, and ignorance." Notably Deng was attacking isolationism, not touting cultural or political reform. Nevertheless, the reform movement was on the verge of accelerating at a breathtaking pace.

Before the end of the year, the party had announced a sweeping liberalization of the urban economy, ended compulsory procurement of grain and declared a "smashing" of the wage system. Hu and his supporters also carried the reforms once again into the cultural field. Hu indirectly endorsed a national writers congress attack on past restrictions on artistic freedom and an official promise that writers and artists would never again be punished for their creative efforts.

In 1985 and 1986 the mood was reminiscent of the days of the early Chinese reformers who tried to spur modern ways in part by urging their countrymen to adopt foreign customs. Domestic fashion shows displayed sport coats and evening dresses. The Chinese Body Building Association decreed that in competition all female participants had to wear bikinis. *People's Daily* urged Chinese families to give up eating out of the same bowl, and Hu Yaobang even suggested Chinese abandon chopsticks for forks and spoons. Articles appeared praising Meiji Japan's example of modernization by the wholesale absorption of Western learning and by putting Western-educated intellectuals in charge.

But most striking of all was the call for political reforms. The party's propaganda chief, a Hu supporter, urged progress toward democratic pluralism. Liu Binyan, a renowned journalist who had written a 1979 novel attacking corruption in and out of the party, wrote articles questioning the "four principles" and even suggesting Marxism was outdated.

The high tide for the liberal innovators was the September 1986 resolution of the Central Committee plenum on building "a socialist China with an advanced culture and ideology." The document endorsed the necessity for cultural and artistic freedom and the view that Marxism is not a dogma and provides no "ready-made" formulas. It described the opening to the outside as a "basic and unalterable state policy" that applies in cultural and ideological realms as much as economic and technical ones.

Perhaps most important of all, the 1986 resolution affirmed the need to foster "socialist humanism." The neo-Maoists, like Politburo member Hu Qiaomu, who had openly denounced the concept of humanism, remained silent. To Westerners this vague endorsement of humanism seems commonplace. But for Chinese intellectuals it was pregnant with meaning. The new leaders in Peking were committing themselves to the philosophical approach of pre-Mongol China. They were formalizing a Chinese Marxism that rationalized a more plural and tolerant society that pursued human needs, not empty dogmas. They had redefined communism to mean human happiness.

Putting ideology in its theoretical place, the resolution explained that communism is a long term goal of party members, but that the nation's efforts must focus on the common goal of the vast majority—the building of a modern socialist country with a high degree of democracy and advanced culture and ideology. Creating a socialist culture and ideology is the task of all the people, not just the party. By implication, the future role of the party would not be to transform society but to serve as a modernizing elite.

The concept of humanism also implied checks and balances to protect against the concentration and abuse of power. In 1986 Chinese in fact began openly to talk about "human rights abuses" in their country. Newspapers reported cases of extortion and torture by local officials, and a senior member of the Supreme People's Procuracy called publicly for a crackdown on "serious abuses of human rights." How all this would be achieved was uncertain. But the Party Congress due in 1987 was tasked with formalizing and promulgating the long awaited political reforms as well as concrete guidelines on the new relationship between the party and society.

It was too good to last. When the "hundred flowers" slogan revived in the fall of 1986, the intellectuals should have known they had again gone too far. Following the student protests at the end of the year, Hu and a number of his associates were canned. Deng and the more cautious of the reformers joined with the conservatives in ousting China's Dubchek and putting the quietus on another "Peking spring."

Metamorphosis of Indian Politics

Chinese political culture has been non-democratic, but so has the Indian; nevertheless, the Indians of today do not seem ready to abandon their right to "kick out the rascals" at the top. Since 1967 they have in fact bounced two-thirds of incumbent members of parliament standing for re-election.

The major communist parties in India dutifully pledge to preserve parliamentary democracy. The Communist Party of India (Marxist) (CPM) won re-election in West Bengal in 1982 on the slogan of resisting "authoritarianism," referring to Mrs. Gandhi's period of "emergency" rule in 1975–1977. Although the emergency was initially welcomed or accepted by a wide range of Indian opinion—"things got done, bureaucrats went to work"—within two years the majority of Indians realized that authoritarian rule would not cure the political evils of the day, but make them worse.

Liberal observers in India and abroad deplore the loss of idealism and the corruption of political life. "India has a ramshackle democracy . . . a facade," lamented one editor. True, said another, but it would also have a "ramshackle dictatorship." However rickety it may be, Indian democracy has twice accomplished a feat rare in the Third World: the peaceful transfer of power by free elections from one government to another.

In the early years of Indian independence the Indian Congress Party, under Nehru, enjoyed the support of a broad national consensus embracing conservatives and democratic socialists. Nehru, himself, was committed to socialism; he admired the economic and social achievements of the Soviet Union, but he was also a democrat. Moreover, the holocaust of partition and the fear of disunity encouraged him to pursue a policy of compromise and to avoid confrontation. At that time, the Congress leadership was composed of the educated elite and was overwhelmingly upper caste. The rural establishment—the dominant land-owning castes—delivered the votes of the newly enfranchised masses who, to the extent that they were aware of a choice, were largely enthusiastic supporters of the Congress, the party of Mahatma Gandhi and the party which promised to support the downtrodden and the minorities. The critical vote in that period was restricted to the cities. It was a time of lofty goals: rapid industrialization, reform of the social structure, uplifting the poor, and equality of opportunity. Congress Party workers were dedicated servants of the party, veterans of the independence struggle. Congress MPs were educated and sophisticated. It was politics of an elite selflessly serving the people—or so it seemed.

Now all this has changed. Politics has become mercurial, expensive, and corrupt. Businessmen back all the parties and expect something in return. Winners must make hay while the sun shines. Limited patronage drives the ambitious to form their own parties. Parties splinter left and right, each identified with the initial of its leader's name, including Mrs. Gandhi's Congress (I), the Congress (S), Congress (J), Congress (W), etc. Amoeba-like, the Indian Communists have also divided into three. Idealism has been replaced by office-seeking; noble causes have been lost in the whirlwind; and elections are won or lost on the basis of who can promise the most short-term rewards to the most voters or the largest castes.

Much of the blame was heaped on Mrs. Gandhi for her centralization of power and for putting personal loyalty to herself above all else, and also on her late son, Sanjay, for wrecking the Congress organization and bringing in his untutored followers.

But however more astutely Mrs. Gandhi might have managed the Congress Party, the factionalism and other maladies that afflict Indian politics are the symptoms, not the cause, of basic changes taking place in Indian society, and the consequence of a populist democracy in a very large and very poor country. The apparent deterioration of Indian politics, even the increasing political violence in some states, are a reflection of India's greatest achievement—the creation of a working, albeit chaotic, democracy.

In one generation, the Indian masses have become highly politicized, with voting turn-outs of 60–80 percent. "Voting banks," controlled by the rural gentry, are disappearing and more of the landless poor and untouchables are voting according to their own—usually meaning their caste—interests. In 1969 Mrs. Gandhi split the conservative wing of her party and two years later nationalized banks, insurance companies, and coal mines, and ended the privileges and privy purses of the former princes. The old Congress machine was, by and large, against her, but she swept the elections on a leftist and populist platform. For the first time, a national election was won by appealing directly to the people. But in 1977, with government and police organs under her control and in possession of more funds than her opponents, Mrs. Gandhi was thrown out by the voters because of the abuses of the emergency, especially Sanjay's forced sterilization program. Then, again in 1980, fed up with the fractured leadership of the Janata government, the voters returned her once again to office. But in January 1983 two southern states that had stuck with her through the 1970s, Karnataka and Andra Pradesh, unexpectedly voted in non-Congress state governments which advocated greater states' rights. There was much talk that she and the old Congress Party were again slipping badly. Then after her assassination, a mass sympathy vote in the December 1984 elections returned her party to power with an unprecedented majority and a new leader, Rajiv Gandhi.

"Hindu Democracy"

In India the political and developmental processes intermesh. Political parties compete for the votes of the poor, promising welfare measures such as free lunches for children and old people, more schools and clinics, guaranteed work, and subsidized food prices. The better off farmers, who exercise predominant political as well as economic influence in the villages, must be lured with promises of more irrigation and paved roads, higher produce prices and fertilizer subsidies, and more credit, extension services, and government-backed cooperatives.

Indian politicians must also attempt to find the right balance between promising to extend affirmative action programs and placating those who are neither untouchables nor members of a "backward caste" and who want education and job reservations and other forms of social assistance given on an economic need, rather than a caste, basis. Obtaining jobs for the families of influential caste leaders is another way of winning support, and thus the Indian bureaucracy balloons. Advocating greater state autonomy and promoting sectional and linguistic interests are additional appeals that political parties effectively exploit.

Carrying out the promise is another matter. As Myron Weiner observed, even after the 1971 elections Mrs. Gandhi's more leftist Congress Party "continued to be dominated by members of the local rural gentry and the state ministers were in no position to push through and implement any land reforms that would take land away from land-owing peasants."[62]

Land reforms, economic assistance, affirmative action programs, and other legislated efforts to re-distribute resources are strained through political and governmental layers and, in the final stages, implemented by local bureaucracies and established elites who shift some of the benefits away from the poorer half of the population. In Karnataka, for example, a sociologist claimed that in redistributing "excess land" under the state's land reform act, 70 percent went to the better-off half of the villagers—the current landowners. In Madras, another student of rural affairs believed that 30 percent of those benefiting from poverty programs were not in the poorer half of the population. However effective an administration may be, limited funds sharply restrict what the states can do in terms of populist relief measures. West Bengal, for example, has had to cut back sharply on its Food For Work program because grain allocations from the center for the project have been reduced. The Communist government of West Bengal claims this was a political move by Mrs. Gandhi, but their opponents charge that Communist officials blatantly used the program to reward local supporters and pro-CPM villages.

The campaign rhetoric, however, is not all empty or cynical. Benefits do trickle down to the lower half of the population. Reservations are slowly bringing members of the lower castes into the mainstream. At Bombay University, for example, untouchables averaged 45 on the admission exam 20 years ago, while upper castes averaged 85; but today the former average scores of about 72. The land reform acts have sharply reduced the phenomenon of absentee landlords and, in a number of states, have provided some measure of security to the landless agricultural laborer; for instance, providing title to hut land. The Integrated Rural Development Program (IRDP), the National Rural Employment Program (NREP), and Operation Flood Dairy Development Program are targeted at the poorer half of the rural population. At the same time, a minimum needs program has set specific targets for increasing access by the rural poor to family planning, health and nutrition services, water supply, sanitation, and education. While the goal of reducing the "poverty ratio" to as low as 30 percent has fallen by the wayside, there is steady political pressure for populist welfare programs and progress in most areas of human development is being made.

In the U.S., class-consciousness and class politics have never taken hold because thousands of local, regional, economic, institutional, and one-issue-oriented interest groups prevent polarization and require politicians, if they are to succeed, to compete for the center ground. Likewise in India, the competition of thousands of castes, regional and linguistic interests, and communal and minority blocs results in non-class-oriented politics of the center, shifting alliances, and factionalism. State leaders as well as the central government must play constituency politics. The Communists in West

Bengal, and also in Kerala, where they are once again in power, must take expedient positions to avoid alienating important vested interests. For example, although the CPM favors affirmative action programs on an economic basis it has had to support allocation of such advantages strictly to lower castes and minorities, in order to appeal to the large bloc of Moslem and low-caste or untouchable voters.

Elections in India are sometimes rigged and voting rolls are tampered with. A professor, who has served as presiding officer at elections in Bihar, said that in his polling district there might be 1,000 voters on the rolls, but only 100 people would be casting all the ballots; there were ways, he claimed, to remove the indelible stamp placed on voters' hands and, besides, "the presiding officers did not want to get killed." This is not the norm, but buying of votes for a few rupees or a blanket is a feature of many Indian elections.

Manipulation of the electoral process is, of course, one of the evils to which democratic systems are subject. Such tactics were not uncommon in the U.S. not too long ago, and have still not disappeared. "Politicians cannot win on money alone," a legislator commented; "but they cannot win without it." Still, in India as in the U.S., it is difficult to buy millions of votes and, where there is strong competition, the presence of poll watchers keeps fraud to a limited and usually non-decisive level. The Indian Election Commission, which certifies elections, reports directly to the president and enjoys a high degree of popular credibility.

For many intellectuals, catering to the voters' immediate caste and parochial interests is not so lofty as offering ideological choices of socialism, Marxism, or capitalism. Ideological appeals can still have effect in India, as witness the 1971 election and the popularity of Mrs. Gandhi's slogan, "End Poverty." But there is skepticism at the moment toward grand-sounding proclamations. "People don't expect too much, anymore, although they still like to hear the promises." Reflecting the mood, the Communist state government in West Bengal has shied away from its revolutionary programs of the 1950s and 1960s and, instead, has concentrated on carrying out more effectively the reform measures which other parties purport to support. In any event, virtually every party in India has adopted the rhetoric of social justice, equality, and ending poverty.

Political affairs have become more vulgar and corrupt in India because politics is becoming less elite-directed and there is more mass participation. Very likely, a large percentage, even a majority, of Indians still do not vote as fully autonomous actors, and only a small portion of the population is politically organized. But the common man, illiterate and barely able to maintain his family at a subsistence level, has become aware of certain rights which politicians left and right keep telling him he has. The ubiquitous Indian movies have made him fully aware of the life of the elite and, for the first time, he entertains, often vaguely but sometimes more keenly, the prospect of future progress. His neighbors go to work in Calcutta, Bombay, or the Punjab and return with impressive little nest eggs. His sons join the army; a few make it through high school, receive government jobs, and become living proof that a life of poverty is not fated. Education spreads slowly. Yet there are 100 million more literate Indians today than in 1950. There are also more illiterates than ever before, but the percentage of families touched by education has grown; and for those who cannot read, almost every village has at least one transistor radio and, in places like the Punjab, most have a TV or two.

The extent of politicization and the degree of autonomy among the poorest half of the population varies greatly from state to state. In the Hindi-speaking cowbelt, semi-feudal relationships continue in much of the countryside. Agricultural laborers in these areas by and large vote the way their employers, the landowning farmers, direct. Increasing violence against untouchable communities and individuals after elections in states like Bihar and Uttar Pradesh suggests that untouchables are breaking the old rules of subservience. In West Bengal, most of the south, and in many other states, the poor and landless generally vote according to how they see their own interests and that of their castes.

Although the Congress (I) still commands the support of the majority of untouchables and Moslems, some observers believe that despite the 1984 election victory, this constituency has begun to erode as the feeling spreads that the party has not adequately lived up to its promises. "The Indian voter has a certain common sense about politics," commented a New Delhi intellectual. "The concept of probity—of what is right and proper behavior—greatly influences his or her vote." Mrs. Gandhi's dynasty building, the squabbling of the Janata leaders in the 1977–1979 period, and the switching of parties by elected legislators have all offended the sensibilities of the Indian voter. Consequently, elections have often confounded the polls, the entrenched establishment, and both Mrs. Gandhi and her enemies.

Traditionally, religious rituals and taboos were the cement that held the caste system together. Today, caste has a political imperative, and caste-consciousness, rather than caste-identification, has increased.

No important political party is based on caste, but all of them give the greatest weight to caste and sub-castes in selecting candidates and, indirectly, in their campaigning. Rivalries between sub-castes often overwhelm common political and economic interests. The landless untouchables and the landless backward castes do not always unite. The untouchables are themselves divided into occupational groups that sometimes split politically. In Karnataka there are two rival groups of untouchables, the "Left Hand" and the "Right Hand" factions. The poor marginal farmers may also see different interests from those of the landless and often resent the special privileges given to the untouchables.

A striking example of the complexity of Indian politics, and the interplay of caste, communal and class interests, is the state of Kerala.

Kerala

Kerala, the original home of pepper and some of the hottest food in India, is a slim strip on the western side of the southernmost tip of India. It was here at Cochin that Vasco da Gama, seeking to cut the Arab middlemen out of the spice trade, landed in 1498 and found to his amazement both Christian and Jewish communities. Today, Christians, including those from the original Syrian church but mostly Roman Catholics and Protestants, make up about 30 percent of the population. That is one of several reasons for the remarkably high literacy rate in Kerala (69 percent), almost double that of the rest of India. Hindus may be close to a majority in the state, but only barely so, as the Moslems have 15–20 percent of the population. As usual in India, below the major Hindu divisions are a myriad of sub-castes and groups. In addition, there are small but important Jain and Buddhist communities.

Politics in Kerala center around the balancing of these communal and caste interests. The largest caste among the Hindus are the *ezhavas*, a poor and backward farming caste who are mostly "toddy tappers" (toddy is a fermented drink made from the coconut palm). Below them are the untouchables, who comprise about 20–30 percent of the Hindu community. As elsewhere, the untouchables are divided into various occupational groups. The *pulayas*, for example, are agricultural laborers and the *ganakas* are coconut-pluckers, a different and more lowly occupation than the toddy-tapping of the ezhavas.

The most important land-owning agricultural caste are the *nairs*. Until recently, the nairs were a matrilineal clan in which a man's obligations were to his sister's children and they inherited his property. The nairs lived in an interesting familial symbiosis with a brahman caste, the *namboodiripads*, who customarily allowed only the eldest son to marry. Younger namboodiripad brothers would establish relations with nair women, and their offspring would be taken care of by the maternal uncles and would not become members of the brahman family, nor fragment the wealth of the namboodiripads. These mores have generally been abandoned by the younger generation of nairs and namboodiripads.

Land reform has been carried out fairly effectively in Kerala, particularly during the years of the coalition government formed by the Communists and Mrs. Gandhi's Congress (I). The nairs, who themselves did not till the land, are no longer dominant land-owners, but have gone into government service and business, taking advantage of their relatively high educational standards. Politically, the nairs are divided into supporters of the National Democratic Party and the Nair Service Society. The ezhavas also have their own political party, the Socialist Republican Party, but many ezhavas support the Communists or the Congress (I). The untouchables have generally backed the Communists and, to a lesser extent, the Congress (I). The brahmans, being only a tiny group, have no party of their own. The national president of the Communist Party Marxist is, however, a namboodiripad. Many of the namboodiripads have fallen on hard times. One nair journalist said that although a brahman may be extremely poor, "he is never a crook—or, if so, a very fine one." But most have moved into the modern elite, the government service and professions. Most senior officers in the State Secretariat are brahmans.

Christians in Kerala are also a varied lot. Like other Keralans, most are poor, but they have the highest literacy rate in the state; many Christians own plantation estates, big trading and transport firms, and are also into the professions. The "Syrian Christians" generally vote as a bloc for the splinter Kerala Congress. The "Latin Christians" are divided, but many support yet another party called the Kerala Congress (Joseph). Protestants go for the Congress (I) or the Kerala Congress.

The Muslims represent the most cohesive communal bloc; the great majority support the Indian Union-Muslim League (IUML). The IUML frequently carries the balance of power in the elections and it has joined in coalition governments with the Communists as well as the Congress (I). The Congress (I) obtains most of its support from the nairs, the Christians and, to a lesser extent, the untouchables. The Communists, however, receive most of the untouchable vote and the largest bloc of voters from the ezhavas. Rounding out the confusing spectrum are extremists on both sides; Maoist Naxalites are still lurking about waiting for violent opportunities, while the revivalist Hindu RSS is busy recruiting a fanatical paramilitary force.

Neither the Communists nor the Congress (I) have been able to form a government without support from one or more of the local parties. Thus they must play factional and communal politics, a constant process of bargaining and coalition-making and un-making. Except for the 1970–1977 Communist-Congress (I) coalition, no other state government in Kerala has lasted its full term since the early 1950s. After the 1982 elections, the Congress (I) led a new front, controlling 77 out of 140 legislative assembly seats. Jockeying for position, however, immediately ensued. The IUML, as a key member of the front, pushed its demand for a separate Moslem majority district in Kasargod; it also demanded old-age pensions for mullahs and appointment of another Moslem on the public service commission and the high court bench. The Congress (I) government agreed in principle to set up the new district. This provoked the Kerala Congress (Joseph) party to push its own demand for a Christian majority district at Moovattupucha. To strengthen its hand, the IUML was said to be discussing a merger with the All-India Moslem League and to have formed a coalition within a coalition with the ezhava SRP to promote their common interest in full implementation of reservations "for the weaker sections." In early 1983 the Congress (I) was strengthened when a splinter group, the Congress (Anthony) rejoined it. Meanwhile the Kerala Congress (Mani) and the nair-dominated NDP were said to be working closely together within the front government to strengthen the position of their communities.

The land tenure situation in Kerala has also undergone considerable change over the last several decades. According to a local economist, about 20–22 percent of the rural population is landless, mostly untouchables. Under a land reform act, they now at least own the land on which their huts are situated. Thus they cannot be evicted and their bargaining position as agricultural laborers has somewhat improved. Many of the untouchables and the "backward" caste ezhavas own a few coconut trees and this provides a small guaranteed income. Another 20–22 percent of the population in the countryside are marginal farmers who must also work as laborers to feed their families. The big absentee landowners, nairs and brahmans, have largely been divested of their holdings, but the prime beneficiaries have been the middle-sized landowning families. Local observers in Kerala from a wide range of political opinion agree that the poor, rural population vote according to their own interests, as they perceive them. This seems borne out by the fact that the majority of the landless and marginal farmers in the countryside have continued to support the Communist Party.

Kerala, in sum, is the most varied and pluralistic state in India and in many ways the most progressive. The situation in Kerala suggests that democracy is more vibrant and effective where there is a relative balance among cultural groups, literacy is high, and there has been a tradition of populist politics.

Provincial politics in China are on the public level devoid of interest group organization and coalition making. Shifts in policy and the ups and downs in personal fortunes are the result of maneuverings behind the scenes and, most important of all, of changes in the central leadership balance. A brief sketch of Fujian province will amply reflect the fundamental difference between popular politics in an Indian state like Kerala and bureaucratic and factional politics in a Chinese province.

Fujian

The striking feature of the 200 mile road trip from Fuzhou (Fuchow) to Xiamen (Amoy) is an endless human procession pushing, pulling, pedaling and toting enormous loads on wheelbarrows, two wheel carts, bicycles, and bamboo shoulder boards. Buffalos and horses supplement human muscle, along with three wheeled tractors driven like motorcycles, and ungainly monsters enclosed in canvas and plexiglass. World War II vintage trucks, buses crammed with market-going peasants, and occasional Shanghai cars and new Japanese trucks careen past the thin line, padding, jiggling, struggling on its eternal course to make a penny or two.

The queerest thing is that everything seems to be carried in both directions, including long blocks of granite, sugar cane, bags of grain, logs, piles of firewood, vegetables, bricks, fish, and trussed pigs. It is uncertain in which direction Fujian is headed, but it is on the move. The Fujian countryside appears not only busy but healthy. Conditions vary, however, from subsistence farming in the mountains, to the poor but scenic villages along the

Min River, to the rich coastal area north of Putian where overseas Chinese and entire villages of relatives have erected two-story, white residences with tile roofs that from a distance seem like clusters of California townhouses. One is reminded of the gaudy houses in Kerala built by oil workers returning from a Middle Eastern stint.

Fujian is a small mountain province on China's southeast coast. Only 5 percent of its land is cultivable. Isolated by mountains from the rest of China, in the nineteenth century Fujianese living in the densely populated coastal area had more connections with overseas communities than with the hinterlands of China. Fujianese (or Hokienese) migrated in large numbers to Taiwan and Southeast Asia. Seventy percent of families in Xiamen claim to have one or more relatives overseas.

Fujian like Kerala is one of its country's pooret provinces. Yet like Kerala, its overseas connections and traditional emphasis on education in some ways make it the envy of the nation. Fujian students score the highest on the national college entrance exams, continuing a pattern that dates back to at least the Ming Dynasty when Fujian ranked first nationally in the number of top-rank scholar officials per million population. Also like Kerala, Fujian has had a relatively large number of Christians, the legacy of American missionaries who flocked to the treaty ports when the province was forced open in the nineteenth century.

Fujian politics, however, are distinctly different from that of Kerala. Fujian does not have a dozen political parties appealing to different interest, caste, and religious groups but only one party with many factions and sub-groups. The political struggle in Fujian has always mirrored political strife in Peking and ideology has been the favored weapon of combat.

From 1981 to 1986 the province was run by party First Secretary Xiang Nan (Hsiang Nan), a strong Dengist reformer. Xiang was a native Fujianese but until his return in 1981 he had not worked in the province since he departed in 1951. Thus he was relatively free of involvement in the confusing and convoluted factional scene and one of his major goals was to end the often violent intraparty infighting that has been endemic in the province. Prior to Xiang's return, the province had been under the domination of the so-called "Red Faction," which by 1978 had taken over from the provincially oriented "Black Faction," which in turn had emerged in control after the Cultural Revolution.

Other groups that over the years have formed components of the two major factions or at times have competed independently include: "the Fujian-Zhejiang-Jiangxi group" of bandit and guerrilla leaders who were absorbed into the CCP's Third Field Army during the war against Japan; "the Shandong faction" of Third Army commanders who liberated Fujian in 1949; "the Central Guerrilla (or Underground) faction" of native Fujianese guerrillas who had stayed behind in the mountains fighting the Japanese during the war; and "the Shanxi faction" of "southbound" party cadre from

Shanxi province who had accompanied the Third Field Army into Fujian in 1949 and had organized local communist governments.

After liberation, some native Fujianese took leading roles in the government, but until the mid–1960s most senior posts were held by outsiders with Third Field Army or "southbound" cadre backgrounds. As elsewhere in China, the Cultural Revolution created a power vacuum in Fujian and allowed disgruntled groups and office seekers to seize positions at the local level and eventually to drive out the post-liberation provincial leadership. The military, under the regional commander Han Xianchu (Han Hsian-ch'u), however, took executive power in its own hands. Han came under a cloud in 1971 because of his ties to Lin Biao, although he was not implicated in the defense minister's plotting. Some purged old guard officials returned, but were put in subordinate positions, as those factions which had sided with the radicals continued to receive strong support from the "gang of four" in Peking.

In January 1975, the moderates in Peking temporarily gained the initiative, and a friend and colleague of Deng Xiaoping, Liao Zhigao (Liao Chih-kao), was appointed Party chief in Fujian. Liao, supported by the Red Faction including the Shanxi group and other old Third Army and "southbound" cadre as well as an establishment wing of former Red Guards, began to remove the Cultural Revolution beneficiaries, mostly native Fujianese. But in April 1975 Deng fell once again, Liao was suspended, and those he had purged were reinstated. Street fighting broke out among the factions and again the army had to restore order. Six months later, Mao died and Madame Mao and her "gang" were arrested. Liao promptly returned to office and the Black faction was again on its way out of town. A number of executions reportedly took place in 1977.

The Red faction dominated by the Shanxi clique was in the driver's seat, but in 1978 as the contest between the Dengist and the neo-Maoist supporters of Hua Guofeng heated up, the Red faction reportedly split into a right (pro-Dengist) group and left (pro-Hua) group, which included some Third Army elements, most notably the leader of the Shanxi faction, Governor Ma Xingyuan (Ma Hsing-yuan). Hua Guofeng was a Shanxi native and this presumably strengthened the political link between Ma and Hua.

Ma had accumulated strong organizational power in the party and again seemed to gain the upper hand in 1980 when Liao became seriously ill. But by the end of the year, Deng had triumphed over the Hua forces in Party Central and in 1981 he dispatched Xiang Nan to take over control of the Fujian party. Xiang transferred local cadre, rehabilitated others, including some members of the Black Faction, and put several new outsiders in senior positions. In 1983, Xiang was able to replace Ma as governor with a professional economist and administrator, Hu Ping. The following year, the vice governor who had succeeded Ma as head of the Shanxi Faction was also removed.

Xiang seemed to be making headway. Under his administration, factional infighting appeared to diminish and Fujian began to prosper. In December 1985, however, the Hong Kong paper *Ming Bao* reported that central had criticized the province for serious unhealthy tendencies. These included the charge that government and party organizations had collaborated in the manufacture and sale of counterfeit TV sets, bicycles, and other products, as well as adulterated wine, honey, tea, and bogus medicine. Other offices were said to have speculated in goods and contracts and to have blindly established business enterprises.

Whether or not Xiang was responsible for this outburst of entrepreneural spirit, he was transferred to Peking in 1986. His replacement, Chen Guangyi, was another native Fujianese who had spent his career away from the home province and mostly in technical jobs. Chen reportedly continued the struggle against the Red and Shanxi factions in particular but against all cliques in general.

At the end of 1986, Fujian appeared securely in the hands of the Dengists, who were focused on a hard-headed drive for economic development. But the old factions and probably new ones never seen lay like like hidden faults waiting for future tremors from Peking.

Political Expression

In terms of freedom of expression, India ranks among the top of a small number of Third World democracies. Intimidation of political critics and censorship of the press have occurred and, during the two-year emergency, tough police-state controls were applied. After returning to power, Mrs. Gandhi passed the National Security Act (NSA) of September, 1980, which authorizes detention without trial for up to twelve months for those "acting in any manner prejudicial to the security of the State." Although several thousand people have been detained for various periods under the NSA, there is "no evidence that the Act (has been) used against political opponents of the administration in the absence of some other allegation such as inciting to riot."[63] Nevertheless, the Act has obvious potential for unlimited abuse.

Despite travails and threats, real and potential, to civil liberties, freedom of expression has still triumphed in India. The manifold Indian press and a plethora of journals and intellectual broadsheets constantly pepper the reading public with critical assessments of society, political leaders, and government policy. In few other Third World countries are the intellectual community and the press by nature so hostile to the incumbent government. It is rare to find independent observers or writers who have anything good to say about the government of the day. The attacks range from the far left to the far right. Political graffiti is widespread in India and usually also unkind to the establishment: "Parliament is a pig-sty!" "Army out of Assam!" "Protest curriculum—Support Council Students on Fast."

Inspired by Gandhi tradition, fasts, demonstrations, and going to jail are all part of the Indian political scene. Indians go on a protest fast at the drop of a hat, although no prominent figure has yet died for the effort. The popular Chief Minister of Tamil Nadu, M. G. Ramachandran, upset with the central grain allocation to his state, launched a seven-hour fast, squatting on the marina beach in Madras. Following the set routine, the New Delhi minister concerned contacts the Chief Minister and pleads with him to end his fast; talks at the center are proposed. The question will be looked into. The fast is broken.

Going to jail is another modern Indian political tradition, and a period of detention is not entirely unwelcome by politicians. The jailer and the jailed play the game carefully. In 1975 Mrs. Gandhi put the opposition into comfortable detention and later they did the same to her. The Indians seem to be able to deal with political enemies and to accept vitriolic criticism in a more ambivalent manner than do Chinese. Indian politicians and lawyers exchange heated attacks in public, then have a cordial drink together.

Traditionally, neither the Indian nor the Chinese political system included the concept of legal opposition, and neither society encouraged the settlement of disputes through legal disputation. Over the past 150 years, however, India's adaptation of the concept of a loyal opposition and its even more enthusiastic embrace of litigation suggests that the spirit of the Indian is at once more contentious and less dogmatic than that of the Chinese.

Over 10 million court cases in India remain undisposed of (compared to 8 million in the U.S.). Reformers and leftists, as well as defenders of the status quo, also make use of the judicial process. Recently, liberal Indian lawyers have begun to file "class action suits" against government bureaucracies or the police. On the other side, landowners have filed hundreds of thousands of court cases holding up redistribution of millions of acres of land deemed excess in terms of land-reform acts.

After more than a decade of having no formal legal system, China under Deng's guidance has steadily rebuilt its judicial structure. The economic reforms have sparked a flood of new laws, regulations, and decrees. Since 1979, the NPC has enacted about 100 laws, the State Council has promulgated more than 300 administrative regulations, and local legislatures have passed in excess of 700 laws and local decrees. In 1985, Chinese courts heard more than 226,000 economic lawsuits. There were only about 20,000 Chinese lawyers—only half full-time and less than a third fully trained—to deal with these suits as well as with the growing number of criminal cases. But while litigation is increasing significantly in China, it seems unlikely to become a form of political activity or expression as it is in India.

Because politics has been the core of Chinese life, embracing all cultural and social values, a political enemy in China has traditionally been viewed as a mortal threat to be forced to repent or else cut into a thousand pieces. Chinese charm and graciousness can easily disappear in the face of a political foe. Political enemies are a threat to social order and to the preservation of orthodoxy. The preference not to destroy, but to humble the enemy, was reflected in Mao's treatment of successive challengers in the party. The ruthlessness of the Cultural Revolution toward its perceived enemies, and Peking's difficulty in the past in dealing dispassionately with disagreements with foreign governments, also suggests the trouble which Chinese still have in accepting the notion of legitimate opposition, whether political, judicial, or international.

During a question and answer session after a criminal trial in Shanghai, a judge explains that "Naturally, 99 percent of defendants plead guilty." To do otherwise is only to assure heavier punishment. Likewise, except for the brief democracy-wall period and the even more brief budding of the "hundred flowers" campaign in 1957, public criticism of the powers that be has rarely been permitted in the People's Republic. The torrent of "big character posters" during the Cultural Revolution was directed at Mao's enemies, including the bureaucracy, or else they reflected local feuds between rival Maoist factions. The Red Guards knew better than to attack those really in authority in Peking. Likewise, despite the impressive liberalization of culture and art as well as the economy under Deng, the reform regime has made clear in its "four principles" that government and party leaders and the doctrine they formally embrace are not to be criticized. The student protesters that took to the streets of Shanghai, Peking, and other cities in December 1986 were, with rare exception, careful to criticize the absence of real democracy and not the leadership or socialism.

Agitation

No day passes in a major Indian city without a demonstration of some sort. A local union, a student organization, a group protesting something, another group supporting it, and bands of disgruntled citizens wanting this or that done or not done by the government parade daily down the streets of India with banners flying, chanting their demands. No one in the streets pays much attention. Squads of riot police with wicked-looking clubs called *lathis*—and sometimes automatic rifles chained to their bodies—are usually present. Generally, it ends peacefully, but sometimes it explodes into bloody violence, as in continuing Sikh agitation in the Punjab since 1984 and the bloody riots in Assam in 1983.

Labor unrest also occurs sporadically. The 1981 Essential Services Maintenance Act empowers the government to ban strikes in critical sectors of the economy such as defense, energy, steel, irrigation, etc. A general strike, called to protest the act, resulted in the arrest (under the act) of 6,000 strike leaders and the death of twelve people. Despite the new act, strikes increased, including prolonged agitation in Bangalore and Bombay, and at the Bharat Oil Refinery. The proliferation of unions—the average membership is only about 600—makes it difficult for the government to stabilize industrial relations, but also undermines efforts to organize regional or national strikes and agitation.

Sometimes the police themselves have taken to the streets to assert their demands. A mutiny of the Provincial Armed Constabulary in Uttar Pradesh in 1973 was suppressed by the army, which shot 100 of the strikers. In Gujarat, the Punjab, Maharashtra and other states, the army has also been called in to put down illegal protests or strikes by police, and several hundred Sikh soldiers mutinied after the 1984 attack on the Golden Temple.

In Hyderabad, civil servants angrily demonstrate because the new state government has decreed they must sign a check-in book by 10:30 A.M. every morning. In Trivandrum the Kerala Frog-Catchers Association gathers in a mass demonstration before the state secretariat, protesting the government's decision to bring frogs under the Wildlife Protection Act and to regulate the trade—a controversial government action which had, itself, followed earlier protests by Kerala farmers over the upsurge in frog slaughter which the farmers claimed was resulting in the proliferation of stem-borer pests in the paddy fields. About the same time, lawyers in Bihar stage a strike protesting police lathi attacks against a group of Patna lawyers who had been meeting to protest an earlier police charge on a demonstration parade by lawyers. Meanwhile, a "national conference of backward castes" in Madras calls for rallies throughout the country as part of a country-wide movement to promote greater reservations of government jobs and university placements for "backward castes." Subsequently, bucking the trend, the Chief Minister of the State creates a storm by calling for extension of the concessions given to "backward castes" to all poor people, regardless of caste. Earlier, the same chief minister had had to back down from a proposal that backward caste members and untouchables with an annual income of more than $900 should not be eligible for reservations. Students unhappy with the extension of reservations and what they see as a lowering of educational standards have gone to court on the matter.

Between the "democracy wall" outburst of 1978–1979 and the end of 1986, only a handful of labor strikes or student demonstrations took place in China, including September 1985 protest marches against Japanese "economic aggression." On a few occasions, minority students made brief public protests of government policy toward their respective regions.

The December 1986 demonstrations in Shanghai, Peking, and a number of other eastern cities, however, were much more serious. In the biggest such event since the Cultural Revolution, university students demanded genuine democratic reforms and in some cases tens of thousands of marchers chanted slogans such as, "no democracy, no modernization!" The students in large part were reacting to calls for political reform and democracy that the intellectual innovators around Hu Yaobang had generated over the previous year. There was speculation that Hu's people had encouraged the demonstrations in order to provide momentum to their announced plans for political reform.

If the Hu liberals had in fact encouraged the demonstrations, it was a grievous mistake. Whatever it was, it was not an India-type political affair. Rather it ended in a Chinese style purge. The leading liberals lost their jobs and some intellectuals their party membership as well. It was a purgative meant to clean out those in prominent positions who had been too tolerant of disorder and of agitation against the political establishment—a neo-Confucianist as well as a communist sin.

Once again intellectuals and artists, during a period of liberalization, had rushed over the bounds of what was intended. For the third time since the ascendency of the Deng reformers in late 1978, the intellectuals had been directed back to the borders of the permissible. Most of the students were apparently concerned with being suspended or given undesirable job assignments at graduation. The agitation quickly died out, the youth returned to their studies, and the liberal Marxists' dream of fundamental political reform seemed to have been given a serious if not fatal blow.

While the general impression of foreigners is that India since 1950 has been afflicted with endemic civil disorder and China has generally been more peaceful, the fact is that more Chinese have been killed in domestic violence during this period than have Indians. By Peking's official count 34,000 Chinese were killed as a direct result of the Cultural Revolution and more than 700,000 were "persecuted." The actual figures could well be higher. The number of victims has not been estimated for the 1957 anti-rightist campaign, but a good number of Chinese must have died indirectly because of imprisonment and "persecution" at that time.

One might insist on counting the 250,000 or more killed by mobs in India and Pakistan during the 1947 partition, but in that case it would be appropriate to add the hundreds of thousands and possibly more than a million Chinese executed by kangaroo courts during the land reform campaign of the early 1950s. If we included all domestic violence in the two countries since 1947, we would also have to include the millions killed in the Chinese Civil War. In gross figures, life and limb was in more danger in China over the past 40 years or so than in India. Presumably this has been the culmination of almost a century and a half of chaos and now China is settling down to another few hundred years of serenity. We will have to wait and see.

Fear of violence in daily life, however, is greater in India. Conflict in Indian villages between castes has no counterpart in China. Typically, the waves of violent death in modern China have resulted from political movements, while in India they have reflected religious and communal conflicts.

Another form of political activity in India that has its roots in the Gandhian tradition is the individual agitator and organizer who acts independently and remains relatively untainted by political ties. Two examples of this phenomenon gained national attention in recent years. Dr. Datta Samant, a medical doctor, started out attempting to help hutment dwellers and quarry workers in Bombay and then moved into organizing workers in industrial units. His confrontational tactics were successful and workers flocked to him. Samant, who has spent time in detention, has had little or nothing to do with the Indian National Trade Union Congress or with any established political party. He became a folk hero in Bombay, and at one point pulled out 65,000 workers on a prolonged strike of the ailing Bombay textile mills. Samant is typical of the socially committed leader of mass movements that India traditionally has produced.

Another leader of this type is Sharad Joshi, a retired civil servant from Maharashtra who took up farming and the cause of the Indian commerical farmer. Joshi, also avoiding ties with established political parties, has railed against exploitation of the countryside by urban India and with notable success he has led farmers to agitate for fair prices for their produce, lower electricity and irrigation charges, and concessions on overdue bank loans. Farmer unions are active in 8 of India's 22 states. In 1984 Joshi held a national conference attended by 50,000 farmers from across the country.

While there are today no effective national, or even state-level landless peasant organizations, and labor unions are splintered and weak, Samant and Joshi represent the potential for the gradual emergence of class politics in India to compete with caste and communal interests.

As we have seen, the organization of vested interests for political purposes is not permitted in China. Whatever political reforms the Dengists may have in mind, it is unlikely that they intend to allow the type of organization that Samant and Joshi have carried out in India. While they intend to expand the autonomy of individuals in cultural and social life and of separate units in the economy, the performers like the neo-Maoists believe that mobilization of interest groups for political purposes would bring instability, loss of control, and eventually chaos.

CHAPTER 8

Changing Pace in Industry

Seeking Power through Industrialization

India and China could have chosen development strategies that stressed agricultural production and development of labor-intensive industries. If they had done so, there is little doubt that both would have achieved more in the way of eliminating poverty, raising general standards of health and welfare, and reducing the gap between the "two Chinas" and between the "two Indias"—rural and urban. It is a moot question whether they would now be in a better position to launch an industrialization drive. A communist regime and a democratic government each gave higher priority to nationalistic and ideological objectives than to raising consumption and living standards.

The new leaders of India and China were determined to end poverty in their countries, but their programs were not designed primarily to raise living standards as fast as possible. The drive for national power and the force of ideology shaped their respective development strategies far more than did the simple objective of improving the general welfare. Long periods of subjugation had made both Indians and Chinese determined to free themselves from dependence on the West, and to build self-sufficient nations. Both sought to restore their pride and sense of greatness by creating an economic base for national power that would not only predominate in its region, but would also be a major, independent actor on the world stage.

In both cases defense was an immediate priority for the allocation of resources; and defense industries required heavy industry. India had fought a war with Pakistan immediately after independence, and China had swept into a conflict with the U.S. little more than a year after the establishment of the People's Republic. Moreover, China at the time saw itself allied with the

Soviet Union in a militant struggle with world capitalism, headed by the United States, and thus building China into an industrial and military power was a primary ideological goal. For its first 15 years, India, emphasizing peaceful coexistence and non-alignment, would give considerably less priority to military spending than China; nevertheless, security as well as independence was a major rationale of the Indian focus on industrialization.

These emotional, intellectual, and ideological inclinations convinced New Delhi and Peking that building a modern industrial infrastructure had to be the first order of business if they hoped to safeguard their sovereignty and national independence and to play the roles they saw for themselves on the world stage. Operating with different political economies, the two countries set off in the same general direction of economic self-sufficiency and industrialization.

Under the leadership of Jawaharlal Nehru, India sought to pursue a democratic socialist path to development, stressing heavy industrial and infrastructure growth with an emphasis on expanding the state sector and achieving self-sufficiency through import substitution. In agriculture, Nehru emphasized structural and social reforms, rather than accelerated investment.

Despite a socialist ideology, the Indian economy was to continue to operate within a free, although highly regulated, market and a representative democratic system. Meanwhile, China, set on a more revolutionary course, intended to re-build the nation on the Soviet model, including a command economy, a collective agriculture, and a central plan replacing the marketplace. Even retail trade and services would come under the public sector.

Although there have been gigantic problems of inefficiency and mismanagement and appalling waste of capital, India and China can boast of impressive accomplishments in carrying out their strategies of self-reliance through industrialization.

Both countries have built a wide range of basic industries, including electronics and heavy engineering, that few other developing countries can match. By the 1970s China and India were manufacturing almost all the important durable consumer goods that they required, plus a wide selection of producer goods. Over 50 percent of India's and China's exports are now manufactured items, a much higher proportion than that enjoyed by other low-income countries. Chinese and Indian cars are made from ancient molds, but they have been largely local products. Both countries have built large electric power stations, dams, and steel presses. Their engineering industries can supply the great bulk of the power-generating, railway, and road-transport equipment that their economies require. India, as well as China, has also managed to construct an extensive petroleum industry, including development, in cooperation with foreign corporations, of offshore technology. Building on Soviet assistance, China has constructed its own refineries, and India has achieved considerable self-reliance in this field.

The successes of self-sufficiency, however, were at the cost of comparative advantage, a principle that the most successful developing countries—like South Korea—have pursued. This has resulted in a large loss of return on investment in both India and China, countries which can sorely afford such losses.

To achieve their goals of modernity and power, India and China each showed an impressive ability to put off present consumption for future growth. In India, the domestic savings ratio rose from 10 percent in 1950 to an estimated 23 percent in 1983–1984—a remarkable rate for a very poor and democratic country.[64]

In China savings have been even higher—25–30 percent of gross domestic product. As in India, most of this capital has been devoted to heavy industry. As Wilfred Malenbaum indicates, for 30 years China was putting almost as much into heavy industry proportionally as the average low-income country was channeling into total investment.[65]

The problems that the heavy industrial sectors of India and China eventually encountered were similar in their causes but different in their effect. China faced runaway production with enormous waste; India, stagnation with great inefficiency and underutilization of capacity.

Growth and Stagnation in India

Indian industry grew rapidly until the early 1960s, when India ranked tenth (or twelfth, depending on the yardstick) in the entire world in industrial production. Between 1950 and 1965 industrial production grew in India by 9 percent a year. Nehru's goals of nationalizing heavy industry and bringing the "commanding heights" of the economy under the public sector were achieved. The public sector in India now accounts for 40–60 percent of capital formation, holds three-fourths of the country's industrial assets (including the ten top industrial firms in the nation, which, together, are bigger than the top 100 private firms), employs over 12 million people, and is responsible for one-third of industrial production. Ninety percent of banking is now in the hands of nationalized banks.

In the mid–1960s, however, industrial growth in India began to stagnate, averaging only 3 percent a year. The Indian government's policy of capital-intensive investment, its stress on the inefficient state sector, and its failure to encourage either export industries or foreign investments created relatively few urban jobs. From 1965 to 1975 the industrial labor force grew only 1.9 percent annually, or only 0.3 percent more than the number of new job-seekers coming on the labor market each year. While industry's share of the gross national product grew from 15 percent to 26 percent in three decades, the share of the labor force employed in industry remained at about 11 percent.[66] With agricultural production only staying even with population growth, the internal market could not energize the economy sufficiently to create self-generating growth.

Industrial stagnation in India in the late 1960s and through the 1970s also resulted in part from increased controls on private-sector investment. In addition to nationalizing coal, insurance, and banking, the central government in 1971 adopted even more restrictive measures to control the private sector, with the professed goals of avoiding monopolies, discouraging the over-concentration of power, and encouraging the establishment of industry in backward areas. Large private firms now had to seek government approval for expansion or diversification of their production. "This is the only country where a businessman can go to jail for increasing production," noted the managing director of one of India's largest manufacturing firms.

Elements of the private sector, however, came not only to live with high regulations and a closed and protected market, but also to love it. Profits were made not through increased production, sales, turnover, or higher productivity, but "through creating a regime of shortages with a built-in incentive to produce well below capacity." Large firms could make high profits operating at only 40 percent of capacity.[67] The number of small industrial enterprises increased to over 300,000 (near the comparable Chinese figure) but some of these were established by big business houses to escape regulation.

India's large-scale private industries ceased to expand. In 1966 the public sector employed 9.4 million workers and the "organized," i.e., large scale, private sector, 6.8 million; in 1975 there were 12.5 million workers in the public sector but still only 6.8 million in the "organized" private sector.[68]

There were several other results of the tough regulatory policy: corruption began to grow rapidly; productive investments declined, and wealth was channeled into real estate and other speculative investments and safe havens, such as gold. The last phenomenon caused the black-market price of gold in India to rise substantially above the international price, and smuggling of gold into Bombay became a major problem.

In another move intended to firm up its leftist image and its support among urban workers, the central government, under Mrs. Gandhi, began the practice of nationalizing large firms that were on the verge, or in the process, of bankruptcy. Thus, workers in a company with marginal profitability developed an interest in the company's failure, because they would then enjoy the benefits and security of employment in the state sector. The government takeover and maintenance of sick companies resulted in both a drain on the general budget and a further decrease in industrial productivity. Meanwhile, all industry began to suffer from power shortages and transportation breakdowns.

These factors combined to generate high inefficiency in the industrial sector and a very low rate of return on capital investment compared to most other developing countries. According to an unofficial World Bank estimate, if the incremental capital output ratio in India had not worsened in the 1960s, India could have obtained an average 5 percent annual growth in net domestic product.[69]

China's Industrial Boom and Readjustment

While India in the mid–1960s seemed to stumble over basic inefficiency in its industrialization approach, China's production, especially in heavy industry, appeared to plunge ahead. According to pre–1979 estimates by the U.S. government, Western academics and the World Bank, Chinese industrial production grew by about 10 percent every year from 1957–1959. Heavy industry reportedly grew even faster, at 13 percent, compared to 9 percent for light industry.[70] Overall, China in 1980 was said to be producing 13 times the industrial product that it had turned out in 1950. This apparently stunning record was achieved despite the economic disruptions caused by the successive upheavals of the Great Leap Forward in the late 1950s, the withdrawal of Soviet advisors with their blueprints in the early 1960s, and the Cultural Revolution in the mid and late 1960s. Even the Japanese had not equalled such a sustained growth in industry.

If China's industrial growth rate since the 1950s had been as high as outsiders, and presumably the Chinese, believed in the 1970s, then Peking should have been very pleased with its policies. But, beginning in 1979, Chinese official statements stressed the serious imbalances that existed in the Chinese economy—very similar to those in India—and the irrational aspects of China's industrial production.

Concerned about the serious flaws in the economy and by budget deficits and inflation caused by large food subsidies and wage increases, Peking at the end of 1978 proclaimed a long period of economic retrenchment, and in 1981 further tightened its economic belt and announced that the "readjustment" would last throughout the 1980s. The thrust of Chinese economic policy in the 1980s has been to try to limit the expansion of heavy industry and capital construction, and to attempt to hold down overall industrial growth to a moderate rate.

Why did the Chinese leaders not wish to repeat the rapid growth of industrial production that the nation supposedly recorded in its first thirty years, and instead plan to keep overall economic growth rates down to modest levels? The answer given by the Chinese themselves is simply that a great deal of industrial production in China in the past had been unusable. Premier Zhao Ziyang told the 1982 NPC that industrial growth from 1953 to 1980 had not been "low" but that the economic results of this growth were "very poor." Waste in industrial production, he said, had been "appalling."[71] Because of priorities followed over the previous years, heavy industry in China had become a monster, consuming the savings of the country, but producing machinery and new plants simply to serve its own expansion.

In China's command economy, in which management performance had been judged by output and capital had been used to expand production facilities whatever the demand for the product or its quality, unmarketable inventories piled up. Premier Zhao told a Science and Technology Awards Conference in Peking in October, 1982, that China's economic system had two fundamental short-comings: (1) "It cannot very effectively encourage enterprises to concern themselves with technical progress," and (2) it has difficulty "in producing usable products."

Chinese media, citing one example of wasteful production, reported that the inventory of electrical machinery in 1980 was valued at over $30 billion, one-quarter of the planned value of all heavy industrial production for the year. The stockpile of steel products was nearly 20 million tons that same year although high quality steel imports were increasing.

In his address in June, 1979, to the National People's Congress, then-premier Hua Kuofeng, expressing the views of the dominant reformist group led by Deng, stressed the poor quality of industrial production. Hua also stated that 24 percent of China's industrial enterprises were run at a loss. In 1982, Premier Zhao said the figure was 30 percent. The Chinese also reported that 43 percent of major industrial products from key enterprises were qualitatively inferior to the best produced in the past, and 55 percent of enterprises used more raw and semi-finished materials than during their best past periods.[72]

Complaining of blind expansion, Zhao told the 1982 NPC that industrial enterprises, not including those run by production brigades, had increased from 195,000 in 1971 to more than 377,000. According to Zhao, many advanced enterprises could not operate at full capacity because the energy and raw and semi-finished materials they needed were being used by backward enterprises which consumed these valuable supplies and turned out sub-standard products.

Net production per industrial worker in China had increased over the years by a fairly respectable 3.7 percent per year, similar to a comparable figure in India of 3.4 percent. But capital investment in Chinese industry had expanded even faster than in India, and with labor and capital inputs combined together, there was no increase in Chinese industrial productivity. In China's planned economy, capital was essentially costless for managers, as it was obtained through bureaucratic lobbying for higher allocations. China thus continued to expand industrial production by pouring in more capital—and, to a lesser extent, more labor. The large capital inputs into industry were, in turn, accummulated by holding down investment in agriculture as well as restricting domestic consumption.

Bottlenecks

India and China have encountered similar kinds of physical bottlenecks, primarily in transportation and in shortages of input materials and energy.

India, for example, has been importing steel, cement, and fertilizer, a good deal of which it could produce itself if it could operate its present plants at full capacity. A major constraint on production in Indian steel plants is the erratic supply of power. Electric power plants in India produce at less than 50 percent capacity due to (1) poor maintenance and inefficient use of equipment, resulting in part from squabbles between unions affiliated with different political parties; and (2) shortages of coal at power plants caused by labor disputes, by violence at the pit-heads, and—completing the circle—by a shortage of electric power at the mines. The deterioration of Indian railway service in the 1970s also contributed to the coal-supply problems as deliveries fell behind schedule. The quality of the coal actually delivered has also been low, usually consisting of a good deal of rock and other debris which breaks down power-plant boilers.

While India's problem in energy is one of inefficient use of power-generating capacity, in China it is staggering waste. China's energy consumption per capita (in kilograms of coal equivalent) in 1980 was 835—as compared to India's 242. China's energy consumption rate is four times that of the average low-income country and its energy-to-output ratio is more than double India's. Even with such a large output of energy, much of Chinese industry operates at 25 percent of capacity because of power shortages. In both countries coal accounts for over 60 percent of energy consumption, so the relatively low inefficiency of coal does not explain the higher energy-to-output ratio. China's cold winters increase its per capita energy consumption compared to that of India. But the main reason for the high Chinese consumption rate appeared to be the lack of incentives to conserve energy on the part of industrial consumers, who were concerned with output rather than profitability.

Transport has been another major infrastructure problem in both countries, but it is an even bigger bottleneck in China than it is in India. China's transport system remains significantly less developed than that of India. Both countries still use animals, human-pulled carts, and, particularly in China, wind-powered vessels for a great deal of transport. But the superficial impression is that there is a good deal more of these primitive ways of moving things about in China. The figures on modern transport tend to bear this out.

China has 5 kilometers of railway track for each 1,000 square kilometers of land area, and .05 kilometers per 1,000 population. In India the comparable figures are 15 and .09. China has doubled its railways to 50,000 kilometers of track, but it is still behind India which has 60,900 kilometers, serving one-third the total land area.[73]

India is even further ahead in motorable roads, with 1,604,000 kilometers to about 900,000 kilometers in China, which has one of the least developed road systems in the world. India is clearly more motorized than China, which has 16 motor vehicles per 10,000 population, to India's 58 per 10,000, including motorcycles (or 22 per 10,000 excluding motorcycles). Chinese urban streets are dominated by bicycles and buses, whereas in India the motorcycle middle-class is much in evidence. But in long-distance travel, the Indian people are also much more mobile. In China, trains average 200 passenger kilometers per person per year, while in India the figure is 710. This great difference in train travel, which in both cases is overwhelmingly second-class travel by everyday workers and peasants, reflects in part the artificial immobility imposed on most of the Chinese and in part the pattern of migratory workers in India.

The Informal Economies

In countries where there is an environment of scarcity combined with comprehensive government controls, it is inevitable that efforts will be made to get around the system. An extensive informal economy has grown up in China, different from but somewhat similar to the pervasive "underground" or "parallel" economy in India—which may be as high as 10–15 percent of gross national product.

In India, the parallel economy consists of businessmen and individuals who hide income profits or business activity from government tax collectors and regulators. An entrepreneur will, for example, run a number of small sweatshops making, say, clothing—rather than one factory which cannot so easily escape taxes and regulations. Small factories, when they need to expand but wish to avoid the controls that go with being classified as an "organized" (i.e., large-scale) industry may simply cut another gate in the fence and treat the expansion as a new, separate company.

Understating assets is also an Indian game played by the giants. In 1979 the Indian government estimated the assets of the Tata group at more than $1.3 billion (U.S. dollars), but in December of that same year Tata placed an ad in the Paris-based *International Herald-Tribune* which claimed assets of 1.3 billion pounds sterling, which would be equivalent to more than $2 billion (U.S. dollars). After this became a public issue in India, Tata placed another ad in the *Economist* which claimed assets of only 550 million pounds, or less than $1 billion in U.S. dollars. Some Indian observers maintain that if the parallel economy was included in official economic estimates, India's industrial performance in the last twelve years would look much better.

The supply of input materials at the right time and the right place has been an even greater problem in China than in India because of the more centralized bureaucratic management system and the less well-developed transport network. Since shortage of materials is the biggest constraint in meeting output quotas, plant managers in China have tended to hoard such materials. Barter trade has also grown up in which two or more companies swap their products.

Chinese provinces have tried to retain raw materials for processing at home because of the threat of shortages and the enormous profits to be obtained by processing. At one time, the Shanghai cigarette industry ran out of tobacco because local administrations in tobacco-growing provinces had opened their own cigarette factories.

The competition among Chinese enterprises for financial allocations and for material supplies leads to banqueting, gift-giving, and other forms of public relations that have often developed into outright bribery. In a crack-down on corruption in China, 136,000 cases of "economic crimes" were dealt with in the first nine months of 1982. A July, 1983, report by the party's central Discipline Commission raised the total to 192,000 cases, ranging from petty bribery to million-dollar smuggling rackets condoned by officials. Thirty-thousand offenders were given jail terms and $205 million in illegal gains were reportedly recovered.

In 1984 and 1985, following institution of liberal reforms in commercial, industrial, and financial management, another even larger wave of corruption swept over the scene. The head of the Hainan People's Government and a number of his colleagues were dismissed or jailed for importing tax free 89,000 motor vehicles and over two million TV sets and reselling the goods all over China at double or triple the price. According to the official report, 872 companies and 88 departments under the regional government participated in the scandal. Schools and banks were involved; even the *Hainan Daily* pocketed 4.3 million yuan in illegal foreign exchange dealings and declared huge bonuses for its staff. Four people were found guilty of pocketing more than 1 million yuan. A farm worker in Qionghai County, in a manner left unexplained, made 2.09 million yuan.

Corruption in India, of course, has long been a way of life. While anti-corruption squads still go about their work uncovering dramatic cases, little or nothing is done about the pervasive corruption that has infected the whole bureaucracy—from government ministers and officers of the Indian Administrative Service down to village officials. According to a university professor, his colleagues must pad various vouchers and make up other expenses in order to make ends meet. Villagers tell a foreign visitor that the doctor or medical worker in the government clinic requires *baksheesh* before he will prescribe an injection or medicine, otherwise he will simply dole out an aspirin. If a traveler wants a seat or compartment in a crowded train, he has only to offer a gratuity to the conductor. This sort of petty corruption and a great deal much worse involving the police and the courts has become much more internalized as a part of Indian society than it has in China.

India demonstrates the observation that corruption of the people as distinct from corruption of the ruling circles is much greater in a populist democracy than in an authoritarian one. The more total control a government exercises the less opportunity there is for private interests to invade the public domain. But the most profound corruption is the concentrated perversion of power by the ruling circles of an absolutist regime of the right or the left. As China has become a more pluralistic society, not surprisingly the problem of corruption has grown.

Managerial Talent

Efficiency in Chinese industry has also been handicapped by a lack of managerial and technical expertise among its enterprise managers and senior officials; in 1980 only 7 percent of the managers of China's 377,000 industrial enterprises had college degrees—350,000 were former PLA officials with an average of only a junior high school education. The Cultural Revolution not only traumatized existing management, but also set back for a generation the process of training more competent industrial cadre.

India has produced a much larger number of accountants and engineers over the past 30 years than has China. In India there is no shortage of college-educated applicants for engineering and management positions. According to businessmen the quality is not always high. Nevertheless, most Indian enterprise managers today have had either university training or entrepreneurial experience in the private sector.

During the Dengist reforms there has been an enormous shakeup in the ranks of China's industrial managers. By 1986 more than 90 percent of those holding top positions in the 3,000 most important factories in 1982 had been replaced. These factories account for 45 percent of the nation's gross value of industrial output. The new managers reportedly average less than 47 years of age and nine of ten are college educated.

The Problem of Pricing

Another common problem has been the de-stabilizing effect of administered prices which do not reflect relative scarcity, quality, or production costs. Premier Zhao, in December 1982, told the NPC that prices of various commodities in China were "for the most part irrational," and that reform of the price system and conscious use of the law of value were imperative. Some items in China have been grossly underpriced, such as coal and oil, a situation which discourages conservation. On the international market 3 tons of coal in the early 1980s could buy one ton of wheat. In China it took 15 tons of coal to do so.

Other products have been greatly overpriced, in particular processed and producer goods. The domestic price of Chinese fertilizer, for example, is four times the world market price. In manufacturing extravagant cost and large mark-ups are added at every stage of production. Thus the outdated and inefficient Shanghai sedans cost as much or more as current Japanese or American models. Consumer prices were set with little regard to quality or demand. For example, popular Flying Pigeon brand bicycles have been almost impossible to buy, while less desirable brands have stacked up large inventories in warehouses.

In India durable consumer goods have been competitive in pricing, but a number of other products have been administratively under-priced, reflecting popular pressures. For example, demands from farm groups have usually kept fertilizer prices below the international level. This has resulted in irrational distribution and higher government deficits, although it has also encouraged greater fertilizer use.

Reforms in the Industrial Sector

In the 1970s Indian and Chinese leaders became seriously concerned over the imbalances and inefficiencies in their industrial sectors. Even more painful was the stark reality that large areas of extreme poverty continued to exist in both countries. In 1973 in India and in 1978 in China, policy direction shifted to those who believed that future growth was linked directly to progress in agriculture and to increases in the purchasing power of the peasant masses. These reformers also recognized that future economic expansion would have to come from enlarging the return on investment and the efficiency of labor, rather than on withholding heroic amounts of resources from consumption for investment purposes. They also knew that increased productivity could not take place without access to international technology and that this, in turn, required an expansion of exports. Deng's "bean curd" or "consumer communism" and India's "chipati" or "semi-deregulated socialism" were both based on the concept that higher investments in light industry, including locally generated rural industries, and increased production of consumer goods could yield rapid returns, raise domestic living standards, and at the same time open new export markets to help pay for imported capital equipment and technology.

Since 1978 the reformers around Deng have been determined to redress structural imbalances by redistributing national income to allow for more consumption, particularly in rural areas, and by directing the larger share of investment into light industry, energy, and infrastructure and, where possible, to more labor-intensive production. Other major goals of the Deng group have been to increase labor discipline and productivity, decentralize and enhance management responsibility, and drastically reduce and energize China's huge bureaucracy. The innovators have also launched various schemes to reorganize, consolidate and amalgamate enterprises and to overhaul the administration of the industrial system. Their objective is to devolve authority over all but key enterprises or national corporations to the municipal level and to encourage collective and even privately-run enterprises in light industry and commerce.

Directives from Peking have attempted to strengthen worker discipline and apply the principle of "more pay for more work, less pay for less work, and no pay for no work." Efforts have been made to adapt the successful incentive reforms in agriculture to industry, setting up various "responsibility systems" throughout industry at all levels. Bonus payments are being tied to individual shop and enterprise productivity.

Meanwhile, a transition has begun to substitute taxes on enterprises for direct remittance of profits to the state and to substitute bank loans for direct government allocations.

Not only has small-scale private enterprise been encouraged but a few state firms have been privatized or returned to their previous capitalist owners, such as the Minsheng Shipping Company on the Yangtse River.

At the same time, efforts to break the various physical bottlenecks have focused on increased investment in transportation and energy and a major campaign to force energy conservation measures and conversions from oil to coal. The greatest bureaucratic shake-up of all time also began with wholesale retrenchment of the central government bureaucracies in Peking and the replacement of a large number of senior cadre with younger and better-educated persons.

Beginning on October 1, 1986, all new workers in state enterprises were to be employed on a new contract system. Regulations set out the procedures for recruitment and dismissal as well as establishment of a new unemployment insurance system. New workers who lose their jobs can receive 60–75 percent of their average wage for the first twelve months they are unemployed and 50 percent for an additional year. How the system will work in practice is of course a big question, but another revolutionary change was the provision for direct recruitment of workers by each enterprise rather than through assignment by local labor departments.

In a major opening to the marketplace, China in 1986 also decontrolled the prices of a number of consumer goods, including bicycles, sewing machines, electric fans, watches, black and white TVs, cassette players, and some textile goods.

India got a three or four year head start on reform. Mrs. Gandhi began liberalizing government control over business activity during the 1975–1977 emergency period. The Janata administration (1977–1980), stressing rural development and maximization of employment, extended Mrs. Gandhi's reforms. New Delhi loosened up on import licensing, including the purchase of technical know-how, and tax and other incentives for up-dating technology were introduced. The Indian government also tried to rationalize and improve the efficiency and profitability of the public sector, which in 1979–1980 was still running at a net loss of 1 percent, compared to the average after-tax profit of large private companies of 14 percent. As in China, a productivity-linked bonus scheme was begun in the public sector, including the railways.

When Mrs. Gandhi returned to office in 1980 she continued the process of liberalization, further relaxing licensing procedures for private company expansion, diversification, and external borrowing. Twenty-four industries "reserved" for medium- or small-scale enterprises were exempted from licensing requirements and certain automatic expansion was allowed in 19 industries open to large industrial houses and foreign firms. Large production increases and plant expansion still required government license, but these were now approved more liberally than in the past.

Further encouraging the private sector, Mrs. Gandhi's government took a generally harder line on labor agitation as, for example, in the Bombay textile strike, and the top income tax bracket was reduced from 97.5 percent to 66 percent. Meanwhile, the government announced it would henceforth only nationalize "sick firms" that promised an early return to viability.

To end budgetary subsidies, the prices of some public-sector products, including steel, were raised in 1981 to more closely reflect production costs. To help meet the energy problem, private Indian firms like Tata were permitted to build electric-generating plants. More resources were also devoted to increasing efficiency and productivity in the coal mines and in petroleum production. Finally, a new Economic Administration Reform Committee was established to recommend other reforms.

Looking for Foreign Capital

In recent years India and China have also moved away from import substitution and instead have sought to spur the growth of exports and to recruit private foreign investments and joint ventures. In the early 1980s Peking promulgated a Joint-Venture Law and a Foreign Enterprise Tax Law, and established New Economic Zones where foreign firms could construct tariff-free assembly and manufacturing facilities. Eventually, the regulations permitted some wholly-owned foreign ventures and the partial retention of foreign exchange earnings.

Foreign businessmen, however, continued to complain of bureaucratic frustrations and disincentives to growth and expansion. Nevertheless, from 1979 to 1986, according to unofficial figures, China absorbed $4.6 billion in private investment and another $12 billion had been committed. China also joined the World Bank and the International Monetary Fund, and by 1985 had signed loan agreements with the Bank totalling over $3 billion. In 1986 Peking made its third drawing from the IMF. That year, China's external debt rose to over $20 billion.

Under Rajiv Gandhi more policy initiatives were taken to streamline investment procedures and licensing requirements to encourage upgrading of technology. Gandhi exempted 25 broad industrial categories from all licensing requirements, allowed 28 industrial groups to integrate their product mix horizontally, and quintrupled the asset threshold above which companies automatically come under anti-monopoly sanctions. Other reforms in taxes, trade, and banking policies also attempted to stimulate investment. The number of foreign joint ventures rose from 752 in 1984 to 1,024 in 1985. Total foreign investments in 1981 had been only $8 million, but since 1985, foreign companies have pumped in over $100 million a year, spurring sectors such as automobiles, leather and oil field servicing.

While this has been a significant gain, China, despite its late start, has had more success than India in attracting foreign investment. The main reason for this is that 80 percent of such investment in China comes from overseas Chinese, principally in Hong Kong. In addition, China with its system of command politics may be able to be more flexible than populist India in coming to terms with foreign capitalists. China, for example, in the early 1980s signed 23 contracts with foreign oil companies for exploration and exploitation rights in the South China Sea. India at about the same time engaged in a similar negotiating process with Western companies for rights in the "Bombay High," but could reach agreement with only one.

China also has confounded most expectations and passed India in terms of the role that exports play in its economy. The value of China's exports is now more than three times that of India and represents 9 percent of China's gross domestic product, as compared to 5 percent in the case of India. Oil has been the main single contributor to China's dynamic trade picture. Even with the drop in prices beginning in 1985, oil accounted for about one-fifth of China's total foreign exchange earnings.

Since 1978, China's foreign trade has developed at a dizzying pace and in different directions. First, between 1978 and 1982, yearly exports more than doubled in value to about $24 billion. In 1983, due to declining oil exports, China's trade earnings rose only marginally, but then spurted ahead another 14 percent in 1984.

Imports ran significantly below the value of exports until 1984 when China relaxed controls, imported a large amount of capital goods and technology, and thus experienced a small trade deficit. In 1985 matters seemed to careen out of control. Peking relaxed its management of commerce, the banking system, and foreign exchange. Capital development, particularly in the rural areas, whirled upward. By 1986 total domestic investment was double that of three years before! The rush of imports that year, including Japanese cars and other consumer goods, was partially deliberate to sop up excess buying power, but mostly it seemed to result from factories and government and even party offices with access to foreign currency going on a buying spree.

Controls were reimposed during 1985 but only gradually began to have effect. That year China experienced a staggering trade deficit of $14 billion. Peking reined in imports, and the deficit was expected to drop below $10 billion in 1986.

In contrast to the situation in China, petroleum has been a very negative factor in India's trade picture. India has rapidly expanded its domestic oil production, which in the 1984–1985 period met 70 percent of its domestic needs, reversing the ratio of several years ago. But despite its shrinking oil import bill, India has been running increasingly large trade deficits, estimated at about $5.6 billion in the 1985–1986 fiscal year.

As part of Rajiv Gandhi's approach to modernization, imports of foreign technology have leaped ahead, accounting for part of the trade gap. Another element of the problem has been that with indigenous refining capacity coming on stream, India has decreased its crude oil exports which were sold for hard currency (and which were offset by imports of Soviet refined oil products denominated in rupee counter-trade). Non-oil exports did rise by 8.4 percent in 1985–1986, but the increase was largely in primary products.

In the last two years India has seemed to follow a more cautious financial and international trade policy than China. If its trade gap continues, New Delhi will presumably also move to cut back on imports. Indian businessmen hope it will not be in the capital goods sector.

Another unique foreign exchange asset for Peking is Hong Kong, where over 4 million Chinese pay hard currency for Chinese cabbage, water, and other food and consumer goods. China has gained another 25 percent of its foreign exchange from this convenient and irreplacable market and, as noted, 80 percent of its foreign investment! In recent years, China has earned more than US $700 million annually in remittances from overseas and Hong Kong Chinese to relatives on the mainland. Keen not to lose this source of foreign exchange, China in 1984 concluded an agreement with the U.K. under which Hong Kong will remain a separate entity for another half century, although nominally, beginning in 1997, under Chinese sovereignty.

China also has a major advantage in its economic complementarity with Japan and the prospect that Japanese capital and technology will play a major role in China's development. As of 1984, Japan had already committed more than $14 billion in concessionary and commercial loans to China and Sino-Japanese two-way trade had grown to more than $10 billion.

India has no foreign exchange earning asset comparable to Hong Kong, although "non-resident Indians" provide some investment funds. India, however, has continued to benefit in a major way from the remittances of Indian contract workers and other residents abroad as well as from Indian construction projects in the Middle East. These and other "invisible receipts" amounted to over $5.1 billion in the peak year, 1980–1981; but, unlike China's Hong Kong market and petroleum sales, this source of foreign exchange for India could dry up or even disappear very quickly. Indeed these invisible receipts nose-dived to about $3 billion in 1983–1984. Likewise, India does not have a nearby, culturally related, capitalist dynamo like Japan that is keenly interested in exchanging capital and high technology products for raw materials and light manufactures.

The group of Western nations called the Aid India Consortium, however, has had a special interest in India's healthy development. While the availability of concessionary loans for India from this group as well as from the World Bank were diminishing in the 1980s, the two institutions as of 1982 had provided India $17.7 billion in economic loans and grants. While the U.S. and Britain in this period scaled back their contributions, Japan and West Germany increased their aid in hopes of gaining trade advantages.

Toward Mixed Economics

The Chinese Communist Party Plenum that met in October 1984 approved a wide-ranging course of reform in industrial management and economic organization. Although the party document avoided specifics and many of the reforms listed had already been introduced on an experimental basis, the plenum put the stamp of approval on the type of market socialism favored by Deng and his supporters.

While retaining a basically centrally directed economy, the principles approved by the plenum authorized a greatly expanded area of activity that is decentralized and influenced by market conditions as well as a reliance on fiscal and monetary policy. The goals of the program included price rationalization and stimulation of efficiency and quality through autonomy and competition for some state enterprises (for example by allowing several competing regional air carriers), reform of the wage system, and profit and loss incentives. The regime also began to experiment with price reform. Production above quota in certain enterprises could be sold at market prices. Likewise optimum energy consumption levels were set for enterprises. Prices of consumption above the set limits were considerably higher. The promotion of some private enterprise was also reaffirmed.

The central government, under the reform plan, will retain command over production and distribution of 60 major industrial products and 10 agricultural goods, which probably will account for about half of the gross national product.

Assuming these reforms are in fact carried out and maintained, China's economy will still be considerably more centralized than that of India, and the great bulk of all Chinese capital as well as land will remain under state ownership. Nevertheless, there are increasing similarities between the two economies.

The Communist Party's 1984 reform decision suggests emergence of a mixed economy in China containing: a strong state sector controlling heavy industry and major infrastructure; a substantial element of competitive, decentralized state capitalism, mostly in light industry and commerce; a smaller private sector mostly in retail commerce and services; and a sort of state tenancy in agriculture, i.e., the contract system of household farming.

The Dengists are trying to synthesize socialism and capitalism by employing the dynamic elements of the latter in a Marxist framework, while the

Indians continue to adjust their own mix of the two systems within a democratic framework. One of the basic assumptions of the Dengists, however, is that an efficient economy as well as a healthy polity requires more pluralism and autonomous elements in the society than Leninism, Stalinism, or Maoism have allowed.

Consequences of Chinese Reforms

The consequences of Chinese reforms in the industrial and bureaucratic fields have to date had mixed results. The bureaucratic and industrial monsters in China have not been nearly so susceptible to structural change as the agricultural system. The reason seems simple: The changes made in agriculture have appealed to the self-interests of the peasants, whereas the bureaucratic and industrial management reforms are viewed by many cadre and workers as striking at the core of their interests—that is, their authority in the case of cadre, and their iron rice bowls in the case of workers.

But the quality of life has nevertheless advanced rapidly as seen in the growth of service industries and employment. By the end of 1985 China had ten million registered private businesses of which 5.8 million were in commerce, 1 million in food services, 650,000 in miscellaneous service trades, 750,000 in general repair trades, 46,000 in house repair work, and 800,000 in transport. In 1985 in Peking about 36 percent of the city labor force was in the service sector. In that year alone entrepreneurs opened 1,300 restaurants and food stalls and the same number of small hotels or inns.

By 1986 Chinese industrial production had leaped far ahead of the planned figures, alarmingly so. With decentralization, capital construction expenditures multiplied. More than half of the investments were in non-budgetary funds raised by local enterprises. Capital spending in 1985 was 32 percent above the 1984 record figure. Peking had found it very difficult to use macro-economic tools to regulate non-budgetary investments under the new more liberalized system of industrial management.

Industrial growth scored over 20 percent in 1985. Much of this growth was presumably wasted production. A survey of 400 state-run enterprises in December, 1984, showed that about 20 percent of stockpiled consumer goods were unsalable either because of price or poor quality. Meanwhile, the surge in the money supply and the shortage of basic materials for industry resulted in an unprecedented inflation of over 10 percent.

Following the October 1984 approval in principle of price reforms in the urban economy, Chinese rushed out in a spate of panic buying and withdrawal of savings. Other repercussions were also immediately felt, including a surge in reported corruption, gift buying, back door dealing, and excessive granting of bonuses by managers. The foreign exchange deficit soared. Despite organizational reforms and the retirement of perhaps a million cadre, the size and cost of the bureaucracy continued to grow.

The pains and the shortcomings of reforms were obvious. But China by 1986 had made a substantial shift toward "consumer communism," rapidly increasing the availability of consumer products, including both durable items and foodstuffs. The production of bicycles, sewing machines, TVs and washing machines had multiplied several times over the previous five years. Some heavy industries had re-shifted to making consumer goods. A tank factory, for example, was turning out mopeds. Urban housing construction had also kept up with an ambitious plan to add an average of 62 million square meters a year, or 2.6 times the average construction in the previous 28 years. The number of rationed commodities had dropped from 73 to 9, and even the 9 rationed items could be purchased at higher prices in the free markets. Urban income had reportedly increased at an average annual rate of 4.7 percent in real terms from 1981 through 1986. By mid–1986 Peking had cooled down the industrial boom, and officials predicted that they would meet their more moderate but still very healthy growth target of 8 percent.

Reform Results in India

The industrial reforms in India have also shown both positive results and continuing problems. Since the Indian difficulty has been one of industrial stagnation rather than exorbitant waste hidden by high-production figures, the rate of industrial growth is a more accurate measure of progress than in China.

During the 1970s industrial growth averaged about 4.2 percent, but this included wide swings from a high of 10 percent to a minimum growth one year of only 0.7 percent. From 1980–1981 through 1985–1986 industry grew at an average 5.7 percent per year, including the drought year of 1982–1983 when the industrial sector still managed a 3.9 percent real growth. With the easing of regulatory controls and a more flexible pricing policy, capacity utilization in industry also increased. Public enterprise profitability markedly improved, although primarily in the oil sector. As the result of a partial decontrol of prices, cement production grew an average of 11.3 percent from 1979–1980 through 1984–1985. Growth in domestic fertilizer production was also impressive, almost doubling over this period. Following three years of stagnation, coal production also began a steady increase after 1980. And thanks to better utilization of capacity and greater efficiency, Indian railways began to move more tonnage.

Under Rajiv Ghandi, more policy initiatives were taken to streamline investment procedure and licensing requirements in several industries, to encourage upgrading of technology, and to increase investment limits. These moves have given special momentum to the electronics, energy generation, and bio-technology industries.

Tax collections also increased in 1985 despite a reduction in tax rates. Private sector companies issued nearly twice the amount of stocks and bonds in 1985–1986 as in the previous year. Small-scale labor-intensive industries, as in China, led the way in India with a 12 percent jump in production. Serious bottlenecks, however, continued. Power generation capacity was up 50 percent from 1980 to 1984–1985, but the gap between power supply and consumption demand continued to hover around 10 percent. Despite growth in demand, the public sector utilities could not increase their rate of capacity utilization beyond the 40–50 percent range. The few private sector plants, however, were operating at 85–90 percent of capacity.

Aggregate Comparisons

Aggregate and per capita production figures indicate that Chinese industry has far out-produced that of India. The advantage for China is not only true for basic sectors such as coal, steel, and cement, but also for important consumer goods as well. China's coal and crude oil production is five times greater than India's; pig iron, steel, and cement all are larger by 3.5 times or more; its per capita production in these areas is more than three and two times respectively that of India.[74]

Given China's wastefully high rate of energy consumption, some substantial portion of its advantage in coal and electricity production would not be economically meaningful. Steel, cement, and pig iron production is also inflated by an unknown, but probably high, percentage of low-quality product, much of it turned out by small plants in the countryside.

Nevertheless, even an extremely liberal compensation for relative waste would leave China with a substantial per capita advantage over India in these fields. In 1976 an Indian economist, Subramaniam Swamy, made a computation of 1973 comparative production by volume.[75] Judging by current figures, China's advantage in electricity, oil, and steel production was significantly less in 1986 than in 1973. China's production advantage in fertilizer also went down while its advantage in coal production increased. Finally, China doubled its margin in cement production, reflecting the boom in its housing construction.

Meanwhile, the surge in light industry in China has ballooned its relative production figures in consumer products. China turns out more than 3 times as many bicycles as India, produces 22 times the number of radios and 34 times the number of sewing machines.[76] Paradoxically, per capita cotton cloth production is about equal in the two countries. The explanation for this anomaly is that traditional Indian clothing, saris for women and dhotis and simple sarongs for men, still worn by the great majority of the population, require little cutting and sewing at home.

In sum, since 1973, except for cement, India has somewhat narrowed China's large advantage in per capita production in basic industry and in electricity generation. At the same time China has improved substantially, and in some cases dramatically, its comparative production of major consumer goods.

CHAPTER 9

The Greening of the Revolutions

A Back Seat for the Peasant

In both India and China agriculture for many years took a back seat. This was ironic as the Indian National Congress and the Chinese Community Party both owed their successes to peasant support and both had come to power promising to improve the lot of their rural populations and to redress the great imbalance between the countryside and the cities. In reality, both governments pursued urban-oriented development policies. In the case of the People's Republic, this policy would further entrench the existence of the two Chinas—urban and rural. Likewise, in the sub-continent, divisions would grow between Bharat, the countryside, and India, the land of bustling cities.

In India's first five year plan (1951–1956), 37 percent of public-sector outlays went into agriculture; but this fell to 23 percent in the second plan. In rural policy, the stress in the Nehru years was on limiting the size of land-holdings and increasing political consciousness and receptivity to change among the peasantry. The very largest land-holdings were broken up, especially those controlled by absentee landlords. Landowning cultivators or peasant entrepreneurs in most states, however, found ways to avoid the new limitations on the size of their holdings by putting land deeds in the names of relatives or even pet animals. Credit cooperatives also had some success in curtailing the role of moneylenders, although this primarily benefited the more productive farmers.

While treated as a poor cousin to industry in terms of investment, agriculture in India, helped by unusually good weather, did reasonably well in the first two five-year plan periods. From 1949–1950 to 1960–1961, grain production grew on the average of 2.8 percent per annum, while population growth averaged 1.9 percent. This growth was achieved primarily through expansion of the amount of cultivated land, from 118 million hectares to 140 million hectares, by employment of known technology, and by a steady increase in irrigation coverage.[77]

By the mid–1960s the initial momentum of growth in Indian agriculture seemed to have been exhausted and a succession of bad harvests required record importation of millions of tons of U.S. grain aid.

Unlike India, China in 1949 had virtually no scope for expansion of the land area under cultivation. The total cultivable area in China today is about 100 million hectares, or about the same as it was in 1949, and 40 percent less than the total available in India. This means that each hectare today must feed 10 persons in China compared to 5 persons in India. Consequently, increased production in China from the very beginning had to come from more intensive application of fertilizers and pesticides and more rapid development of irrigation. As in India Chinese agriculture also received a relatively small percentage of state investment resources. In the first five-year plan it was under 8 percent; or, including investments in agriculture-related industries, slightly over 14 percent. Major state investments in China did go into expanding the irrigation system, improving road and transport facilities in the countryside, and building a modern fertilizer industry. Resources also went into agricultural research and, as in India, new high-yield varieties were introduced. But the most important official inputs into Chinese agriculture were organizational changes, political mobilization, and officially ordered alterations in the cropping pattern. The inherent disincentives to production in these non-material and political inputs into agriculture reduced the effect of increased irrigation and other physical changes.

Following its 1949 victory, the CCP at first moved step by step but then remarkably quickly to accomplish a drastic reorganization of economic, social, and political life in the Chinese countryside. Land was distributed in small plots to the peasants, who were then organized into producer cooperatives. In the early 1950s, following a mass political campaign marked by execution of former landlords, the farmers were organized into collectives. In 1958 Mao, stimulated by his budding ideological quarrel with Moscow, became excited by the vision of a superhuman breakthrough to both modernization and achievement of the ideal egalitarian society. The consequent disruption of agriculture caused by the Great Leap Forward led to the severe food shortages of 1960–1962 and, according to mortality figures published in Peking in 1981 and 1983, the premature death of 12 to 24 million people through malnutrition.[78] In 1959 population growth fell by half to one percent and in 1960 China actually lost population.

Mao was forced to step back temporarily, pragmatic leaders accorded a higher priority to investment in agriculture, and disincentives to production such as controls on free markets were relaxed. But in a few years, radicals in the party, with Mao's support, were back in the driver's seat and agricultural policies were again influenced by political considerations. Although organizational upheavals were avoided on the farms during the Cultural Revolution, egalitarian models such as the now-debunked brigade called Da Zhai were again ballyhooed. Rural free markets were closed, the policy of insisting on grain self-sufficiency was instituted, and restrictions were placed on peasants's side-line endeavors, such as hog raising. In some areas private plots were reduced. Output targets were set without regard for costs, comparative return, or income for the production teams. According to a Chinese economist, Xue Muqiao, the output of cash crops dwindled, the peasants earned less and less, and grain output showed little increase. Some once-prosperous areas were classified poor.[79]

Running to Keep Up

From 1955 to 1977 China and India kept agricultural production just barely ahead of population growth. But by the end of 1977 neither country had actually achieved a significant increase in per capita food production. Keeping up with the population explosion, however, was no mean achievement for either country. The rate of China's population increase from 1952 to 1977 was about the same as the rate of increase in food grain production. Thus Chinese per capita production of unmilled cereals was about 239 kilograms per person in 1977, versus 234 kilograms in 1952. Beginning in the mid–1960s, China began to import food grains to supplement domestic production.

India's population, however, rose even faster than China's in the twenty-five years between 1952–1977. Thus India required a higher growth rate per annum in food grain production to stay even with its per capita level of 1952.

By 1977 the average income of Chinese peasants had increased only slightly and labor productivity on the farms had actually diminished by 12 percent. The productivity of Chinese farm workers was still well above that of their Indian counterparts, as it was before Liberation, but until 1978 the advantage had actually been diminishing. World Bank studies show that, while agricultural production in India and China from 1960–1978 increased at about the same rate, agricultural labor forces in the two countries grew by 1.6 percent and 2.0 percent per annum, respectively. Thus, according to the World Bank, the average annual growth in net output per Chinese worker was only 0.3 percent, while the growth figure for Indian productivity on the farms, though low, was more than double that of the Chinese at 0.7 percent per annum.

The popular image abroad of rural China during the most intense period of collectivization, 1957–1978, was of great masses of enthusiastic peasants building dams and irrigation canals. Some writers have suggested that although low productivity marked this period, it established the infrastructure for future growth through the construction of a large number of communal projects, particularly irrigation works.

In fact, during this time India expanded its irrigation system faster than China. Today India has about 66 million hectares of irrigated cropland and China only 45 million. India, not China, can claim to have carried out the largest irrigation construction program in the world. In addition, some of the communal labor projects in China were hastily and badly designed. Large areas of north China, for example, are suffering from soil salinity because the irrigation system does not include sufficient drainage.

In addition to the expansion of cultivated area, another reason for the relative improvement of Indian labor productivity on the farms compared to that of China was the more rapid increase in the Chinese agricultural labor force that resulted from strict controls on migration out of rural areas.

India's Green Breakthrough

In the 1960s, the Indian government began to reassess its farm policies. Soon a new strategy evolved that focused less on social reform and more upon incentives and increased inputs to spur production. Major factors in this strategy were intensive use of high-yielding varieties (HYVs) of wheat and rice, and increased application of fertilizers and pesticides. The result was the "Green Revolution."

Incentive measures were as important as technology in turning around Indian agriculture. Indian farmers now sell their output at guaranteed prices, which are close to world prices. The government subsidizes their output, including seed, credit, fertilizer, and a farmers' extension service that provides free advice. They pay no taxes and in effect are guaranteed a profit.

Food-grain production in India had increased at only about 1.8 percent per year from 1960–1961 to 1969–1970, but in the 1967–1968 to 1977–1978 period it recovered to 2.6 percent per year.[80] Then, despite disastrous droughts which resulted in a 17 percent drop in the 1979–1980 harvest and a 2 percent drop in 1982–1983, agricultural production between 1979 and 1986 grew at an average rate of about 5.4 percent or somewhat less than the rate in China, which did not suffer an extreme or extensive drought during this period.[81]

India is now self sufficient in wheat and rice and occasionally sells grain abroad and even makes emergency contributions. In 1985, for example, India contributed 150,000 tons of wheat to Ethiopia. By mid–1986 food grain stock reached 30 million tons, well in excess of suitable storage capacity. Indian cotton production also far exceeded consumption. In grain and cotton, however, India's prices exceeded international levels and export potential was limited. But other farm exports such as jute, tea, coffee, and spices enjoyed bumper harvests after a period of lean years.

Rural Revolution in China

Faced with the stagnation of agricultural productivity, the CCP in the third Party Plenum (of the 11th Congress) in December, 1978, adopted incentive- and production-oriented agricultural policies, which would ultimately bring about sweeping changes in the collective structure of agriculture. As with the new agricultural strategy in India, the Chinese reforms represented a shift in priorities from political to economic goals and new measures to bring about an income transfer from urban to rural areas. In China as in India, the new pragmatic approach would encourage productive farmers to "get rich." The policy accepted the possibility of a widening disparity in incomes in anticipation that the bulk of the countryside would follow and the entire economy would be better served.

China's new agricultural strategy was based upon a recognition that so long as agricultural productivity did not increase, the country could not escape from the poverty trap, no matter how much its heavy industrial production expanded. It was also an acknowledgment that the lack of incentives and initiative had resulted in ineffective farm management and gross errors. The new strategy in China involved:

- Increased procurement prices for farm products and reduction of agricultural taxes.
- Encouragement of sideline production by farmers and the reopening of free markets, which led to the rapid expansion of handicraft, as well as hog, poultry, and egg production. Virtually all pork, for example, is now produced privately and pork rationing has ceased.
- Increased availability of fertilizer. In 1977, China was applying approximately 64 kilograms of chemical fertilizer per arable hectare, compared to 25.3 kilograms per hectare in India. By 1980 the Chinese figure had doubled to 128 kilograms, while the Indian figure was up to 32 kilograms.[82]
- Implementation of the so-called responsibility systems which, in effect, resulted in the decollectivization of Chinese agriculture.
- Encouragement of rural industry by localities, collectives and private individuals to absorb the enormous surplus labor in the countryside.

The most important and, within China, the most controversial of all these changes was decollectivization. By 1985 the great bulk of Chinese farm land was being worked on a household basis. This was the largest scale transformation of an economic system in history. Under the new program each household signed a contract to produce so much of a certain crop or crops for state procurement. Any production above the quota may be retained by the farmer or sold, either to the state at a 50 percent premium or on the free market. By 1985 signing a procurement contract was supposedly no longer compulsory.

Other types of responsibility systems involved groups of four or five households signing similar contracts for production. In order to provide incentive for land improvement by the tillers, the government in 1983 decreed that contracts could assign land use to specific householders for up to 15 years or in some cases 30 years. The right to use the land could also be inherited. Moreover, if a peasant family decided to spend full time in some sideline production or to take jobs in local enterprises, it could sell its contract to another family.

The results have been startling. Of all the changes instituted by the pragmatists around Deng Xiaoping during the past eight years, agriculture is the area of most dramatic success. From 1979 through 1985, real growth in agricultural production averaged about 7 percent a year. Despite a 6 percent drop in the area of land sown to grain, total grain production in 1984 was 100 million tons more than that in 1978.

In 1985 grain production dropped 53 million tons primarily because another 12 million hectares less were sown to grain as farmers switched to more lucrative crops. With overflowing granaries, however, there was no shortage of either wheat or rice. Meanwhile, cash crops increased at a remarkable pace. The cotton harvest, for example, tripled in 6 years! In 1980 China was a major importer of cotton. By 1986 it was exporting cotton as well as substantial proportions of its corn and soybean harvests. In a six-year period, oil seed and sugar production also surged over 100 percent.

Meanwhile, in history's greatest job program, over 60 million rural workers between 1980 and 1986 left full time field work and took up sideline occupations or jobs in small-scale local industries. In 1984 peasant households specializing in transportation and farm implement rental business owned about 120,000 motor vehicles, 2.78 million tractors, and 230,000 boats. There were also six million township and village enterprises, generating 40 percent of the gross value of rural output. Over 40,000 rural markets sprung up.

Rural households engaged in sideline occupations or employed in local industries can now rent the land allotted to them to "grain specialized households." Because of the large differences in income between industrial jobs in the countryside and agricultural work, local governments have begun to pay farmers an additional subsidy for growing grain.

With the shift of surplus labor out of cropping and into rural industry, labor productivity in the countryside between 1979 and 1984 rose about 8 percent compared to the 0.5 percent loss in productivity from 1957 to 1977.[83] The overall effect on the standard of living has been dramatic. Since 1978, peasant income in real terms has been increasing about 14 percent a year!

This surge in income is seen in the construction all over China of new farm-houses, with brick replacing mud walls, and tiles for roofs instead of thatch. Fifteen billion square meters of rural housing was added in one year alone. The Chinese government has, in fact, become alarmed with the rapid absorption of arable land for farm housing and "unplanned development." One village in Guangdong, for example, was said to have used up 12 percent of its farm land for new housing within two years. The outburst of factory construction in the countryside also has consumed a significant amount of agricultural land, which nationwide diminished 5 percent between 1978 and 1984.

Equations In Agriculture

India did as well or better than China in agricultural growth until 1978. While Indian agriculture, despite the vagaries of the monsoon, has also performed comparatively well since 1979, Chinese food productivity has moved further ahead with the introduction of the incentive system and the quadrupling of fertilizer application over the past decade.

The figures present an interesting equation:

- India has 1.4 times the net amount of land under cultivation (not counting multi-cropping) as China.
- India has 1.3 times the net amount of irrigated land.
- China manufactures 3.0 times the amount of fertilizer as does India.
- China applies 4.0 times the amount of fertilizer per hectare.
- China produces 2.1 times the amount of grain as does India.

It is apparent that China's greater grain harvests today, as a thousand years ago, are due in large part to the much more intensive use of fertilizer, including organic waste.

The Risk of Reform

Some academic observers, Western and Indian, predicted that India's new agricultural strategy would benefit only rich farmers and would lead to a greater concentration of land and an ever-widening disparity in income distribution. The argument was that only large commercial farmers could afford the more extensive application of fertilizer and chemicals required by the HYVs. The more prosperous farmers, it was feared, would reap much bigger harvests than poor farmers and, as prices fell, the small farmer would be forced to sell out to big-time operators and become part of the landless proletariat. Initial statistics seemed to bear out this thesis. Robert L. Hardgrave, Jr., writing in 1975, commented that "by emphasizing growth as growth, rather than growth as long-range development, India opted for production without social change, a policy that implicitly accepted the growing gap between the haves and have-nots."[84]

A similar argument has taken place over China's incentive- and production-oriented reforms in agriculture. Defensive statements in the official Chinese press rebutting the criticism of "some comrades" indicated that opponents, in this case conservatives or neo-Maoists, have warned that by treating the Chinese peasant as an economic rather than a political creature, the regime will foster income disparities, erode political and administrative control of the countryside, and set the stage for the return of capitalism, first in rural areas, then in the cities. Peking's unabashed appeal to the materialistic instincts of the Chinese peasants and the eulogizing of well-to-do peasants for their greater contribution to national production is seen by party conservatives as nothing less than embourgeoisement.

A Soviet view of these reforms in the pre-Gorbachev days is enlightening. When asked, a senior Soviet diplomat in Peking explained privately that Chinese incentive reforms in agriculture, like Lenin's New Economic Policy in the 1920s, were necessary short-term spurs to production, but they could not last more than five years. "The Chinese are bad Communists," he said, "but they are Communists." In other words, he did not believe the system could long tolerate 80 percent of the population working under an individualistic incentive-based economy in which the most productive are allowed to get "rich," while the cities and industry remain highly regimented with much stricter limits on disparities in earnings.[85]

Critics of the production- and incentive-oriented strategy in India are liberals, while opponents of the same approach in China can most appropriately be called "conservatives." This reflects the different ideological directions from which the two counties have moved toward incentive policies. Liberals in India and conservatives in China both stress the priority of political and social goals over the simple but concrete objectives of production and growth.

The Punjab

The Green Revolution in India's Punjab has sparked a big debate on whether social goals are compatible with a production-oriented agricultural policy. The Punjab's success in raising agricultural production is undeniable. In fourteen years total grain production in the state increased over 380 percent. In ten years rice production went up almost 600 percent. With only 1.6 percent of the total area of India and 5 percent of the population, the Punjab produces over 50 percent of rice and wheat procured for public distribution in the entire country. Fertilizer use has grown from 10 kilograms per hectare to 105 kilograms; tractors have increased from 4,900 to 120,000.[86]

The Punjab's per capita income in 1977–1978 was 1.7 times the national Indian average and only slightly below the rate of middle-income countries like South Korea. Despite wide provincial differences in China, the most successful of China's rural provinces has not equalled the growth rate of the Punjab. Only 12 percent of Punjab's rural population is below the official poverty line, compared to 40–50 percent for the whole country. The only other state with less than one-third of the rural population below the poverty line is neighboring Haryana, which has also enjoyed a sharp increase in food grain productivity. Statistics, as well as a road trip throughout the Punjab, verify that the state is much more prosperous than other parts of India, and there is a much smaller proportion of the population living under the poverty line, although the imbalance in wealth is as lop-sided, perhaps even more so, than in other areas.

The Punjab success is due to social factors as much as to technology, including a tradition of peasant proprietorship and few absentee landlords; a social system based on Sihkism, which promotes a way of life relatively open to mobility and change; and consolidation of the usual myriad of farm patches. The average Punjab farm is divided into only two parts, while in the state of Orisa the average peasant-holding is scattered among nine small patches. (Consolidation took place when Punjab was split between India and Pakistan.)

In addition, Punjabi farmers have been more politically conscious and active than farmers anywhere else in India. In the Punjab's legislative assembly, rural representation increased from 73 percent in 1972 to 79 percent in 1980, and the number of actual cultivators among the legislators rose from 44 percent in 1969 to more than two-thirds in 1980.[87]

The Punjab state government is therefore heavily oriented to the interest of the farmer, and every village in the Punjab has electricity (versus 35 percent throughout India and about 65 percent in China); irrigation covers 80 percent of Punjab's agricultural land (versus 43 percent nationwide in India and 45 percent in China); advisory services are widespread including an excellent agricultural university at Ludhiana; and cooperative credit associations are located in every Punjab village.

Critics, however, focus on the highly skewed distribution of the cash benefits of the Green Revolution in the Punjab, and charge that disparities are widening and the number of landless laborers is increasing. Indian academics who believe that the Green Revolution has resulted in "pauperization" of the masses seem to suggest that India would have been better off without the increased production. But if pauperization of small farmers and the landless in the Punjab has actually occurred, it is hardly the fault of the technology of the Green Revolution. Nor would such a condition mean India has not benefitted immensely from the enormous increase in food grains which the Green Revolution has produced.

In fact, nothing like pauperization has occurred in the Punjab. The better-off farmers, those with 20, 40, or more acres (held in different names) are getting the lion's share of the income benefits; but the rest of the rural population is not worse off than before. These others have either remained at the same level or, apparently in some cases, somewhat improved their real income standards. Despite an increase in the number of tractors by almost 30 times since the early 1960s, increased productivity and double cropping have required the expansion of human labor on Punjabi farms and in ancillary occupations by about 66 percent.[88] As a result, a quarter- to a half-million migrant laborers, mostly from Bihar and Uttar Pradesh, now come to the Punjab every year during the peak seasons, when they constitute about 8 percent of the labor force. Farm wages rose 59 percent between 1967–1968 and 1979–1980, only sufficient to keep up with inflation; but the migrants who pour into the state, jammed into and on top of trains, are happy to get Punjab wages which they could not begin to equal back home. In six months they may save 1,000–2,000 rupees ($100–$200).

Local Punjabi farm laborers have not been displaced by the migrants, but are moving into services and small-scale industries which have been spurred by the increased demand for farm input materials and mechanization. By 1979 Punjab had 29,000 small-scale industries. Statistics show that despite the sharp rise in total income generated by agriculture, since 1971 the industrial and service sectors in the state have increased their proportion of net domestic product to 52 percent, and their share of the total labor force to 41 percent.[89] This trend can also be confirmed firsthand. Untouchables in Sikh villages report that increasing numbers in their communities are moving into non-agricultural jobs. In one village near Ludhiana, for example, about 200 of 500 untouchables in the community were engaged in non-farm jobs. Studies show that the middle-sized landowner in the Punjab with 4 or 5 acres or so of irrigated land has also been able to afford the inputs and exploit the technology of the Green Revolution. Some evidence indicates that small farmers cultivating more intensely can even obtain greater results from the new technology and irrigation than can the large farms.[90]

As population in the Punjab has risen, the average size of land-holdings, as elsewhere in India, has been diminishing, not increasing. At the same time the number of farm laborers has been growing much faster than the number of owner-cultivators. Landless agricultural laborers were only 9 percent of the total Punjab labor force in 1961, reflecting the basically owner-tiller traditional society in the Punjab. By 1981 farm laborers constituted 22 percent of the labor force, while the percentage of cultivators fell from 46 percent to 36 percent, although their actual numbers rose from 1.6 million to 1.7 million.[91] Thus, while the concentration of landownership as such is not increasing, the proportion of landless laborers in the Punjab countryside is growing. This is a result of population growth and is happening everywhere in India, including those very poor states where the Green Revolution has made little or no impression.

Criticism of Rural Reform in China

Can a society be truly socialist if its agriculture relies on a system of self-interest? The Chinese reformers believe it can and point to Yugoslavia, Hungary, and Poland. The neo-Maoists, however, think it is corrupting and will increase social tensions. They point to Lenin's thesis that peasants farming individually are "small commodity producers" who constantly "produce capitalism and the capitalist class." A November 20, 1983, article in *China's Peasant News* rejected this thesis, saying it was not applicable to Chinese peasants.

City-folk in China now grumble about "rich peasants." It is not unusual to hear cadre and teachers in Peking and Shanghai complain that some peasants in properous areas outside the cities are earning a great deal more than they and, in addition, own their own houses. In 1984, *People's Daily* proudly reported the first purchase of a private car by a peasant family. Meanwhile, in the countryside there have been isolated reports of jealous neighbors sabotaging the crops of newly prosperous families, and of local cadre imposing various levies on well-to-do farmers. Households with only older people or little labor-power have found themselves disadvantaged by the responsibility systems, and some peasants working on prosperous, mechanized and relatively large-scale production teams apparently preferred to retain some form of work-point or collective system.

Nevertheless, talks with peasants in markets and villages in many parts of the country and the rapidity with which 90 percent of all villages have opted for the reforms suggest that the new system is, in fact, exceedingly popular. In five years (1980–1985) rural income in real terms reportedly grew by a remarkable 70 percent.

The devolution of decision-making on the farms to the household or small-group level, and the tying of income to production have, however, also weakened party authority and control over the peasants. The number of local cadres has reportedly declined by over 20 percent and, as peasants have dramatically increased their cash incomes, the ability of the authorities to apply sanctions to win compliance with various programs has deteriorated. For example, the rural birth-rate went up sharply in 1981, although it was subsequently brought down again by stern measures.

With greater efficiency in the fields there is now more surplus labor available. One peasant was quoted in a Chinese newspaper as saying that, under the old work-point system, everyone lolled around in the field in order to log their 8 to 10 hours, but now they can do in 2 hours what used to take 8. Some farmers, however, are short of labor at peak seasons and have taken to hiring temporary workers. Chinese press and other reports have highlighted other side-effects which have occured in some areas:

- Reduction in control of plant diseases and pests;
- Appropriation of collective property;
- Illegal buying and selling of land allotted under the responsibility system;
- Cutting down of trees and forest;
- An increase in gambling and extravagant weddings;
- A decrease in PLA recruitment;
- A revival of feudal practices and violent land disputes; and
- A decrease in the area sown to grain.

Most upsetting of all is the neglect of water conservancy infrastructure. From 1980 to 1985 irrigated land is said to have decreased by about 2.43 million acres or close to 5 percent of all irrigated land. Although by 1985 fifteen-year leases were common, peasants were still tending to invest more time and resources in maintaining their private plots and viewing their allotted collective land as a medium-term asset to be exploited with less care for the long term.

While taking measures to try to counter these and other undesirable consequences, the innovators in Peking have pushed relentlessly ahead with implementation of the responsibility systems. So far, the remarkable achievements of the reforms in raising production and peasant income have overridden ideological and political objectives.

Maintaining the reform momentum, Beijing, at the end of 1984 announced the end of compulsory grain procurement from farmers. As in India, prices of grain and agricultural inputs such as fertilizer would henceforth be partially controlled through government intervention, including the setting of procurement prices and government purchase and storage of surplus grain in years of bumper harvests.

Guangdong

Guangdong, like the Punjab, is booming, and similarly it is the greatest source of worry to those of its countrymen who are concerned with the social and political effect of growth.

Cantonese (referring to the people of all Guangdong), like Punjabis, are considered eccentric by their compatriots. Like Punjabis they have historically had considerable exposure to foreign contact, they have numerous relatives abroad, and they are considered good businessmen, if unsophisticated compared to the more worldly Shanghai types. Cantonese are also known as mavericks and rebels; many secret societies and revolutionary movements, including those of the Taipings and Sun Yat-sen, had their beginnings in the provincial capital of Canton (or Guangzhou).

Forty-seven million of the 58 million people in the province are peasants, but agriculture accounts for only 27 percent of the GNP. Typhoons and floods continue to make life uncertain for many peasants but rural income in Guangdong, as elsewhere in China, has soared with introduction of the "responsibility systems." Fish production has leaped ahead as households have been permitted to establish their own fishponds. The surge in the vegetable harvest has in some area at times led to an unmarketable surplus which has been dumped in the rivers. The variety and quality of goods and produce in the local markets have returned to that of the best days before communalization.

New houses are popping up in every village in the delta and TV antennae sprout from almost every house (unlike prosperous areas in the Punjab where each village will sport only a few such masts of modern well-being). In small towns and larger market centers, Guangdong farmers are thronging restaurants and shops engaging in the traditionally favored pastime of conspicuous consumption. Elaborate wedding ceremonies have returned and there is a mad rush to buy appliances, even washing machines. A tiny number of "10,000 yuan" households have purchased pianos and private autos.

The provincial press reported that in the fishermen's village in Shenzhen Special Economic Zone, one-third of the families have housemaids. A very wealthy village outside Canton in 1984 reportedly put up the capital for a 26-story hotel in the city. The money came from the village's industrial enterprises, settlement fees for land requisition by the state, and the peasants' individual savings.

As elsewhere in rural China, the Guangdong boom has been due not only to the decollectivization of agriculture, but also to the virtual explosion of local industries. In some counties, in 1985 alone rural industrial production soared 30 percent as latent entrepreneurs among peasants and local administrators rushed to open small factories and workshops. In the Pearl River delta, the *average* per capita income rose to over 500 yuan, a figure considered "well off" in the rest of China.

Given the freedom to do so, a substantial percentage of the rural labor force in Guangdong has moved out of field work. Fifteen percent of the peasant population have become so-called "specialized households" engaging in animal husbandry, fish culture, handicrafts, or some form of individual commerce such as transport services.

Another 12.5 percent of the rural work force are now employed in small-scale rural industries which by 1984 had grown to 80,000 with a total income double that of 1980. In some counties in Guangdong, 40 to 50 percent of the rural labor force is now engaged in either local industry or specialized occupations. As in the Punjab, a sharp increase in grain productivity in Guangdong has provided the basis for the expansion of small scale industry and commerce, which in turn provides an increasing share of employment for the expanding population.

In the most vibrant area of Guangdong, the Pearl River delta, the industrial output of rural enterprises grew over 500 percent from 1979 through 1985! Overall industrial production in the delta area rose to over 70 percent of the gross value of total industrial and agricultural output. While still a small minority, an increasing number of privately owned rural enterprises were in operation, including even textile factories. In six years, some areas of the delta had become so prosperous that the labor flow had reversed. Workers were coming from the cities to take jobs in rural factories and workshops. Small-scale collective and village enterprises also have led the way in Guangdong's remarkable export boom. In the first half of 1986, exports grew 40 percent over the same period the previous year to U.S. $1.76 billion. Guangdong thus became the number one exporting province in the country.

Guangdong has experienced another type of of Green Revolution which has set it apart from the rest of China—the inflow of foreign money and foreigners. Given significant autonomous authority since 1979 in arranging foreign investments, Guangdong has attracted $2.6 billion in pledged investment from abroad. This represents 90 percent of the total pledged foreign investment in all of China. The largest foreign ventures have been established in the Shen Zhen New Special Economic Zone near Hong Kong, but the greatest foreign impact to-date has been the 13,000 small-scale assembling and processing projects established throughout the province by outside investors, mostly Hong Kong and overseas Chinese. These ventures have generated 220,000 new jobs and considerable foreign exchange. Lacking the raw material and energy base for heavy industry, Guangdong has not suffered the irrationalities of production in that area. Led by light industry, overall industrial production in the province has grown by over 10 percent annually in the last few years.

As Punjab receives a large share of overseas remittances in India, so most of the funds sent by overseas Chinese to relatives on the mainland flow into Guangdong. Likewise, a large percentage of the 6 million Hong Kong and overseas visitors to the mainland each year are returning to see relatives in Guangdong. Canton, which has a population of 2 million, itself receives over 1 million such visitors each year. The daily trains from Hong Kong to Canton are overflowing with tourists on their way to visit relatives and ancestral villages and tombs in China; they are usually loaded down with appliances, color TVs, stereos, and stylish apparel for their relatives. This traffic has led to a black market in such goods, large-scale smuggling, and corruption. Peking's concern with runaway corruption in Guangdong was a prime reason for the massive anti-corruption and anti-smuggling campaign that was begun in 1981.

Of all Chinese provinces, Guangdong has also become the most infected with other forms of bourgeois contamination. Presumed accoutrements of Western culture, such as bell-bottom trousers, jeans, and sun-glasses initially proliferated in Canton, which became the first city in China where one could not always distinguish between local and overseas Chinese youths. Soft rock music inevitably worked its way in, and dozens of "music tea parlors" opened.

Hong Kong television also became the major entertainment medium for the great majority of Cantonese and others in the province who lived in range of the colony's UHF transmitters. Fish-bone antennae capable of receiving the UHF signal sprouted from the roofs of Canton like a growth of unruly hair. Unofficially it was estimated that over 80 percent of Canton's TV sets on any one night were tuned to Hong Kong stations. Beginning in 1981 sporadic efforts were made to discourage this pastime, which was several times declared illegal. Resourceful Cantonese put their antennae on hinges and raised them only after dark. In 1983 the government finally began to jam the reception of Hong Kong TV broadcasts with its own new station, which as a concession also featured Hong Kong Kung Fu movies and Japanese serials.

Superstitions and religion are also flourishing more in Guangdong and neighboring Fujian than anywhere else in China. Ancestral altars, temples to the earth gods, elaborate funerals as well as marriage ceremonies, magic potions, and even secret societies and other feudal remnants are making a visible comeback in the province.

In addition to back-sliding in proletarian culture, it also seems clear that there is a growing gap between better-off and worse-off peasants, and also between those with overseas Chinese relatives and those without. The provincial media frequently carry stories of well-to-do farm families whose rights have been unjustly violated by jealous neighbors. In one such case, the local party committee assigned a cadre to act as legal advisor to the harrassed household.

No figures are available on recent changes in income disparities in Guangdong, but as in the Punjab one suspects that the poorest 20 percent are also improving, although at a slower rate than the top 20 percent. Conservatives in Peking, however, are worried less about statistical changes than about the long-term political and social consequences of the new prosperity and the culture it brings in tow.

Production and Social Goals

Whas has happened in India and China suggests that, even if income disparities widen, the welfare of all groups in the population, including those living in poverty, can increase faster under production-oriented programs than under strategies that stress principles of equality over concrete improvement in overall consumption. A World Bank staff working paper in 1978 made a lengthy statistical analysis of Indian agriculture and came up with what would seem to be the obvious conclusion, that "improved agricultural performance is definitely associated with reductions in incidence of poverty."[92]

In almost any social system, benefits of increased production will, to some degree, trickle down, and this is happening in both countries today, where a minority comprising the most efficient farmers spearheads growth. Whether these farmers are getting too much of the cash benefit is a separate, political question. Peking and New Delhi have ways available to redistribute the cash-flow from their Green Revolutions, which would not involve disincentives to high production by efficient farmers. In India the peasant-proprietor class has paid relatively little tax; in 1975–1976 collections from land revenue and agricultural income tax together constituted only 6.2 percent of the tax receipts of state governments.[93] In China, well-to-do farmers still do not earn enough to pay income taxes and there is only a small agricultural tax.

The results of the agricultural reforms in China highlight the potential advantages of family farming, even on very small holdings. Under the new responsibility system, some Chinese households are working—successfully—as little as one-quarter of an acre. In India, however, it is not clear whether dividing up the land more equitably would in the short- to mid-term improve production. In West Bengal and Kerala, where land reform has been more thoroughly carried out than elsewhere in India, it has not yet resulted in increased productivity.

There are two explanations for the success of small-scale household farming in China, and the possibility that it would be less successful in India. First of all, individual productivity on the farms in China had been suppressed for three decades. With the new incentives, a surge in productivity occurred which may now level off unless there is increased capital investment in agriculture. Second, with a long tradition of peasant land ownership and intensive farming, the great majority of Chinese peasants, including the poorest group, have always been potentially efficient individual farmers. On the other hand, the poorest one-third or more of rural Indians—the untouchables, tribals, and some other "backward" castes—have been landless laborers and culturally deprived since the beginning of time and would probably be less efficient as individual farmers working tiny holdings than are the poorest one-third of the Chinese peasantry.

The Nutrition Gap

The turn to household agriculture in China, together with grain imports and the quadrupling of fertilizer use have had a dramatic impact on China's food consumption and nutrition. By 1983 each Chinese on the average was consuming over 2,600 calories, up 24 percent from the level of 2,100 calories that had persisted until 1978.[94] The Chinese were eating 44 percent more meat, 50 percent more fat, and daily protein intake increased from 70 grams in 1978 to 80 grams in 1983. The new calorie intake in China is above the average for low-income countries (2,336 calories) and compares favorably with middle-income countries such as Brazil and Malaysia.

The Green Revolution has also had an impact on consumption in India. According to official estimates the percentage of the Indian population below the poverty line, defined in terms of a consumption level of 2,400 calories daily in rural areas and 2,100 calories in urban areas, declined in the countryside from 54.1 percent in 1972–1973 to 50.8 percent in 1977–1978. The overall national decline in the poverty figure was from 51.5 percent to 48.1 percent.[95] Nevertheless, food availability between 1978–1981 provided an average intake of only 2,021 calories—a figure which, despite expanded grain production, had increased only slightly since the 1960s. By 1983 it had increased to 2,115. Although Indian agriculture, in terms of growth, has continued to do almost as well as that of China, the Indian nutritional level has not increased proportionally because of greater population growth, the reduction in food assistance from abroad, and India's grain import/export policies, which in turn result from its foreign exchange position.

While even in recent years of bountiful harvests the Chinese have continued some grain imports, in good crop years India has reduced or eliminated grain imports. In four of the six years between 1978–1982, India actually exported grain when productivity dramatically increased. The importation of about 2.25 million tons annually from 1982 to 1984 served to maintain reserve stocks, despite the 1982–1983 drought year. At the same time, China, enjoying uninterrupted good harvests, continued to import grain. From 1978 to 1983 grain imports averaged about 13 million metric tons per year.

The continued imports on top of bumper harvests allowed the Chinese to increase grain consumption and also to divert more domestic grain in rural areas to livestock feed, which has led to the sharp rise in meat production and consumption. In addition, continued grain imports reflect a decision to allow farmers to shift sown areas into cash crops such as cotton resulting in a sudden end to large cotton imports and in 1984 substantial exports. Likewise, continued sugar and vegetable oil imports, on top of a dramatic rise in domestic production, have contributed to the growing calorie count in China.

The following figures reflect the mathematics of China's higher nutrition level: China produces 2.1 times the amount of grain as does India; China's population is 1.4 times that of India; China has imported grain equivalent to 1 to 4 percent of its annual harvest; Chinese per capita daily calorie consumption is about 1.2 times that of India.

The importance of grain imports to the improvement in the Chinese diet, although imports are a fraction of domestic production, is seen in the World Bank's calculation that a 9 percent increase in food grain availability in India in 1979–1980 (or about 12 million metric tons, which is less than China's grain imports for each of those years) would meet the minimum calorie requirement for the Indian population. The additional amount would, of course, have to be distributed to the poorer half of the population to alleviate the human, rather than the statistical, problem.

Petroleum is a major reason China was able to double up on good domestic harvests with continued large imports of grain and other foods. The sharp rise in oil prices until 1985 was a heavy burden to India and a blessing to China. A few years ago India was importing over 60 percent of its oil needs and oil imports then cost India about $6 billion. The amount of foreign exchange that India spent on importing oil and that China earned from exporting oil from the early 1970s to the early 1980s were in the same range, and both figures were larger than China's bill for its sizable grain purchases from the U.S. and other countries. The rich harvests produced by China's new system of household farming has allowed it to reduce grain imports while continuing to improve the nation's diet. In 1985, however, China still bought over five million tons of foreign grain. Given its steady if low rate of population growth, the PRC may continue to require some imports if it is to maintain an improving nutritional record particularly in terms of meat consumption.

Feeding the Poor

Despite China's relatively high average calorie intake in the last few years, there is still considerable undernourishment in the poorest rural areas of China, affecting 150–200 million people. The Chinese government provides a safety net for the poor one-third of its rural population, selling, or if necessary loaning, sufficient grain to poor communes or those in areas hit by natural disasters to guarantee 200 kilograms of unmilled grain per person in wheat areas and 150 kilograms in rice areas. This provides an undernourished subsistence diet, but in most cases it is presumably supplemented by production from private plots. Except for the early 1960s, the grain-relief system in China has apparently worked fairly well and there has been no significant chronic malnourishment, as distinct from undernourishment. Foreigners, however, are rarely allowed to visit communes in the poorest areas and no surveys have been allowed in these areas. It is not clear, for example, what happens in the case of a village or commune that is persistently short of grain for subsistence and, thus, cannot pay back its previous loans. According to the State Statistical Bureau, 2.43 million peasant households in 1984 received government aid.

The Indian government has also attempted to protect the consumption level of low-income groups. The food corporation of India procures and manages buffer stocks of grain and other foods which it sells on a rationed and low-cost basis to the poor through 276,000 "fair-price shops." As of 1982 the Indian government was procuring and distributing approximately

13 million metric tons of food grains per year, about 10 percent of the total harvest.

In China the state procures and distributes about 50 million tons, or approximately 19 percent, of the (milled) grain harvest. In other words, in China the state sector's role in distribution of the grain harvest is about 58 percent larger proportionally than in India. The Indian system limits the sale of subsidized, low-price rationed grain to the poorer section of the population, urban and rural. Seventy-eight percent of the fair-price shops in India are located in rural areas. In China the urban population feeds on state-procured and, since 1977, heavily subsidized grain rations. Only state employees in the countryside can purchase from procured stocks. The result is an enormous subsidy by the Chinese government of urban and cadre consumption. Agricultural production in China still remains undervalued, but another rise in procurement prices is not likely soon, due to the likely inflationary and budgetary impact. The effect of higher prices to producers has been demonstrated in both India and China. In 1983 New Delhi announced an 8 percent increase in wheat support prices and a 7.5 percent reduction in fertilizer prices. This resulted in a 12 percent rise in fertilizer use and a 15 percent increase in grain production.

India's safety net for the very poor varies from state to state. In addition to running the fair-priced food shops, the central government helps to finance various "food for work" programs in the states. A few states have guaranteed employment programs in the countryside, and others have free lunch programs for children or old people. Essentially, however, the hungry who cannot afford the subsidized grain must turn to the wider family for support or to money-lenders, land-owners, or employers for consumption loans. While the nutritional level is low for half the Indian population, and there are great gaps in the safety net, the fact is that India has not had a famine since Independence, while China has had one major famine—the 1960–1962 food shortage. It is probably accurate to say that in the past 35 years many more Indians than Chinese have died indirectly because of poor nutrition; but more Chinese have died because of famine.

Overall Economic Growth

It should be apparent by now that it is difficult to arrive at precise comparisons of economic growth and per capita income between India and China, and that such figures must be accompanied with numerous caveats. Aside from the relative quality and utility of the goods produced, basic problems arise from different concepts used in market and non-market economies in preparing national accounts. Differences in prices also distort the value of production and one can choose any number of imperfect formulae to compensate for this factor. Chinese producer goods are considerably out of line with international prices and this has distorted the relative value of production. Official exchange rates also do not convey the real differences in purchasing power of the two countries.

Numerous scholars, the World Bank, and the U.S. government have all tried their hand at calculating Chinese per capita gross domestic product and the rate of overall growth. In December 1978, U.S. government and World Bank estimates indicated that China that year had a per capita GNP of US $422. In 1980, however, the World Bank drastically lowered its estimate of China's per capita GNP to US $230. In its 1986 report, the World Bank calculated Chinese 1984 per capita GNP at US $310 and India's at US $260 or about 16 percent less than the figure for China, a significant Chinese advantage but far from the 150 percent difference which some pre–1980 figures had suggested. By 1984, the yuan had also significantly devalued against the dollar. On the other hand, aggregate production figures for steel, grain, and other major items, as well as China's much larger exports and electricity generation, suggest that the real difference is probably higher than the latest World Bank figures show.

Irving B. Kravis, of the University of Pennsylvania, who has worked on the UN International Comparison Project, has produced an estimate of relative gross domestic product per capita for China and several other countries based on price comparisons and expenditures.[96] According to Kravis' computations, the relative standing of China to other countries in 1975 GDP per capita as a percentage of U.S. per capita GDP was as follows:

India	6.6%
China	12.3%
Pakistan	8.8%
Thailand	10.6%
Philippines	13.2%
South Korea	16.4%
Malaysia	18.2%
U.K.	62.2%
U.S.	100.0%

Kravis concedes that his informal collection of Chinese prices during a delegation visit to China is subject to considerable error. Nevertheless, his figures again suggest that the latest World Bank calculations may underestimate the difference in per capital GDP or GNP between India and China.

In terms of the rates of growth of GNP per capita between 1950–1978, the World Development Report of 1980 estimates 3.7 percent for China and 1.4 percent for India. The bank's special 1981 report on China, however, calculated a 3.5 percent per capita GNP growth for China for the years 1957–1979, but further adjusts this to take into account unusually high industrial prices in China and emerges with a net per capita average growth of 2.7 percent. Wilfred Malenbaum in 1982 calculated China's overall growth rate at 4.3 percent, against India's 3.7 percent.[97] Taking into account population growth, Malenbaum's figures would translate into a long-term per capita growth rate up to 1980 of 2.5 percent for China and 1.5 percent for India, close to the World Bank figures.

Over the past several years both India and China, as we have seen, have been growing at a faster rate than in the previous twenty years. Since 1980, India's overall growth rate has been over 5 percent and in China, according to official statistics, including the probably distorted high rates for 1984 and 1985, it has averaged about 7 percent or about the same relative advantage over India as in the past.

One has the feeling that we are getting close to the truth—about a 40 percent Chinese advantage in overall growth rate compared to India. This advantage, until recent years, has been largely in industrial output and, if we arbitrarily discount 20 percent for the probably greater unusable product in China, the figure would reduce to about 32 percent. To be safe, we can guess that Chinese growth has been 30–40 percent greater than that of India.

What accounts for the difference? The World Bank suggests that about 40 percent of the difference is attributable to China's lower population growth. Thus, if population had grown at equal rates in the two countries, China's advantage in per capita growth would have been reduced to 18–24 percent.

The productivity of industrial, as well as agricultural, workers in China and the efficiency of Chinese capital investment, as we have seen, had not up to 1980 surpassed the growth achievements of India. Thus the remaining difference in per capital growth in the first three decades was largely due to greater savings in China and a greater investment in industry, rather than more efficient use of either capital or labor.

It would therefore be difficult to make a case that central planning or state control of industry or collectivization of agriculture had provided China any significant advantages compared to India, in terms of growth. China's advantage has not been its economic policies, structure, or organization. It is China's command society, rather than its command economy, which has been the source of its relative progress over India.

China's highly organized way of life and its disciplined political structure has enabled it to achieve unprecedented success in birth control and also to keep a tight lid on current consumption. If the country had not been diverted by flights of fancy for long spells, its growth would have been much more impressive.

While China's growth has been quite good compared to India and to the average low-income country, its per capita 1984 GNP was still below that of other poor Asian countries such as Pakistan ($380) and Indonesia ($540); China's GNP is even further behind middle-income countries such as the Philippines ($660) and Malaysia ($1,980). More than 20 Third World countries or areas including Singapore and Hong Kong have per capita GNP four to ten times that of China's. The eccentricities of exchange rates and domestic prices cloud the value of such comparisons, but there is little doubt that these countries are more prosperous than China on a per capita basis. As in the case of an India-China comparison, there are historic and cultural factors that explain these differences as much or more than the successes or failures of government policies.

CHAPTER 10

Love: Yen and Yoni

The Hindu Obsession

In India God was a phallus. "Unlike any other ancient culture of the world, sexual union occupies the most central place in ancient Indian cosmology, religion, philosophy, and culture. It marks the beginning and the end, the be-all and the end-all of the entire Indian view of life."[98]

Womanhood in India took many forms, but essentially an overpowering ambivalence and duality existed, represented in the images of the mother-goddess and of Kali, the destroyer. In China the duality was that of the yang and yin, less vivid symbols than the lingam and the yoni of the male and female principles. In the Chinese Taoist tradition, women and men both embodied elements of yin and yang and, while Chinese differentiated between a woman's maternal and sexual roles, Chinese sexual attitudes were not so complicated as the schizoid outlook of the upper-caste Indian.

In India, sexuality, like everything else, was seen in the religious context. The Aryans were preoccupied with the mysteries of death and procreation and, for their Hindu descendants, sexuality was symbolized in Shiva's erect lingam, the creative force of the universe. But death and destruction were an essential component of creation and, thus, of sexuality. Shiva was creator, preserver, and destroyer, and Kali, clad in a garland of skulls, was the essence of the power of female sexuality.

Hindus did not see sex in the Christian manner as sinful, but rather as all-powerful, all-consuming and, in the end, a destructive as well as a creative force. But it was never to be suppressed even by the yogi or the wandering ascetic. Indian celibates were preoccupied with their sexuality; not with self-denial, but with concentrating, transforming, and channeling sexuality into the service of achieving that transcendental state of fusion called *moksha*.

Gandhi was always fussing over his sexuality whether as a young bridegroom or a celibate older man. He tells us—rather curiously—that he was making love to his teenage wife when he should have been tending to his dying father. After years of celibacy, Gandhi took to sleeping chastely in the same bed with young girls, including his niece, and giving them enemas. This was quite in keeping with the tradition of holy men, some of whom concentrated their powers of chastity by rubbing in oil the naked bodies of nubile maidens.

In few countries would politicians expect a record of celibacy to enhance their popularity. But Morarji Desai in 1977 at the age of 81, and then Prime Minister, publicly boasted of having abstained from sexual intercourse since he was 33. Equally admired by his countrymen, however, was Jawaharlal Nehru, who while negotiating the terms of independence with Lord Mountbatten during the day, was making love to Lady Mountbatten at night—with the apparent approval of the lord. A fitting and poetic end to India's tempestuous, bad but beautiful affair with England. Not surprisingly, Nehru, understanding the habits of the Anglo-Saxons, permitted their clubs to remain exclusively white if they chose—and they did until the 1960s.

Hindu gods were riotously promiscuous, flaunting all taboos, like characters in a Joe Orton play. But maternal goddesses were usually conventional. In the Sakti cults the supreme power is conceived of as a woman, either the benign Durga, the righteous Chandi, or the naked ogress, Kali. All are worshipped at once. There is nothing in Chinese mythology comparable to the imaginative parade of sexual adventures in Hindu myths or to the strong feminine character of Hindu religion. Goddesses were fewer in China and there were no erotic sculptures except in Llamist temples which had been influenced by Tantric schools of Indian Buddhism. There were also no temple prostitutes in China "married to the gods," and no worship of the male lingam and the female yoni.

If the reader wishes to pursue the subject in depth, Wendy Doniger O'Flaherty provides more than 300 intriguing pages recounting the sexual themes in Hindu mythology. One citation from her book will give some hint of the fertile imagination of Hindu myths:

> Death, as an erotic release, is a recurrent motif in Hindu mythology on various levels. It appears in the ancient ceremony in which the Queen copulates with a dead stallion, in the medieval myth of Shiva dancing with the corpse of Sati, and in the Tantric image of the goddess (Kali) holding a severed head while she engages in intercourse with the corpse of Shiva or straddles a copulating couple. In many of the images of the goddess and the corpse the only part of her partner that is alive is the erect phallus, which has become animatedly separate from the rest of the body (just as the head that she holds in her hand has become, literally, separated from its body). . . . The goddess, herself, provides a further parallel for the motif of the animation of the separate

phallus in the myth in which her amputated yoni becomes a shrine where Shiva dwells forever with her . . . a still closer example is the castrated phallus of Shiva which first wreaks havoc upon the sages responsible for its severance, and then becomes the instrument of universal fertility.[99]

Kali's triumph suggests the dominance of the female principle over the male, and Shiva's fate that of the angler-fish consort. In this connection, a popular legend about Koka Pandit, a classical Indian writer on sexual love, describes what is at once the greatest dream and the greatest nightmare of the Indian male: to make love to an insatiable female partner. According to the legend, one of the most attractive women in India let it be known that no man could satisfy her, but that if anyone did, she would become his slave. If not, he would become her slave. Many men tried and failed, and thus became her servants. For a long while no one else dared make the effort; then Koka Pandit accepted the challenge. Within a few days he thoroughly exhausted the woman's sexual appeptite; she cried in anguish, begged his forgiveness, and for the rest of her life she worked as Koka's slave.[100]

To the Hindu, all women are lustful. According to the Mahabrarata they enjoy sex eight times more than men. "The Vedas say, 'Fire is the woman, the fuel is her lap; when she entices, that is the smoke; and the flames are her vulva. What is done within is the coals, and the pleasure is the sparks. In this Vaisvanaha fire the Gods always offer seed as oblation.' "[101]

Understandably, with this sort of literature around the house, there was a powerful male compulsion to cloister his libidinous women, but also to mate with them and any other female and, by satisfying their lust, to conquer them. A wife's sexuality was regarded as a threat, "either as the erotic woman who will drain him of his life or as the maternal woman who conjures up the spectre of maternal incest. Indeed, these two roles merge in the figure of a sexually aggressive mother, a recurrent image in myths and a persistent stereotype in conventional perceptions of Hindu family relationships."[102] Fear of the sexually mature female, of "the vagina with teeth," was one factor in the emergence of the custom of child-brides and in the Indian male penchant for adolescent girls.[103]

Yin and Yang

Compared to all this, the Chinese outlook on sex and women was quite ordinary and matter-of-fact. As the Chinese early on developed art for art's sake, so they also practiced sex for sex's sake. True, the Taoists saw the mixture of sexual fluids as the human equivalent of the interaction of the essence of yin and yang, and the sex act was often described in cosmic imagery. Moreover, some Taoist sects considered public orgy as a way to achieve immortality. Nevertheless, the treatment of sex in Chinese culture is essentially as a natural act, necessary for good health and happiness. The original *Joy of Sex* was written by a Chinese sometime in the first or second century before Christ, when a number of books classified as "art of the bedchamber" material were in existence.

Still, this sort of material was kept out of sight in respectable households. Chinese scholars and the best poets and painters considered it uncouth to refer to sex directly. In translating explicit sexual descriptions in the Indian sutras, Chinese Buddhists would often sanitize the language. For example, an Indian passage describing how a dragon had concealed her female organs and displayed a phallus would be changed by Chinese translators to say simply that the female dragon had changed her figure to become a male dragon.[104]

The famed Indian Kamasutra appeared probably between the third and fifth centuries. Oddly enough, the Kamasutra is relatively pedantic in its instructions compared to the flowery imagery employed by the Taoist texts. It displays, however, the Indian proclivity—like the Chinese—for classification, describing the eight kinds of embrace, eight stages of oral intercourse, sixteen ways of kissing, and so on.

The Indian sex manuals emphasize the satisfaction of both partners more than the counterpart Chinese manuals; the Indian law books, for example, require a man to have intercourse with his wife within eight days of her menstrual period, and a father who does not find a husband for his daughter shortly after puberty could be found guilty of a crime. Generally, however, Indian and Chinese sex manuals alike were meant for extra-marital sexual union, where full scope for inventiveness and participation of both partners was possible. Indians, in particular, fearing a wife who was too active a sex partner, could more easily enjoy the licentiousness of a young courtesan or a clandestine partner: " . . . a good Hindu wife seldom exhibits sexual passion in the act of copulation with her husband, lest it make her husband feel he is less than a match for her."[105]

Only the upper caste and, of these, primarily the brahman, were literate and could read the Kamasutra. The average Indian did not practice suttee, nor prevent the re-marriage of widows. Nor did the macabre escapades of Kali and Shiva have much effect on their sex lives, which were probably no more ecstatic, humdrum, or perverse than in any other country. Likewise, both the Chinese and Indian peasant woman working in the fields alongside her husband, was far more an equal than her citified, sophisticated cousin. Foot-binding in China, like suttee in India, was an upper-class affectation; female babies and young girls, however, suffered much more among the poor of both countries, who, in hard times, favored preservation of their sons.

Extended Families

Traditional Indian and Chinese family lives were similar in many ways. In both countries the extended family was the core social institution, in which the individual was submerged, and marriage was the most important ceremony. Child marriage or betrothal was not unusual in either society. In both cases, the bride became a subservient part of the groom's extended family; mothers-in-law were tyrannical and numerous sons were to be produced.

Additional wives were accepted in Hindu society if, for example, the first wife bore no sons. Hindu princes and kings, as in China, usually had many wives as well as harems. Reflecting the paradoxical and ambivalent attitude toward women, however, monogamy was considered the ideal in India. On the other hand, after their children were born Hindu men felt quite free to engage in extra-marital relations with prostitutes, younger women, maidservants, and when possible married women. The husband would not normally pursue such affairs before the birth of his children, for fear of losing his semen and his ability to sire sons.[106] In China the ideal was polygamy; if a man could afford more than one wife, he did so, both for the variety of pleasure and the prestige it afforded. The wife's function in both societies was to bear children, satisfy her husband sexually, and to obey and serve him and their sons. The Indian woman, however, was expected to go further and regard her husband as a deity, at least in public.

In neither country did marriage include emotional and intellectual affinity between man and wife, but it was more likely to develop to some extent after marriage in Chinese families. Not only was the Indian wife reluctant to show passion during intercourse with her husband, but "any attachment and tenderness" at all between the couple was (and is) "discouraged by the elder family members by either belittling or forbidding the open expression of these feelings."[107] The birth of a child often demanded an even greater repudiation of an Indian woman's erotic impulses, which disposed young mothers "to turn the full force of [their] eroticism toward [their] infant son[s]."[108]

The rearing of children was likewise similar, but with very important differences. In both societies there was a very close attachment of sons to the mother, and a general indulgence from all the family for the first five or six years; then, suddenly, came a strict discipline, a demanding father-figure, and a transition to identification with the dominating male role. Instruction was through rote learning; and punishment, rather than reward, was the usual stimulus. Girls in both societies were also indulged during the early years; but later, while feminine chores were assigned and dutiful behavior expected, many fewer demands were made upon them.

A comparable pattern of prolonged indulgence and intensive maternal nurturing in early childhood followed by a narcissistic crisis at 5 or 6 years of age contributed to similar Indian and Chinese psychological traits among males, including: an acute sense of dependence on family and authority ties; a fear of isolation and impotence; and a relative lack of tension between the superego and the ego, that is, between abstract concepts of "good" and "bad" outside the family context.[109] The pattern of prolonged maternal intimacy, however, has been more intense in India, given the young mother's required redirection of her sexuality toward her sons. Thus, as the Indian psychiatrist Sudhir Kakar relates, a vicious circle spirals inward in the Indian unconscious: "mature women are sexually threatening to men, which contributes to avoidance behavior in sexual relations, which in turn causes the women to extend a provocative sexual presence toward their sons, which eventually produces adult men who fear the sexuality of women."[110] Kakar suggests that this pattern of infant and childhood development, in addition to the traits listed above, results in a more "feminine" non-aggressive stance toward the world by Indian males, a greater emphasis on primary (sensory) thought processes, and a keener sensitivity to symbols and abstract concepts than to causal thinking.

There were other contrasts in marital and family customs reflecting basic differences in outlook between the two countries. In India a dowry was the tradition among the upper caste. In China, while dowries were given, the expense of a lavish wedding was borne by the groom's family, which also paid a "bride's price." Giving a daughter in marriage in India was considered a sacred act of religious merit, and had to be accompanied with gifts that were as extravagant as possible. In China giving a daughter was deemed worthy of receiving gifts and a feast as well in return—certainly a more businesslike approach and one that perhaps suggested a greater valuation of daughters.

Oppression of women in China served the concrete or sensual needs of exploiting males, but did not include the religiously inspired horrors of some Indian practices, such as suti. The ghoulish Chinese custom of foot-binding was intended to heighten the ornamental quality and sexuality of a Chinese woman and, thus, had some imagined benefit for men, however perverted. Tying a wife onto the funeral bier (they could seldom be counted on to stay put) obviously could bring no tangible or sensual reward to the departed husband. Upper caste Indian widows who lived were shorn of their hair and all ornaments, and remained in seclusion the rest of their lives, treated by all except their children as pariahs. This cruel treatment was also often inflicted on child-brides who were still virgins when their "husbands" died.

In both societies a woman came into her own when her sons were grown and her mother-in-law departed. In India, where the aging husband traditionally was expected to withdraw from daily cares into meditation, a mother's role could even more easily become dominant. Despite the theoretically total obedience to be shown by the wife, the hen-pecked husband was a well-known character in both India and China. In India, however, this position of prestige and power for a woman was short-lived, as it ended when her husband died. Ideally, Indian wives were one-third the age of their husbands at marriage and, thus, the male spouse usually died many years before his wife—who either went to the flames with him or assumed the dreaded role of widow.

Contemporary Sexuality

Among non-Moslem Third World nations, India and China today are the most conventional in sexual mores. Restrictive attitudes in India which were spread by centuries of Moslem rule were reinforced by the Victorian Raj, while in China, conservative Manchus were followed by even more straight-laced Communists.

Indian and to a lesser extent recent Chinese films are full of romance, but until recently Indian as well as Chinese love scenes faded out before the kiss. Recent Indian films have become a bit more explicit, but young people in both countries appear to be generally uninformed about sexuality. Some Indian families still give a young bride and groom the traditional "love book" which describes the mysteries of conjugal life, but today the pages are blank.

Even less instruction in written form has been available to the curious virgins of China. An unofficial Chinese sex manual was finally issued in the 1970s, but it only hinted at the anatomical activities involved; needless to say, *Important Matters of the Jade Chambers* and other erotic classics are not publicly available in the People's Republic. In 1985 a Shanghai magazine inaugurated China's first course on sex education including "basic theory."

All is not what it seems on the surface. India, in fact, remains a sex-obsessed society, more prudish as well as more sexual and libertine than Chinese society. Meanwhile the Chinese attitude toward sex is as uncomplicated as it has always been. The neurotic duality of the Indian view of sexuality and of women continues; Indian women are either cloistered and avidly protected as virgin daughters and faithful wives (and admired as prime ministers), or they are seen as lustful, degraded, insatiable sources of sexual satisfaction.

The Chinese approach to sexuality, whether in the old, more permissive age, or in today's bureaucratic society, reflects a practical, non-emotional, and more consistent attitude than that in India. Restrictions on sexual practices in India today are a reflection of popular social attitudes. The Indian government is not in front of public opinion on the issue. In China, the stern code emerges from the political leadership and any relaxation of current restrictions would not likely meet with significant public protest. Indian surface prudery of today, like its sybaritism of yesterday, is cultural; modern China's sexual Spartanism, like its decorum of the past, is political.

The Chinese regime tries to control and dampen sexuality, not because of deep moral concerns, but in pursuit of social, political, and economic goals. Sexuality is still viewed by the Chinese as neither an evil nor some sort of supreme, hedonistic good, much less as the way to religious enlightenment. But traditional Chinese and modern communists alike believe that to assure social control and order, sexuality, like everything else, must be strictly regulated.

Femininity among Chinese women was discouraged over most of the past 30 years and, during the Cultural Revolution, actively suppressed for political not moral reasons. As in China's past, however, the appearance of propriety is more important than its actuality and there is a considerable gap between the myth of the moral code and the reality.

While the authorities play their Mrs. Grundy role, Chinese urban society has become even more permissive than in the pre-Manchu days. Extra-marital sexuality has become democratized in that it no longer involves only upper-class men and lower-class women. Young couples today publicly cuddle in Chinese parks, something that would not be seen in India where dating is simply not done. In China virginity is no longer the most important quality required of a marriageable young woman and many young urban couples engage in pre-marital sex, although usually with the intended marriage partner. In India, however, virginity is still the most esteemed of all feminine values and this is as true, or perhaps even more so, in the cities and among the middle classes than in the countryside.

Sexuality in India is both more repressed and more available than in China. Western sex manuals, which can be purchased in English at high prices, soft-porn paperback Western novels, and increasingly video cassettes are avidly passed around in middle and upper class male circles. Prostitution flourishes in the big cities, and brothels are often staffed by young girls who have been kidnapped from remote tribal villages or, in some cases, dedicated by their parents to the goddess Yellamma and thus to a life of prostitution. The "Devadasi" system of temple courtesans has been outlawed; but in 1983, a Bombay paper reported that dedication rituals were continuing in a Yellamma temple in a Maharashtra village and that, as a result, 2500–3000 girls were provided to the brothels of Bombay and Pune every year.

In China prostitution has rebounded in recent years. In a 1985 sweep in Canton, police arrested more than 800 sing-song girls. There is a crime in China for women only called "consorting with foreigners." No one in China, foreigner or otherwise, however, goes naked on the beaches. Nevertheless, while young Chinese women unselfconsciously appear in one-piece bathing suits, Indian women are just not seen publicly in swimming suits. At the beaches, Indian females, young and old, wade giggling into the water, fully swathed in their saris.

While most Chinese women still plod about in Mao suits or, in recent summers, increasingly in simple skirts and calf-length hose, every Indian woman, even the poorest, wears an alluring, midrift-revealing sari, jewels in her ears—and often her nose as well—bangles galore, and delicate make up, including the intriguing spot of *tilaka* just between her mysterious eyes. The good news in China, however, is that the long slit skirt or *chi par* has now officially returned.

Romantic songs are also back in China, but these are not nearly as suggestive as the love songs of India. Nor is there anything in China like the erotic movements of an Indian dancer in her harem-like apparel. Nevertheless there is probably proportionally as much or more sex for fun, marital or otherwise, going on in China as in India. In India it is just more visual, exciting and, well, sensual. Current sexual mores in China are primarily the result of arbitrary rules, whereas in India they spring from a much deeper culture of sexuality and the starkly ambivalent attitudes it has fostered.

Indian women are frequently teased sexually by male strangers; in school, girls will be careful about casual chitchat with boys, lest the latter take it as an invitation to sex. Indian boys in their public relations with girls are "pathetically stupid," not knowing what to do or say; but once they find the girls on somewhat isolated roads, "they offer loud, vulgar invitations to sexual intercourse . . . (and) if no one is looking, touch their breasts or pinch their buttocks."[111] Riding alone on buses young Indian women are likely to be pinched and fondled. But such awkward advances seldom proceed on to actual assault or rape, and the rejected male completes his endeavor through fantasy. Given the right pretext, however, some Indian men will carry "Eve teasing" somewhat further. During the Hindu spring festival of Holi, men and women throw colored water and powder over each other, much as Lord Krishna and his female admirers were said to have done in mythical times. On some Indian university campuses, the occasion has led to the terrorizing of women students and sometimes to stripping them in public. Security forces are sometimes called to the campuses to protect the coeds during Holi celebrations.

Indian sexual fantasies are especially stirred by Western women. The knowledge that Western females are frequently divorced, sometimes sleep with men to whom they are not married, and, most astonishing of all, go naked on the beaches at Goa and elsewhere in India has persuaded the male population that all Western women are nymphomaniacs. Indian tour buses from the interior make a bee-line for the shores of Goa and other beaches where young males rush to gaze in amazement at the topless and often bare-bottomed Westerners—some of whom would never go naked in public back home.

Indians allow Western nudity on their beaches out of the indifference and tolerance that they traditionally have shown to beggars, mongrel dogs, and various eccentrics. The display of foreign flesh, white or bronzed, also confirms the Indian belief that Westerners are not really civilized. Likewise, when Indian films show Western society, there is usually a great deal of drinking and loose sexual mores are implied. The same is often true in Chinese film representations of foreigners and overseas Chinese.

This feeds the image of foreign depravity that stimulates sexual harrassment of single Western women traveling in India, and sometimes even escorted ones. A young American lady on entering a Madras cloth store alone is asked directly by the proprietor, "you like sex, sir?" An attractive middle-aged American woman sitting by a hotel pool in Trivandrum is joined by a young cashew-grower who subtly asks if American women do not like to "suck and kiss?" Any Western woman who has been alone in India for any time can relate similar tales. These clumsy overtures are, however, naive and innocent in their way. The Jekyll and Hyde view of women by Indian males is demonstrated by the fact that, despite such harrassment, Western women are quite safe walking the streets of Calcutta at night.

But they are even safer in China, where young Western females hitchhike across the country without encountering a single pass. Only in Tibet, according to one such traveler, did she encounter the wandering hand. The Chinese not only have a deeper sense of decorum, but they also see women as human beings rather than either goddesses or sex partners.

The Indian movie reflects Indian sexual fantasies through its repetitious romantic formula. A young couple meet, fall in love, and promise to marry; obstacles are interposed; but in the end these are happily resolved and the couple are united in marriage. While to the Westerner or the Chinese it all appears very chaste, the Indian movie-goer sees romantic love on the screen expressing a deep thirsting for sexual union. The feast of music, dancing, and pretty girls which every Indian film contains further heightens the erotic imagination.[112] Romantic love is virtually impossible in Hindu society; Hindi and other Hindu languages do not even have an appropriate term for "love" in the romantic sense, and songs and films use either the Urdu or the English word. The Chinese word "ai," on the other hand, like English, can be used to describe love of children and parents, or either romantic or sexual love.

Romantic affairs and marriages are quite possible in China, especially in the cities. While historically Chinese marriages were arranged and unromantic, Chinese tradition embraces the ideal of a romantic infatuation with a member of the opposite sex that includes, but also transcends, the physical attraction. The Chinese classic, *The Dream of the Red Chamber*, is just such a romantic story. But the stereotyped romantic Indian movie stories are more than fantasy: to the Indian movie-goer, they are totally unreal and, thus, he or she feels only the hidden pulsation of anticipated sexual pleasure.

The ideal, as presented in Indian films today, is that sex outside of marriage is degenerate and evil, but in reality the average Indian secretly thirsts for promiscuous and illicit sex, which is the most exciting of all sex. Indian films subtly feed this suppressed desire.[113]

Given the discouragement of adolescent and early adult courting in both countries, it is not surprising that homosexual play and experimentation are not uncommon among Indian boys and young men and perhaps to a lesser extent among Chinese. Young males in both societies, for example, frequently hold hands in public. In India there is virtually no opposite-sex hand-holding. The Indian psychiatrist Sudhir Kakar notes that there is a relative tolerance in India for homo-erotic feelings and fantasies among men who are otherwise normal in their erotic attitude toward women.[114] Although youthful experimentation is winked at, there is a strong social taboo in India against the actual practice of homosexuality. China again is even more conventional and treats chronic or adult homosexuality as a criminal offense, but turns a blind eye to youthful dalliance.

Women's Rights

The elites of both India and China are dedicated to equal rights for women, and the Constitutions and laws of the two countries fully embody this principle. In practice, however, change in this area has come about slowly, particularly in the countryside. Greater strides have been made in the cities and at the more sophisticated levels of society. In terms of university attendance and equal-employment opportunities for college-educated women, India's record is as good or better than that of China. Only 30 percent of university enrollment in China is female, compared to 40 to 50 percent in India. According to the vice-chancellor of Bombay University, which is one of the prestige schools in India, the university has a nearly equally divided co-educational student body. NCNA, on the other hand, reported that Peking University's graduating class of 1980 was only 23 percent female.

Indian women are quite easily accepted into the teaching and medical professions. They provide about half of all Indian doctors. Other women college graduates, however, can have a difficult time in finding a suitable job. For many Indian women a college education is primarily a way to assure an arranged marriage with a college-educated man. All Chinese women college graduates, on the other hand, are appointed into the cadre bureaucracy, of which at all levels they comprise only about 6 percent. Many Indian women run small-scale businesses and cottage industries, but there are few female executives in major industrial or commercial enterprises. Likewise, in China one finds female managers of collective enterprises such as embroidery factories which employ mostly female workers, but it is rare for a woman to head a major state sector company.

In terms of high-level political jobs for women, India has outshone China, if only because of Mrs. Gandhi. Otherwise, there is not much difference at this top political level. There are 26 women among the 544 members of India's Lok Sabha and eight among the 55 cabinet members. Twenty-three women are included among the 343 members of the Chinese Communist Party's Central Committee. There is only one woman among the 22-member Chinese Politburo. Most women who have gained top-rank political influence in China, including Jiang Qing (Mao's wife), have been spouses of leading officials. Although Mrs. Gandhi certainly owed her good start in politics to the fact that her father was Jawaharlal Nehru, her success after his death in 1964 was due to her own skill and drive.

More than as politicians and bureaucrats, Indian and Chinese women are prominent today as academicians, doctors, artists, performers, and writers. A talented and ambitious woman in either country, if born to an educated family in one of the big cities, is likely to make it. The average female rural dweller, however, bright or not, still faces serious obstacles. While virtually all urban women in China are assigned jobs after junior or middle-secondary school, women are often paid less for the same work, and according to the head of the official all-China Women's Federation, 60–70 percent of those who are still waiting for assignment are women.[115]

In India, 78 percent of urban women between 15–59 years of age are not in the labor force. Many, if not most, Indian women prefer not to work out of the home; but because of financial pressures, more and more are doing so. As a generalization it is probably true that in urban areas Indian women are probably more subservient to their husbands than are Chinese women today. Chinese urban wives, most of whom work, must, however, still prepare the meals and do most of the housework. As in other societies, wife-beating is not unknown in either India or China, and divorce is made legally difficult for women in China and socially scandalous for women in India. In addition, India suffers from a particularly atrocious crime—"bride-burning." In a typical suspected case of bride-burning, the husband's family has become outraged over the failure of the bride's family to produce the promised dowry and the new bride's "self-immolation" is arranged. A dowry, although outlawed in India, is still a vital necessity if a good match is to be made for a daughter; consequently, the woman's family frequently promises more than it can deliver. Women's organizations in India have made bride-burning a major target and they vigorously and physically agitate for police action when a suspected case is not being officially pursued. The All-China Federation of Women's Organizations, on the other hand, is an organ of the government and, not surprisingly, it has never organized or demonstrated as an independent advocate of women's rights.

Many more of the old abuses against women continue in the hinterlands of India and China. Child-marriage is one. In India the average age of marriage of females during the 1901–1911 decade was 13.2, and that was an all-India figure; in the countryside it was even lower. In 1971, 13.6 percent of rural girls between the ages of 10 and 14 were married and a few were already widows. In urban India, 3.9 percent in this age group were married.[116] The Chinese do not provide precise equivalent figures, but Fox Butterfield cites an official report on child betrothals in some rural areas of China. In one commune in Shanxi, 43 percent of girls under 5 were betrothed; the report also cited other cases of selling child brides and ill-treatment of brides and abandonment of wives, leading to cases of suicide.[117] In January 1982, five Chinese men were sentenced to prison for kidnapping and selling 115 women into forced marriages. Chinese women in the countryside have also suffered physical abuse and even murder, because they gave birth to daughters. The pressure to have only one child, and the penalties for having more than two, have increased the incidence of this sort of crime as well as the phenomenon of female infanticide in China. Premier Zhao indicated the seriousness of the problem when he told the NPC in December, 1983, that "we must in particular protect infant girls and their mothers . . . the whole society should resolutely condemn the criminal activities of female infanticide and maltreatment of women."

The killing of baby girls is a major, perhaps increasing, problem in China and still rampant in India. It is difficult to say which case is worse. There were 21.6 million more males than females in India in 1981 and 31 million more in China. The differences in surplus males is roughly in the same proportion as the total population difference. According to a 1983 report of the All China Women's Federation, in some parts of China boys outnumber girls by five to one. The reason for these reversals of normal demographic patterns are high malnutrition and death rates among girls.

CHAPTER 11

Art and the Artist

God and Nature

In pre-Moghul India, all art was sacred and its sole purpose was communication with the divine. Indian art was a testament to the Freudian thesis that while the nature and origins of beauty are inexplicable, the concept derives ultimately from sexual feeling, the primordial and most intense of human pleasures. The *Rig Veda* tells us that in the beginning the ultimate reality appeared by its own heat and gave existence to desire (Kama), and then realized all things in the universe using desire as the motivating power. Hindu art openly celebrates sexuality. Chinese art sublimates it in a subtle contemplation of nature and in the graceful though bold strokes of calligraphy.

The cosmologies of Indian and Chinese thought shaped the themes and styles of their art. There is a similarity between the Indian vision, stressing both the sensuality and the transcendence of the human condition, and the Chinese love of nature as reflecting the harmony and one-ness of the universe—the mirror of "the way." But with the important exception of art borrowed from India—Buddhist iconography and accompanying narrative paintings—Chinese art was not religious. Ultimate reality for the mainstream of Chinese art—painting and calligraphy—was natural, not supernatural, phenomena. Chinese artists communed with nature, not with God.

This orientation was consistent with an agricultural society's worship of natural forces and was reflected in very early Chinese hieratic art. Indian arts' emphasis on sexuality as the basic life-force again suggests the herdsman's stress on the supernatural and his concern with animal fertility and regeneration.

Neither Indian nor Chinese art sought to represent the illusion of reality. In China, poetic insight, rather than decoration, early on became the ideal.

Chinese painters and calligraphers strove to represent the inner vibrance of the external world, not its formal appearance.

The first of the six rules of painting set out by Xie He (Hsieh Ho) in the sixth century A.D. was the incorporation of spirit, or *qi*, suggesting nervous energy transmitted from the artist through the brush into his work. In the Chinese view, to paint the essence of bamboo the artist must become a bamboo. Stories were told of painters like Wu Taoci (Wu T'ao-tzu), whose painted horses galloped away or whose waterfalls kept the emperor awake with their cascading noise.

Thus, in an otherwise mundane Chinese society, Taoism had its victory in art. Contemplation of nature, the retreat to the mountains, was the Chinese form of Nirvana; but this subtle Chinese sense of aesthetics also reflected Confucian absorption with the search for harmony—harmony between men, and between man and the universe. Moreover, Chinese artistic expressionism embodied typical Chinese discipline and order. It encouraged free form and originality but strictly within traditional limits. Calligraphy was highly expressive and individual but within tight restrictions of form and method. The calligrapher's subject was limited to words, his colors to black on white, and his technique to the ordered sequence of the brush stroke. The characters, however, could be made to convey an emotion independent of their meaning, and thus calligraphy came to link poetry and painting. The most beautiful and traditional of Chinese art contained all three.

Chinese painters also tended to specialize. A painter of horses would paint horses over and over. Repetition by an artist was not considered bad form but was viewed as we would repetition of a symphony. Moreover, as the Confucianists stressed emulation of models in society, so young Chinese artists meticulously copied the masters. A copy might even be considered better than the original.[118]

Landscape was one of the highest forms of Chinese painting. Yet the subject was nearly always of mountains, rivers, and mist, hardly ever of desert and sea. In Chinese landscapes, man was a tiny, anonymous creature. Portraits were nearly always of emperors, their families, and senior officials, and reflected little or nothing of the individual's psychology or character. Aside from private pornography, of which there was a great deal, Chinese art did not celebrate the human body or man and woman's sensuality. Taoist sects and individuals could express their sexuality in private in very imaginative ways, but in public art, nudes or too suggestive poses violated Confucian decorum.

Indian art, whether drama, music or visual, also was non-literal, its objective being to create a sense of *rasa*, literally "taste," "essence" or "flavor." The rasa which was evoked could be one or more of the eight emotions: love, laughter, sorrow, anger, high spirits, fear, disgust, and astonishment.[119] While rasa is similar to the Chinese artistic concept of *qi*, in that both reflect inner life rather than surface reality, the Indian term directly relates to sensual emotions, while the Chinese concept of "spirit" or "resonance" is less suggestive of human feelings and more of the harmonious reverberations of nature. In ancient Greece, art had to be plausible; in China, intelligible; in India, evocative.

Art in India had both its psychedelic and its somnolescent quality.[120] But always it reflected sexuality as the ultimate spirit of universal creativity. Consequently, while nineteenth-century Westerners were great admirers of Chinese art, they tended to be confused and often repulsed by Indian art. Ruskin, while admitting Indian art was refined, protested that it "never represented a real fact" but either "forms its compositions out of meaningless fragments of color and flowings of line, or if representing a living creature, it represents the creature under some distorted and monstrous form." In Indian art, Ruskin concuded, "flowers do not bloom . . . the creatures of the field and forest do not live, (but) lie bound of their own corruption, encompassed only by doleful phantoms, or by spectral vacancy."[121]

Hegel was not disturbed by the symbolism and exaggeration of Indian art, but still he asserted that "despite all the profusion and extraordinary boldness of their conceptions, (Indian artists) fall into a levity of fantastic mirage which is quite remarkable, a flightiness which dances from the most spiritual and profoundest matters to the meanest trifle of present experience, in order that it may interchange and confuse immediately the one extreme with the other."[122]

It was natural that not only was Chinese art far more popular in Europe than Indian art but that some Westerners became skilled and famous even in China as "Chinese" painters. The most notable example was Father Giuseppe Castiglione, also known as Lang Shining (Lang Shih-ning) (1698–1768), a Milanese priest who worked in China most of his life. There were no parallels of Western expertise in the practice of Indian art. To be a good traditional Indian artist one had to be a good Hindu.

Westerners did not understand the metaphysical and religious basis of all Indian life, including its art. For the Hindu, there was no dichotomy between the profound and the mean, the sacred and the profane. The ultimate purpose of life and thus of art was fusion of the human soul and its driving force of sexualilty with the infinite.

Whether it was "a bull, copulating with a cow, or a man with a woman, the very act of copulation (was) the sharing of a mystical, creative process."[123] It was no wonder that the vivid incessant portrayal of this "creative process" shocked Victorians.

Khajuraho and Konarak

Two of the most famous examples of erotic Indian temple art are those at Khajuraho in northern India and Konarak on the east coast below Calcutta.

Like cosmic symbols whose messages have been forgotten, the main temples of Khajuraho rise from platforms just west of the village of the same name. Similar structures are scattered in the nearby fields of wheat and rape-seed. In waves, ornate towers of triangular or rectangular cones ascend higher and higher, culminating in the unique curvilineal *sikharas*. The top half of the towers are composed of uneven vertical rows of abstract geometric designs that are both baroque and somewhat Aztec. Stone columns fitted together without mortar soar upward and inward to a height of as much as 31 meters, ending in circles of vertical discs, topped by knobs like those found on Buddhist *stupas*.

The famous elements, of course, are the horizontal bands of sensual, mostly naked human sculptures that swirl around the tower as well as inside its inner sanctum. Despite the attraction of close inspection, the best view is from 50 feet away and sitting down. From this position one feels the force of the conception. The mass of men and women, gods and goddesses, which diminish in size from the bottom to the top, throb with both desire and consummation. Some of the erotic *mithuna* couples are among the most beautiful representations in art of the sexual embrace; others are distinctly—and literally—animal, rather than sublime, in character. Above the panorama of humanity and the Gods at play, several decorative, horizontal layers intervene before the abstract designs rise vertically along a convex curve, throwing out a number of random, premature peaks and—in the lower reaches—a few more anthropomorphic figures, but continuing upward toward an apex that is not seen, but hidden by a circle of rings. This is the phallic cosmos, the home of the gods, soaring forever inward toward its beginning, absorbing man's and woman's illusions of desire.

While Khajuraho is a delicate lace tableau of love as destiny, the Sun Temple at Konarak on the Orrissa coast celebrates the plunging ecstatic course of a doomed world. A towering temple on 24 giant wheels, drawn by seven great stallions, rushes pell-mell across the sky. Along the terraces of the 50-foot temple, larger-than-life couples engage in fellatio and gymnastic gyrations of copulation, while three bronze statues of the Sun God, Surya, reflect the solar glow at sunrise, noon, and sunset.

Sitting in the shadow of one of the stone elephants that flank the enormous temple, the traveller contemplates the message that the architect and the patron king, Narasimha, were attempting to convey. It is, among other things, a celebration of the creative force of life and of sexuality, which is its wellspring. It symbolizes the Indian ability to integrate the most mundane with the consecrated, the life of sensual pleasure with the inner life of feeling and spirit.

The Sun Temple also reminds us of the old Hindu story of the man who is hanging by a vine over a well filled with poisonous snakes. The man has no strength to pull himself up the vine, which is being nibbled away above by insects. At this moment, a drop of honey curls down the vine, and, forgetting his fate, the man stretches out his tongue to taste the sweet nectar. Thus do men and gods revel in carnal pleasures.

Monuments and the Grave

The erotic theme is also found in Rajput miniatures, which were the Hindu variation of the Moghul art form, influenced in turn by European Renaissance art. A favorite subject of Rajput paintings were the adventures of Krishna, the eighth reincarnation of Vishnu, and his superhuman romances. Despite the miniatures and the famous cave paintings in India, such as those in Ajanta, the Hindu had relatively little interest in painting. India's sensual culture felt more at home molding solid materials, such as clay, stone, bronze and ivory, rather than working on a two-dimensional plane.[124] Hindus were not interested in observing the world, nature, or people as they actually were, but in the sensual reality underneath.[125]

Tomb architecture was of course missing in India until the arrival of the Moslems. Practicing cremation, Hindu society, unlike China or Egypt, did not have a grave culture. Moreover, in ancient India palaces were made of wood and did not survive. Hindu architecture is concentrated in temples, not palaces.

Reflecting the primacy of the political order in China, however, most of Chinese monumental art is tomb or palace construction. Chinese emperors, compelled to demonstrate that the mantle of heaven remained with them, were driven to ostentatious display in both their mortal and after-death abodes, and these became the focus of Chinese architecture. Sculpture in China was "almost always at the service of the Indian [Buddhist] faith, and when it derived its inspiration from other sources, such as in the monumental figures, human and animal, which decorated the approach to the imperial tombs, it was with certain rare exceptions, formal, stylized, and massive."[126] China's grave culture also preserved for us the most important artifacts and treasures which we have from ancient China, including animal and human statues, bronze figures like the famous "Flying Horse of Gansu," wall paintings, jade burial suits, and Qin Shi Huang's massive terra-cotta army.

The geometrical instincts of India and Chinese monumental architecture reflect a different philosophical base. Indian designers found their ideal in the square, while the Chinese, like many cultures, viewed the circle as the image of perfection and wholesomeness. The perfect curve is the symbol of unrefined nature and fertility. From the egg to the sun to the universe itself it is the primordial state from which all existence begins and ultimately returns. The Chinese pagoda is a repetition of circles and the same theme is emphasized in the Temple of Heaven, the Ming Tombs, the Temple of the Sun, and other famous monuments in China. Chinese spent their lives going in and out of half-circled moon gates.

On the other hand, Indian temples in their design sought to emulate the supernatural not the natural and thus they stressed that symbol of perfection that interrupts and transcends the real world—the square. "Because the Hindu temple, at least in part, seeks to be an embodiment in miniature of a perfect divine world, the square is regarded as basic to its overall form. A temple when completed may have sweeping curvilinear lines and a fluid grace, but it will be based upon a square or rectangle that has been imposed on or carved out of unrefined, raw space."[127]

The Temple of Heaven and the Terra-Cotta Army

The Temple of Heaven in Peking, refurbished by the latest rulers up the street, glistens in primary colors like a huge Christmas toy made to be taken apart and put together by a giant two-year-old. It has the polished look of glaze, lacquer, porcelain, and marble and the geometry of long, straight avenues, circular pagodas in square yards, moon gates, and curving walls.

Auspicious numbers are repeated in the design, especially 9 for the sky and the emperor, and its factor 3. The names are decorous—the Hall of Abstinence, the Temple of August Heavens, the Hall of Prayer for Good Harvest. There is housing for staff and attendants, there are emblems of the dragon and the phoenix, thrones for the emperor, enormous lacquered pillars symbolizing the four seasons, the twelve months, and the twelve hours.

The only mystic aspect to the huge complex, surrounded by a wall four miles long, is the acoustic effect of two locations; one is the circular, echoing stone in the middle of the 3-tiered mound on which sacrifices were offered, and the other is a curving wall that seems to carry one's voice to a listener across the courtyard. Foreigners and Chinese tourists delight in producing these effects, but there is hardly a sense that it is, or ever was, sacred ground.

Instead, one has the image of officials, not of pious believers or mystic priests, scurrying about on the approach of the emperor. Indeed, the temple was never open to the Chinese public until 1911, and it was the Ministry of Rights and the Department of Sacred Music and other bureaucracies, not a priesthood, which were in charge of ceremonies at the temple. The structures were not built to glorify God, but as a symbol of sovereignty, a place for the emperor to engage the heavens in conversation (*jiao tien*) and to offer sacrifices for a good harvest.

Hindus believe that their gods actually live in the temples and that their idols are the gods, not simply representations of them. In India the temple is not only a place of worship, it is an object of worship. In Confucian temples there is no pantheon, nor even a sense of the supernatural; instead, there are the symbols of bureaucracy and the worldly sovereign with only passing acknowledgment of some unknown force that guides human destiny.

When Qin Shi Huang died in 210 B.C. his wife, together with thousands of workers and artisans who had built his tomb, were buried alive with him near the ancient imperial capital of Xian (Hsian). It could have been worse.

Some centuries before, tens of thousands of slaves and war-captives might also have followed the emperor into the next world. Instead, Qin Shi Huang was escorted by a massive terra-cotta army of soldiers, attendants, and horses. Since 1974, the Chinese have been excavating one wing of this pottery army, which marches away from the still unopened tomb. Today, the column parades out of the ground under a gigantic roof, which, so far, extends the length of more than a football field. Toward the rear only the heads of the marchers appear; in the front rows the six-foot figures have been totally exhumed and, when necessary, pieced back together. Their facial features, each individually shaped, suggest the routine of a morning muster—or perhaps it is the calm pride of professionals trooping in the most immortal funeral pageant in all of history. There are swords and bows and arrows for defense, urns for provisions and drink, and carts for transport. There are even underground stables for this vast necropolis. But there are few icons and little acknowledgment of whatever gods might be. The great tyrant went on his last campaign as he had on all the others—neither asking for nor giving quarter. As the entire world had submitted to the Qin, so the heavens, faced with such a force, would also.

Artists and Aesthetics

Artists in China were part of the literati. Some were court artists with titles; others, with private wealth, worked independently. Every gentleman and scholar, whether a member of the court or not, practiced calligraphy, occasionally dashed off a poem and, if at all talented, painted in the impressionist manner. In India, artists and artisans were a caste, not among the lowest, but neither among "the twice-born." Although in the Gupta period, Indian amateurs did take up painting, art in India was dominated by professional craftsmen. They were in service to the faith, whereas Chinese artists, outside the Buddhist tradition, were highly secular. The Chinese penchant for keeping records has left us with identifications of most of the very early prominent artists in China. Even in Xiang times—more than 2,500 years ago—inscriptions were cast in bronze vessels recording when and by whom they were made.

In India, sculptors or other artists rarely signed their creations, but worked closely with brahman priests who described the appropriate costume, ornament, facial expression, posture and gestures for figures to be painted or carved for the temple walls. The intimate relationship between artist and theologian in India demonstrated the underlying purpose of Indian art: "to render visible and in accessible form, the world of the Gods."[128]

The Chinese very early developed the disciplines of both aesthetics and art history. Following Hsieh Ho's work on the principles of painting Zhang Yang-yuan (Chang Yang-yuan) in A.D. 847 wrote the *Record of Famous Painters of All the Dynasties*, in which he classified painters according to their teachers and styles, and surveyed Buddhist and Taoist temple paintings and private collections of the day.[129]

The principal ancient Indian source on painting, the *Vishnudharmottaram*, classified the types of painting appropriate to temples, palaces, and private dwellings and differentiated between "true," "lyrical," and "secular" painting.[130] In the Gupta Period a commentary by Yasodhara on the Kamasutra enumerated the "six limbs" or "essentials" of painting. These essentials included instructions on the proper representation of feeling and mood, as well as the preparation of colors and uses of the brush.[131]

In China, however, there existed more of a consciousness of art and a sense of art for art's sake. India had neither the concept of art as such nor of art history. Akhileshwar Jha points out that India's ancient treasures and monuments existed for thousands of years, yet no Indian document or source, even to the end of the Moghul rule, ever mentioned them. Ajanta, Ellora, Khajuraho and Mahabalipuram were completely forgotten until the British re-discovered them.[132] Sculptures, monuments, and other representational works were viewed in India as religious and ecstatic experiences, not as something in the real world called "art," which could be intellectually analyzed and recorded.

Contemporary Art

The Chinese ability to reject any aspect of their culture and still remain Chinese, as well as the primacy of politics in their culture is vividly apparent in the state of Chinese art today. Meanwhile, India's contemporary art scene confirms the hold of tradition and its union of the mystical and the sensual, as well as the creative artistic environment that exists in India today.

In keeping with the pattern of other Marxist revolutionary regimes, the CCP has not fostered creative departures or experimentation in art, but turned to (1) mechanized political art, and (2) the classics of another society. The Chinese have enthusiastically taken up Western classical music and ballet. There are full-time symphonies in about twenty provinces and ballet companies in a number of Chinese cities, including a professional group in the sprawling industrial city of Shenyang. An extensive system of academies throughout China selects young talent for a life-time commitment to the study of Western performing arts, including piano, voice, and other disciplines. In violin and piano, China already has world-class artists, and in the future it is bound to make a major impact in international music circles.

The Chinese even have Italian-style opera groups which put on good performances of "Aida," "La Traviata," and "Carmen" to appreciative audiences. The regime obviously feels quite comfortable with Puccini and Bizet, although a run of "Carmen" in early 1982 was cut short because party officials were uncomfortable with its sensuality.

By contrast, only a handful of Indians, mostly Parsee and Catholic Goans, have taken up the pursuit of Western music as a profession. In India, Bombay alone has a full-time Western symphony, and there is no professional ballet anywhere in the country. Zubin Mehta, conductor of the New York Philharmonic, comes from the Parsee community, which took readily and enthusiastically to Western culture, and which today is the principal supporter of the Bombay Symphony. Western ballet and classical music are in tune with both Chinese emotions and politics, but they are too organized and unspontaneous to appeal to the Indian heart.

The Chinese concentration on Western classics and socialist realism has not been accidental. In part it reflects the Communist Party's early view of Chinese traditional culture as backward, an attitude which was carried to its ultimate conclusion during the Cultural Revolution. The popularity of "Swan Lake" and Mozart as well as Stalinist-style buildings, statues, and paintings was also shaped by the pervasive influence in China in the 1950s of the Soviet Union, which was seen as a model for everything socialist and progressive.

In China the older generation and country people still thrive on Peking Opera and other forms of traditional music which have been revived since the Cultural Revolution. The younger generation, and intellectuals in particular, however, prefer Western music, either classical or popular. Young Indians, of course, are also enthusiastic about disco, rock, and other such modern syncopations, but most cassettes that are sold in India are Indian love songs, played with traditional Indian instruments or a mix of Indian and Western instruments.

In China rock music and Western dancing enjoyed a brief period of tolerance after Mao's demise. In 1981 they were again declared "poisonous weeds," but by 1984 were once more officially tolerated. Western style popular music and dancing are today sweeping the cities with a proliferation of music parlors and mass dance-ins in public parks, including the Temple of Heaven in Peking.

While the educated elite in China provide the most enthusiastic audience for Western classical music and ballet, the Indian elite throughout this century have led the revival of traditional Indian classics. It is in the metropolitan cities, more than the countryside, where the traditional arts are flourishing in India. Historically, or at least beginning in the Middle Ages, Indian dancers were courtesans or temple dancers, called *asparas*, but early in the twentieth century, as part of the nationalist revival of tradition, the brahman elite not only began to foster Bharatanatyam and other forms of classical dance and music, but to perform it themselves. Today, most of the prominent female dancers are brahman.

While visiting troupes of Peking or Cantonese opera have been well-received abroad, they have not created the same kind of sustained interest as have traditional Indian performers, such as Ravi Shankar, playing the sitar, or dancers like Indrani Rehman and Yamani Krishnamurti. Despite similarities in the music of the two countries—harmony and counterpoint are absent in both—Indian music is more pleasing to most foreign ears and, like Indian dance, conveys an international language of sensuality.

Another reason why Indian traditional classics are relatively popular abroad is that they are a more creative and vigorous force at home than is the case with China's traditional performing arts. The strength of the traditional forms in India lies in the patronage of the cultural elite, whereas in China the traditional forms find their main support among the unsophisticated.

The constraints of political orthodoxy, as much as cultural proclivities, have shaped other areas of contemporary Chinese art. Literature, the representational arts, and music composition are politically dangerous fields in China because the Chinese view the creation of new themes and ideas, whether in words, pictures, or music, as having social or political consequences. The creative interpretation even of classical music or ballet can at times also be controversial in China; but still these are by far the safest art forms. It follows that since liberation China has produced excellent performers in Western music and ballet, but no notable compositions.

Chinese traditional painting, as we have seen, was highly impressionistic rather than realistic. Paradoxically, the regime has not put any restrictions on the promotion of traditional Chinese painting or Chinese calligraphy, both of which stimulate the aesthetic senses through stylistic representation. Because they are traditional and highly disciplined forms of art, such impressionism is not seen as threatening because it does not venture into new ground. Nonetheless, the state of traditional Chinese painting today is depressing. Chinese painting was handed down from master to student and this process was interrupted during the Cultural Revolution. Even in less fanatical times, politics since 1949 has intruded into traditional painting. Elements of social realism, for example, have often been required; thus, a traditional watercolor landscape might include peasants surrounded by Red flags, working collectively on some worthy project, or a modern power plant plunked into an otherwise uninhabited landscape.

Likewise, as anyone in the cultural field in China today will concede, since liberation there has been no great Chinese novel or great Chinese writer. The revolution produced a number of brilliant writers like Mao Dun (Mao Tun), Ba Jin (Ba Chin) and Lu Xun (Lu Hsun), but after 1949 the spring went dry. The reason is clear. Lu Xun and his colleagues could write freely about society, human life, and conflict in their time, but for the past 37 years, Chinese writers have had to follow a political line enforced by a philistine bureaucracy.

While there may be a Pasternak or a Solzhenitsyn secretly at work in China, there is no evidence of it. In fact, good Chinese writers, like Ding Ling, who were purged twice and sent to farm labor in remote areas, did not write anything during their long exiles.[133] "It's not worth it," one writer explained. "It would probably never be published and if it were, it could later get you into trouble." Dissident Russian writers whose cultural identification is Western as well as Russian can achieve fulfillment by publication of their works in the West. Chinese writers, however, have far fewer, if any, emotional and intellectual roots outside of China, and thus the prospect of never being recognized or published at home is more devastating.

India's greatest writers were also produced by the nationalist struggle. Since independence there have been no great literary luminaries like Tagore. Nevertheless, Indian fiction and poetry is vigorous and unfettered. A merger of India and the West has produced superb, usually expatriate writers in English like N.K. Naraya, V.S. Naipaul, and Salman Rushdie. The *New York Review of Books* called Rushdie's *Midnight Children* one of the most important novels to come out of the English-speaking world in this generation. Rushdie deals harshly with India, while Naipaul, who is not India-born, is priggishly disdainful. More important, thousands of writers in Hindi, Bengali, Tamil and other Indian languages are busy writing stories about the tragedies, injustices, foibles, absurdities and glories of Indian life and history.

While most modern Indian literature is not available in translation, Indian novelists are producing honest and often fresh dramatic insights into the human condition, using an Indian setting. In China, "scar literature" or "literature of the wounded" focusing on the suffering and tragedies of the Cultural Revolution first bloomed in 1979 and sporadically thereafter. It began with a short story called "The Wounded" by a young Shanghaiese, Lu Xinhua. Older writers purged during the Cultural Revolution such as Liu Jinyan, Wang Meng, and the poet Ai Qing also began to reemerge. Like the "hundred flowers" campaign in 1957, the relative freedom since 1979 to write about suffering and tragedies in contemporary society has been tenuous. The new literary movement was not crudely stamped out like the "poisonous weeds" of 1957, but has been more gently suffocated. The current crop of Chinese writers, including Lin Xinwu, Gao Xiaosheng, Jiang Zilong, Lin Xinmu and Bai Hua try to walk a thin line between official approval and honest literature. The result proves that literature like man cannot be half free and half slave.

If contemporary art reflects the sensitivity of a society and the times, then Chinese modern art, quite appropriately, is an expression of the bureaucratic state. Chinese officials once again declare that there can be art for art's sake; the painting of a flower or a bee is acceptable, but that art still cannot be separated from politics. Since 1979 there has been a sporadic flowering not only of "scar literature," but also of modern art. Modern painters and sculptors, like Yuan Yungsheng and Wang Keping, have been permitted to show their abstractions and some were even given government commissions. One example was Yuan's stylized murals at the Peking airport, including one with several frontal nudes. Wang's best known work was a Buddha-like bust of Mao.

In 1980 the reform group of innovators around Deng Xiaoping was increasing its pressure on the conservatives, led by Premier Hua Guofeng, and it served their political purposes to criticize excessive control of intellectuals and artists and to allow these groups to denounce Maoist restrictions. In 1981 the Deng group agreed to a crackdown on artistic freedom, once again limiting "pessimism" and "commercialism" in literature and the cinema, and banishing abstract art and other such dangers.

As with the ban on disco music, at the time the liquidation of abstract art was largely a sop to military and other conservatives in the party; but it also reflected the reality that, once secure in the saddle, Deng did not give high priority to artistic freedom. Like the conservatives, many Dengists also saw an unfettered experimental art-form as threatening the party's monopoly of power and its control over society. Yuan's airport nudes were boarded up and he and other modern abstract artists were for a time not permitted to show or even sell their work in China.

Reacting to the renewed anti-modern art line, Chinese bureaucrats in the Ministry of Culture in 1981 insisted that a long-scheduled exhibition in Peking by the Boston Museum of Fine Arts remove abstract and experimental art from the collection. The demand was rescinded but the proscription remained for Chinese, not only in painting but in other art fields as well.

The "spiritual pollution" campaign of late 1983 put another damper on creativity. The liberals, however, rallied their forces and under the patronage of Hu Yaobang appeared to make an important comeback in 1984. In December a congress of Chinese poets, novelists and playwrights called on the party to restore artistic freedom and thereby revive China's leading role in world culture. In only its third congress since 1949, the Chinese Writers' Association heard speeches denouncing the persecution inflicted on writers in the past and calling for cultural freedom.

Ba Jin, the 80-year-old chairman of the association and author of one of the most famous pre-liberation novels, *Family*, in a speech read for him because of illness called for a political atmosphere that would allow modern China to produce "works that can compare with the magnificent creations of our people in the past." Ba declared that the nation should wait no longer for the epic masterpieces that would put China "in the front ranks in the world." Implicitly acknowledging that since liberation no great literature had been written, Ba said, "We yearn for China's Dante, Shakespeare, Goethe and Tolstoy to appear."

Hu Yaobang was in attendance but he did not speak. Instead, his protege, Hu Qili, who then oversaw cultural matters in the party Secretariat, offered some of the most far-reaching assurances ever given to writers by the party. Hu asserted that writers must have the freedom to choose themes and express their own feelings so that they could produce "touching and inspiring works."

Hu Yaobang presumably felt that unleashing the writers and artists against the conservatives would serve his political purposes. At the same time, it is probably true that philosophically Hu also believed in the cause of cultural liberalization more than Deng. Hu's speeches suggest he was convinced that if China's intellectual, scientific, and artistic creativity was to be restored, writers and other artists must also be much freer than they had been from bureaucratic control and the threat of intimidation and persecution. By 1986 it was again possible to show abstract art and discuss it in periodicals. With Hu's fall from power in 1987, it seemed possible that the latest blooming of cultural freedom would prove to be another short season for the "hundred flowers."

In India modern art is very much alive, as a visit to the handsome Museum of Modern Art in New Delhi will attest. The museum has held numerous exhibitions abroad and hosted international shows in New Delhi and other Indian cities. The museum purchases 100–200 new Indian works a year from nearly 2,000 submissions. There are also five or six private galleries of modern art in India, and in universities and numerous art academies Indian students study the modern masters from Van Gogh to Pollock. In contrast to China, where public statuary is usually either of Mao or heroic workers, peasants, and soldiers, Indian parks and public buildings are full of abstract sculpture.

Western critics have been sparing in their praise of Indian modern art, focusing on its failure to reflect a peculiarly Indian element. Responding, probably unnecessarily, to this criticism, some Indian artists paint in an erotic "neo-Tantric" style, which does not do justice to the Khajuraho tradition; others cover the range from surrealism to social realism. Considering its conservative society and the lack of a sizable philanthrophic community or market for modern art, contemporary painting and sculpture is vigorous and quite alive in India.

Movies for the Masses

In both India and China films provide the masses the great bulk of their entertainment and art. But it is India that is the film capital of the world. Indian studios turn almost eight hundred full-length films each year compared to about one hundred in China. Since independence, India has produced seventeen thousand feature films in forty languages and dialects and forty thousand short and documentary films. Twelve million Indians go to the movies each day.

Most Indian films are made by the Hindi-language industry centered in Bombay. The Bombay studios crank out stereotyped escapist movies in which the heroes and heroines are nearly always rich or at least comfortably middle class. Three or more song and dance numbers are included in each scenario, and a lengthy chase episode, a cabaret scene, and a great deal of fighting invariably ensue. Virtually without exception, the story ends happily. Until recently, the dangers and unhappiness that threatened the beautiful protagonists in Indian movies were caused by nature, evil, or accident, not by social or political causes. Still today the average Indian does not want to be entertained with movies which reflect everyday human suffering.

The Chinese counterpart to the Indian film fantasies are the "kung fu" movies mass produced in Hong Kong. The PRC has now produced several of its own "kung fu" movies. But if the Chinese public had their way, there would be many more of these melodramatic "Easterns." Instead, mainland Chinese are treated to whatever their producers decide is: (1) desirable; and (2) acceptable to the government. Chinese film studios can produce a flop and lose money, and so popular tastes to some extent have to be taken into account. But the official guidelines are quite simple—stories should not arouse doubts about the leadership of the Chinese Communist Party or of socialism. In India movies are censored primarily on moral rather than political grounds. Indian laws, however, do prevent movies from satirizing or otherwise portraying living personalities or political parties.

The thirst for glamor in both India and China is evident in the popular adulation of movie stars and the immense popularity of movie magazines which in both countries have the largest circulation of all journals. Even during the Cultural Revolution, Chinese female stars wore make-up that seemed excessive by Western standards. Likewise, male stars were and are allowed to maintain—for China—a semi-Bohemian appearance with longish hair and mod attire. Chinese directors often wear neck scarves and other Cecil B. DeMille paraphernalia of the 1930s.

The Bengali-language studios in Calcutta turn out art films which have received critical acclaim around the world and for which there are no Chinese counterparts. Satyajit Ray is the *eminence grise* of the Calcutta studios. Ray's internationally acclaimed films include *Pather Panchali, Jalsaghar, Debi*, and *Aparajito*. In 1978 the Berlin film festival committee counted Ray along with Chaplin and Bergman among the all-time masters of world cinema.

In contrast to the Bombay genre of movies, Ray's films are imitations of life. His protagonists are caught up in the circumstances of their existence. They may rebel or accept their fate, but it is a human drama which they perform. A recent Ray film, *Ghare Baire*, is about a housewife torn between her politically moderate and rational husband and her lover who is a revolutionary activist. Terrorism leads to violence in the village and to the death of the woman's husband. The story can be seen as an indictment of political extremism. But as Ray himself said in an interview in *India Today, Ghare Baire* is first and foremost a love story. The political allusions and interpretations are there, he admitted, but what is most important is the triangle between the characters.

Unlike Chinese films, in Ray's stories, politics provide the milieu and not the plot. The themes of Ray's movies are social rather than political. Ray portrays poverty but he does not make a film about it. His first film, *Pather*

Panchali (Song of the Little Road), was the simple story of life and death in a monsoon village. In *Charulata*, the beautiful nineteenth-century wife of a wealthy man living in a sophisticated circle of family and friends engages in a reckless love affair.

Ray's movies are not for the Indian masses but they find a sufficient audience among intellectuals and the middle class to pay their way. Recently, another genre of so-called "middle films" has also been gaining popularity that attempt to combine social and political themes and the artistry of Calcutta's cinema with the popular features of the Bombay escapist movies. Unscrupulous politicians are favorite villains of these new films.

A major distinction between Indian and Chinese cinema is the wide range that is available in India, where films provide what directors or producers select as well as what the mass audience desires. In China, politics and the bureaucracy, more than the market place still decide the style, the themes, and the content of cinema.

Concurrent with the period of "scar literature" in China, there also appeared a number of films about suffering caused during the Cultural Revolution. In early 1981, however, the regime once again drew the cultural knot tighter, forcing the soldier-writer, Bai Hua, to pen a self-criticism of his film "Bitter Tears," which had appeared only briefly and was then quickly banned. The hero in "Bitter Tears" is a Chinese artist studying abroad who returns home to serve the motherland after the Revolution. He is soon caught up in the 1957 anti-rightist purge. No sooner does he escape this persecution, than he is enmeshed in the Cultural Revolution. In one scene, his daughter asks if he does not still love his motherland. He replies that his motherland does not love him. In a melodramatic ending, the hero, alone in the mountains, staggers about in the snow and crumbles to the ground. The camera pans away and the audience sees that he has unknowingly stamped out a figure in the snow and that his body forms the dot of a question mark.

This decidedly pessimistic ending was too much for China's conservatives, particularly military leaders, who took the lead in banishing "Bitter Tears." An acceptable portrayal of a somewhat similar story of persecution was achieved by the 1981 movie "The Herdsman" which won China's equivalent of the Oscar—The Golden Cock. The film recounts the story of a youth who was left behind in Peking by his KMT father, who in 1948 had fled the on-rushing Communist army. The young hero grows up under the new regime to become a teacher. Because of his family background he also is swept up in the 1957 anti-intellectual purge and sent packing to a desolate commune, apparently in Inner Mongolia, where he works as a herdsman. During the Cultural Revolution, he marries a young woman who had also been sent to the countryside, and at a critical moment his bucolic friends in the commune hide him out in the mountains to escape Red guards searching for bourgeois victims. After the "Gang of Four" is wiped out, the party redeems itself and the hero is given a job in the commune as a school teacher.

Shortly after, however, who should appear in Peking but the KMT father, who has since become a wealthy businessman in America. The father, accompanied by a Chinese-American woman who is either his secretary or mistress or both, has returned to find his son and take him back to the U.S. After an awkward reunion, the son is torn over whether or not to return with his father to America and a life of luxury. He goes back to the grasslands to talk it over with his wife, who by now has given birth to a son. He then returns to Peking and during a final session with his whiskey-guzzling father announces that he intends to stay in China to serve the motherland. The film closes on a Mongolian run-across-the-fields scene as the hero and his wife rush to greet each other.

In Chinese films, whether a revolutionary opera favorite of Madame Mao, a post-Cultural Revolution production such as "The Herdsman," or even a historical movie, the story is essentially a political one. It is the old Confucian plot found throughout the *Analects* and in the poetry of the *Shi Qing*—the contrast between bad and good officials. This is the theme even when the drama revolves around a factory, a commune, or the housing shortage as in "Neighbors." The struggle for power, the question of correct doctrine, patriotism versus treachery, and the success or failure of leadership comprises the dialectics of Chinese drama. The human emotions of love, greed, self sacrifice, and jealousy are stirred up by and kept in orbit by these political and social forces.

The Rajpath and the Square of Heavenly Peace

There are no public buildings in the world quite so awe inspiring and regal as the Secretariat and the President's Palace in New Delhi. Although built by the English, the red sandstone edifices of government at the end of Delhi's broad Rajpath are still distinctly Indian. Looming over the plaza, the two wings of the colonnaded Secretariat are adorned with Hindu towers and cupolas, as well as a Buddist stupa on each side. The Rajpath rises up between the wings, concealing the palace beyond except for the darkly elongated protuberance of its central dome, which is a very large stupa, but which looks suspiciously like a giant lingam.

The romantic illusion of India is recreated every January 26th in a magnificent Republic Day Parade down the Rajpath toward the India Gate. Even more moving is the beating of the retreat two nights later before the Secretariat. Mounted camels are silhouetted on the high walls, 500 bandsmen curl the bagpipes and play Gandhi's favorite hymn, "Abide with Me." The drums drum, a mournful bugle sounds the end of day, and a spectacle of fireworks lights the night.

The Square of Heavenly Peace in Peking is dominated by the ochre outer walls of the Forbidden City and the multi-storied gate with curving layered roofs that bestride it. Two hundred yards south across the square is the magnificent double front gate that used to be the central portal in the old city walls. The walls have been torn down, so the gates standing alone seem emasculated, but imposing nevertheless. Mao's tomb, a modern structure with a few Chinese flairs around the edges, at his wife's insistence interrupts the great vista between the Forbidden City and the Front Gate. On the west wing of the Square, which is much enlarged from the old days, is the gigantic Great Hall of the People, built in six months in 1959. Its scale, like that of the Secretariat in Delhi, is unstinting. Enormous fluted columns of yellow sandstone give a Parthenon effect, but in its totality it seems more Egyptian than Greek—more pharaonic than Socratic. Across the square the National Museum of History repeats the form.

The government structures in New Delhi, as well as those in Tian An Men, are both examples of authoritarian architecture and a blending of the old and the new. The stupas and the lingam in the government complex in Delhi, the ascending Rajpath, the disappearing palace, and the openness of the setting reflect high grandeur and spirit. The architect seemed deliberately to create an illusion—a merging of India and the West.

The old imperial structures in Peking, flanked by the heavy halls of revolution and power, are more solid; but the combination of the old and the new is more logical. In New Delhi, authority in the Viceroy's Palace, or the President's Palace, as it is called today, was more show than reality, while Peking's Great Hall of the People and the Forbidden City convey a sense of power and its continuity.

Architecture Today

Modern architecture is another area in which China has lagged behind the rest of the developing world, including India. Except for the cavernous influence of Stalinism, China was cut off for twenty-five years from international currents in architecture. Public buildings in China designed between 1950 and 1980 range from Soviet wedding-cakes such as the Industrial Exhibition Centers in Shanghai and Peking to the drab post office style of most government offices. Until recently Chinese hotels with any class or style pre-dated the Revolution. As in other arts, the Chinese have been afraid of the unorthodox in architecture. The bulky and stolid Peking Hotel is the best contemporary Chinese-designed hotel in the north. The most interesting, however, is the Dungfang in Canton, which is an intriguing mixture of the sepulcher and the disco. The latter aspect was an innovation designed to occupy the thousands of foreigners visiting the Canton trade fairs and to draw in a bit of hard currency.

Modern architecture has finally appeared in Peking with several foreign-designed hotels, including an out-of-place replica of the Palo Alto Holiday Inn, a small hotel in the Western Hills by the Shanghai-born Chinese-American, I.M. Pei, and the massive Great Wall Hotel. In India, Frank Lloyd

Wright, Corbusier, and other prominent architects in the modern style have had considerable influence. Corbusier designed the surrealistic city of Chandigarh to be the joint capitol of Punjab and Haryana. Top class Indian hotels compete for opulence and style, and the clear winner is the Tata-owned Taj group, with its Bombay flagship, the Taj Mahal, both its Victorian original and its Moghul-modern annex. Even the government-owned Ashok group has picked private Indian architects, many of whose creations are of world-class standards—for example, the Ashok Kovalam beach hotel.

The Asiad-IX stadiums in New Delhi and some office towers in Bombay and other cities reflect the modernity of the best of Indian architecture. Of course, most new buildings in India, not to speak of the old ones, are dismal designs and, as in China, many of the good new structures rapidly become shabby. Unfortunately this has been the fate of Chandigarh, whose Corbusier buildings now look like the ruins of some long-vanished celestial civilization. Neither India nor China has maintenance cultures, but well-designed and well-maintained buildings, while few, are more numerous in India. I. M. Pei reportedly threw up his hands in despair when the jewel-like hotel he had designed for the hills outside Peking began to decay and run down before his very eyes.

Indian interior and furniture design can also be excellent, but the best efforts of the Chinese tend to be overstuffed or gaudy. One hopes that Chinese architecture and design will be able to move out of its ideological cocoon, but if so, it is likely to do so cautiously. In China the avant garde are not survivors. In addition to its isolation from modern trends and its ideological shackles, Chinese society has lacked the commercial life and competition which caters to middle- and upper-class taste and needs. To some, the social leveling this reflects may outweigh the artistic loss. In any event, Chinese architecture and design have been largely bureaucratic and, at times, consciously inelegant.

CHAPTER 12

Language and Learning

Oral Traditions and Ideographs

The 3,000-year-old unbroken tradition of a written language in China contrasts with the 1,000-year break in the usage of a script in India, following the destruction of the Harappan civilization. During this millennium, Vedic literature was composed and maintained as an oral tradition. Even after adoption in the fourth or fifth century B.C. of a scientifically formulated alphabet, brahmans continued to memorize the sacred texts through oral transmission.

Consequently, in its formative, ancient period, and long beyond, Hindu culture was an oral one; whereas in China the written language—the ideograph—was from the time of the Xiang a central element in Chinese culture.

McLuhan says that oral cultures do not visualize in the same way as societies with phonetic alphabets. The former tend to think through a process of sensual visualization, and in a non-sequential fashion. Thus, as Lannoy observes, Indians seem to reason in a spiral of continuously developing potentialities. The Indian syllogism was of five rather than three parts. And Jain thinkers postulated seven possibilities of existence and non-existence, affirming that:

1. An object, say a knife, exists as a knife;
2. It is not something else, say a fork, thus it exists as a knife and does not exist as a fork;
3. In one aspect it is, in another it is not;
4. Its ultimate essence is unknown and it is thus indescribable;
5. It is, but its nature is otherwise indescribable;

6. It is not, but its nature is indescribable; and thus,
7. It both is and is not, but its nature is indescribable.[134]

This non-lineal thought process may in part explain why Indians were not keen on history, but it is also related to India skill in science and mathematics. Perhaps only a Hindu could think of the zero and the decimal, which allowed numbers to extend to infinity backward as well as forward.

The Chinese were much less taken with the science of logic or with epistemology than the Indians. They translated few of the ancient India books of logic. Instead, they were concerned with logic as a utilitarian tool that could lead to the discovery of moral and political principles for everyday living, not as a guide for understanding the universal or the absolute meaning of reality and knowledge. Indian logic favored the universal positive obverse judgment, e.g., "all books are non-eternal," instead of the Chinese or Western "no books are eternal," or "all books are mortal."[135]

Indian usage emphasizes the negative and the infinite which is neither existence nor non-existence. Indians say "victory or non-victory," not "victory or defeat," "non-one" instead of many or none. It was natural that Ghandi's theme was "non-violence," not "pacificism." In Indian philosophy, the ultimate reality or "atman" can only be described through negative qualities such as "indestructible and incomprehensible." The Chinese, however, portrayed the ultimate in concrete terms.

There is no more developed and complex language than Sanskrit, "the language of the Gods." It is highly inflected for number, tense, mode, and voice. It has three genders, three numbers, and eight cases. Its highly developed grammar and vocabulary, perhaps inspired by the oral tradition of its rich literature, encourages abstract thought and imagination. "The character of Sanskrit and of discourse in it result in a sometimes frustrating unconcern with specificity, with details of time, place, and person."[136] For the Hindus, speech was not a gift of the gods but itself a goddess.[137] A word had objective substance—the essence of the object or act that it named. Thus, Indians revered the spoken word and were more meticulous than the modern French about correct usage. As a result, Indians became pioneers in the sciences of phonetics and grammar.

Chinese language, on the other hand, is uninflected, without gender, number, or tense. Because of the simple nature of Chinese grammar there was less need and inclination to move from a pictographic to a phonetic script. The Chinese writing system has expanded to tens of thousands of characters, but it does not contain the same complexity as Sanskrit. There was no great need for Chinese grammarians.

Because of the ideographic nature of its writing system, the Chinese language also remained relatively monosyllabic. There are many homonyms in Chinese; one syllable may have eight or more meanings, depending on the tone whch it is given, and even with the same tone one monosyllable usually has several meanings. There are thus a great many ambiguities in spoken

Chinese. But these ambiguities are clarified in the written form, as each meaning of any one sound is represented by a very different character. Thus when there is some ambiguity in conversation, Chinese using a finger will often draw the character in the palm of their hand.

Chinese prefer the concrete to the abstract. The Chinese word for "contradiction," for example, is "mao dun" or literally "halberd-shield." Most other attributive qualities and abstract concepts are defined by the Chinese with concrete and literal nouns. The Chinese penchant for using numbers to specify categories, movements, or philosophy is seen in their ancient use of diagrams to explain Buddhism and in the Communist regime's fondness for campaigns such as "the three loves, the four beauties, and the five necessaries." The Chinese create nuances in their language through historical allusions, traiditional aphorisms, and a stress on nouns to create vivid images.

Despite Chinese fascination with numbering things, Chinese nouns and verbs make no distinction between singular and plural. It is not surprising that the Chinese were less interested in abstract mathematics than in its utilitarian and categorizing functions. Chinese language also lacks a cupola, or linking verb such as the English "to be," and thus it cannot "clearly distinguish between the metaphysical principal of substance and derivative attributes."[138]

Sanskrit, on the other hand, did not distinguish between that which possesses an attribute and the attribute itself. In Sanskrit any noun can become an abstract noun. Instead of saying, "the boy becomes fat," Sanskrit would say "the boy goes to fatness." The abstract attribute is endowed with substance.[139] Chinese has no suffix like "ness" in English or "ta" in Sanskrit to denote an abstract noun. In Chinese "fatness" or "obesity" is rendered by a compound "fat sick."

The monosyllabic and pictographic nature of Chinese characters and the repetition of sounds led to the early development of a subtle and refined poetry. A poem in Chinese conveys its effect through form as well as thought. While the Chinese were developing a unique plastic form of poetry—calligraphy—the Indians were composing volumes of poetry purely through invisible sound. Brahman priests even learned to repeat the Vedic hymns backward as well as forward.

The Chinese were probably aware of phonetic scripts very early in their history, but the ideographs by this time were viewed as sacred. Special societies in China tried to preserve scraps of paper on which a Chinese character had been written, and illiterate peasants regularly hung ideographic aphorisms above their huts to engender good fortune or to ward off evil spirits, confident that the gods could read Chinese even if they themselves could not.

China's failure to change to phonetics reflects the continuity of Chinese history and the strong political orientation of the Chinese. Chinese scholars and officials must have appreciated the unifying value of the ideographs. If the Holy Roman Empire had used an ideographic system of writing, there might be a unitary European state today.

India, on the other hand, not only has fourteen main spoken languages, but the script for almost every one of these is different. Although all current-day Indian scripts apparently sprang from the ancient alphabet known as Brahmi, they have so evolved that today Bengalis and Gujaratis cannot sound out each other's scripts, much less understand them. It is as if each European state used a separate alphabet. The scripts of northern Indian languages differ from those of the south about as Roman and Cyrillic scripts differ from Hebrew.[140] Sanskrit as a written language, like Latin, was frozen in time and remained the language of religion. It was a lingua franca, but one known only to the upper castes, and it served to reinforce the superiority and power of the priestly brahmans.

Wealth and Honor

According to the social tenets of Confucianism, in a harmonious and just society, wealth and honor will be possessed according to one's virtue and ability. Confucius observed that poverty and humbleness in a well-governed country are "things to be ashamed of." Confucianism, therefore, encouraged a Protestant-type work ethic that spurred individuals to accumulate wealth. The Hindu caste system, by contrast, promoted a more fatalistic attitude toward material advancement.

Hindus argue that their culture encourages individuals to do their best in their field—in most cases as determined by their caste—but philosophically to accept the outcome. Indeed, upper caste Hindus seem to be as competitive as members of the Chinese elite and, as noted, Indian overseas businessmen are as shrewd and successful as their Chinese colleagues. Peasant castes could also rise in status over generations, but historically the caste system worked to discourage initiative and self-improvement among the great masses of the lower orders.

While conditions in China kept most peasant families close to poverty, it was not unusual to see peasants rise to wealth. Hong Kong and Singapore are full of rich towkays who began as peddlers, and similar success stories were common in old China. But in pre-modern India it was rare although not impossible for members of the sudra or peasant castes, not to speak of the untouchables, to become even moderately well-off or to move into commerce. After the British fostered private land ownership in the countryside, some sudras could and did become well-off landowners, and more low castes than before drifted into trade and, eventually, prosperity.

Brahmans and Literati

For thousands of years, education in both India and China has been a source of wealth and power. Through their education, the upper caste brahmans and kshatriyas in India became "twice-born," and in China education was revered as the path to individual self-fulfillment and career success. Both the India brahman and the Chinese scholar were products of ancient traditions and elaborate educations. These traditions account for the remarkable contributions of both India and China to human knowledge.

Indian rulers relied on Sanskrit-knowing brahmans for advice on matters of state as well as for religious sanction. In China, the scholar notably had no religious authority, but served the emperor as advisor and administrator. Nevertheless, Confucius gave a special aura of sanctity to the Chinese literati that made them qualitatively different from the scribes and administrators of other societies. The scholar, rather than the saint, was the hero of Chinese culture.

But Confucius also decreed that in education there should be no distinction (referring of course only to males). If you plan for a year, said the sage, plant a seed; or if for ten years, a tree; but if you plan for a hundred years, educate the people. The principle that schooling was classless and theoretically open to all has ever since been honored in China. As far back as the Han dynasty, China adopted a system of academic examinations for entry into the bureaucracy. There were 20,000 or so scholar-officials at any one time, and perhaps 300,000 literate clerks.[141] Most successful applicants would be sons of scholars, gentry or merchant families who could afford tutors. But precocious peasant boys could and did make the grade, supported in private academies by clans or perhaps attending one of the charity schools which the Ming government began to support back in the Middle Ages, and of which there were at least 5,800 known in the nineteenth century.[142]

With the advent of printing in the thirteenth century, popular Chinese literature also expanded, and, by the seventeenth century, publishing was flourishing. As a pre-industrial society, literacy in China compared favorably with that in Europe. In the 1930s, Chinese education was surprisingly pervasive. At that time 40 percent of all males, but very few females, had at least four years of schooling. In 1949, 25 percent of all primary-age children—again mostly males—were enrolled in school. Thus even near the end of a century of chaos and disorder, a fair percentage of the Chinese male peasant population had some degree of literacy.

The relatively egalitarian Chinese theory of education contrasted with India's hereditary tradition. Education in India was open only to the upper castes and only the brahmans could perform certain roles, such as teaching. The British regime in India and missionaries broadened the base of education, but it remained distinctly an elite system. By the time of independence only about 2 percent of the Indian population had been educated in the English language. While only a fraction of the Indian population, this English-educated elite numbered in the several millions and dominated Indian politics, government, and the professions.

Characteristically, the Indians surrounded and still surround education with ritual and symbolism. In the jata karman ceremony, a newborn upper-caste male child is fed with *ghee* and honey on a thin gold strip, symbolic of intelligence as well as strength. In the fifth year, when the child is ready to learn the alphabet, another sacrament is carried out; and then, finally, when he is ready to be taken to a teacher to begin primary education, the most important ritual—the *upanayana*—is performed. In this ceremony the child is given a spiritual and cultural rebirth that is considered holy compared to his physical, animal birth. Thus are the upper castes "twice-born." These education rituals originated in the upanishadi period (900 B.C.–500 B.C.), when they were made compulsory. Every Aryan male had to spend some time in the house of a teacher, or in a school where learning and literature were passed on orally until Sanskrit adopted a written form.[143] The high status given to education was not only essential to maintain the voluminous sacred literature of the Aryans, but also as a device to "distinguish themselves from the non-Aryan population around them . . . (even) Aryans who may not (have) devoted the period of youth to education . . . underwent the (upanayana) ceremony . . . put on the sacred thread, (and) were called the regenerate and distinguished from the sudras, the latter-day non-Aryan population."[144]

While elementary schooling was available to a sizable portion of Chinese peasants, higher education in China, as in India, was elitist and tended to produce an aversion to manual labor. Unlike the British landed gentry, neither the Chinese gentry nor the upper castes in India were accustomed to supervising work in the fields, much less actually engaging in it. A traditional interest in science and literature, however, continues down to the present in both countries. By the time of the Second World War, India already had Nobel Prize winners in these fields.

University Education

Modern China has done best at the lower, mass levels of education, while India has developed—perhaps over-developed—higher education. India has over 3 million university students on campus and China ony slightly over 1 million.[145] In 1979, according to reports in the Chinese press, China had trained only 3 million college graduates since 1949 (the World Bank puts the figure at 2.1 million). On a per capita basis, India has 4.5 times as many students in higher education as does China.

Among low-income countries, India has one of the highest percentages of its college-age group in universities—8 percent—and China one of the lowest, about 1.2 percent, or one-quarter of the average for all Third World countries. The main reason for the dearth of higher graduates in China, the original land of scholars, is Mao Zedong. China is still recovering from twenty years of Mao's anti-intellectual policies, the effects of which were as devastating as Qin Shi Huang's book-burning and literati burials 2,300 years ago. There was no higher education in China for five years, 1966–1970, and for the next seven years admission and curricula were heavily politicized. This was the time of "worker-soldier-peasant-students" who were supposedly chosen primarily on the basis of political attitude. Since the leadership of a commune of 30,000 might, for example, nominate one to six students for college enrollment, selection inevitably was determined more by nepotism and local politics than by any objective measure of political purity. The result was a lost decade in higher education, an experience to which no other modern country has ever treated itself, even when at war. In January 1978 a rigorous university entry exam was reinstituted, and the 300,000 plus Chinese who are currently admitted into universities each year represent the cream of the nation's young intellectuals and high achievers. The Chinese university today is more of a meritocracy than that in India, but Indian student bodies represent a more democratic spectrum.

In order to "catch up" with world standards in ten or twenty years, Peking is concentrating its resources on 97 "key universities." One way to catch up is by sending Chinese college teachers and graduate students for advanced study in foreign countries. By 1985, 33,000 Chinese were studying abroad; about 16,000 of these were in the U.S.

The explosion of Indian universities, from 20 in 1950 to 116 today (not including technical schools and two-year colleges), is another reflection of the political power of the middle classes in India and the effect of popular politics. As a university degree, or at least some university education, is seen as essential to success and the prestige of a white-collar job, pressure has continually been exerted on the central government and the states to open more, and larger, universities. Needless to say, the result in India, as in the United States, has been a wide range of quality in institutes of higher education and a mixed bag of graduates.

Caste is also heavily involved in university admissions. Quotas up to 50 percent or even higher are set aside for untouchables, tribals, minorities, and "backward" castes who can enter with lower admission grades than others. The Chinese have a somewhat similar system for minorities, but the proportion admitted on this basis in China is small compared to that in India. Thirteen thousand or 4.8 percent of the 270,000 Chinese college graduates in June, 1982, were minorities. In some states in India, like the Punjab, there are also reservations for rural vis-a-vis urban students, a feature which has apparently not existed in China since the elimination of "worker-peasant-soldier-students."

In other Indian states even faculty appointments are "reserved." In Karnataka, for example, only 32 percent of faculty positions at the university are open on the basis of "general merit"; the majority of faculty positions are reserved for scholars from "deprived" castes and minorities. University appointments in India, thus, frequently revolve around the politics of caste lobbies.

Agitation and strikes by Indian students, and sometimes faculty, also frequently disrupt campus life in India. Political slogans and a collage of old and new posters cover a good many walls of Indian universities. In China, during the "democracy wall" period in 1978–1979, political expressionism on campus burst out in action as well as in rhetorical forms; but today political exhortations are again strictly official, and written neatly on ubiquitous "political" blackboards. With brief exception since the Cultural Revolution, campus radicalism or disruptions of any sort have been as rare on Chinese campuses as fraternity houses.

In some Indian universities student activities, often including quasi-students who have lived on campus for years, have intimidated university administrators into permissive passivity. Indian intellectuals are worried about the erosion of the academic atmosphere on the campuses and increasing attacks on democratic values. Agitators range from radical leftists to fundamentalist Hindus and Moslems to simply incompetent students who oppose efforts to strengthen academic standards. At Aligarh Moslem University in Uttar Pradesh, for example, right-wing Moslem students, combining with academically weak students, brought about the suspension of the dean of the faculty of social sciences for attempting to tighten up examination rules and for pushing through the expulsion of a student caught cheating.

In both India and China university tuition fees are nominal, and in both countries grants are awarded to poorer students who cannot cover these fees or pay room-and-board expenses. Thus an outstanding student from either China or India who comes from a poor, rural background is likely to find the road to a university education fairly open. But a poor rustic who is simply a good—as distinct from a very bright—student is likely to find a greater opportunity in India than in China. Students in China's premier universities are overwhelmingly children of urban intelligentsia or graduates of "key schools" located only in county seats and larger cities. But in India even the prestigious technological institutes must reserve 20 percent of spaces for low castes and minorities. The number of underprivileged in India who make their way to college, however, is only a fraction of the poor community. Moreover, concessions and reservations for poor and backward Indian students are based on certificates issued by local officials and, as one Indian put it, obtaining these certificates is less a matter of being entitled to them than of having the means to procure them.

While there is a great deal of complaining in India about moribund university staffs and the uncreative rote method of teaching, the quality of instruction in Chinese colleges is probably even worse. Professors in Chinese universities are aging and mostly out-of-date in their fields. Because until recently only terminally ill faculty have retired, and those purged were restored to their positions while Cultural Revolution "assistants" were retained, there is a high ratio of students to faculty, about 4-to-1; unfortunately, this does not mean that the quality of education is high. In 1982 less than 10 percent of Chinese college faculty had advanced degrees, and twice that number had no university degree. This situation is improving as new graduate students complete their studies at home and abroad.

China's relatively few college graduates are usually assigned jobs on graduation and, unlike urban high school graduates, there is no waiting a year or more for assignment. Once assigned, however, it is still difficult to change jobs. Under the Deng reforms, graduates are being given more choice and the best are actively recruited.

In India college graduates must scramble for positions and many are unemployed or else take clerical or service jobs. Connections and money are also important in obtaining the most desirable jobs; for example, a university lecturer's post in the Punjab is said to go for US $1,000 and a provincial civil service position for $10,000.[146] One option is to go on acquiring M.A.s and finally a Ph.D. or L.L.B. before "enrolling in a commercial institute for typing and shorthand."[147] Of course, only a small number of postgraduate degree holders follow such a path, but that any do so reflects the surplus of higher degrees in India compared to the shortage in China.

General Literacy

One of China's great achievements has been an increase in adult literacy from 26 percent in 1951 to 77 percent in 1982. This compares to an average literacy for other low-income countries today of 34 percent. Over the same period, Indian adult literacy rose from 17 percent to 36 percent; in other words, Indian literacy rates have increased 111 percent but China's have improved almost 200 percent. Within a generation, China's literacy rate should be over 90 percent, as close to 93 percent of primary-aged children today are enrolled in school.

India, however, appears to be gradually catching up, as about 84 percent of primary-age children in India were enrolled in school as of 1981–1982. Actually, Indian boys are enrolling in primary school at an equal or higher rate than Chinese boys (99 percent according to the Indian Ministry of Education).[148] India's adult education program has been much less successful than that of China, but India's biggest problem in education has been in the continuing gap in female literacy which, in 1981, was still only 25 percent! In some states, like Bihar, it is less than 15 percent; in rural areas of the state the rate for untouchable and tribal women in many areas is below 1 percent. These figures should markedly improve over the next generation as female enrollment nation-wide in primary school, as a percentage of the age group, had risen to 67 percent by 1981–1982. It was still, however, far behind the 99 percent enrollment rate of boys.

There is also a relatively large drop-out rate in India, where 60 percent of starters do not finish the eighth grade. Exactly comparable figures are not available, but Chinese media have reported that 30 percent of Chinese primary students in the rural areas do not finish the first four years of schooling. In both countries official literacy rates may also be somewhat exaggerated, given the ease of slipping back into illiteracy if regular reading habits are not established. This phenomenon is especially prominent among rural women and especially easy in an ideographic language.

China's impressive achievements in basic education reflect the high priority as well as the organizational and mobilization skills which the communist regime has applied to the task. On the other hand, two Asian countries with lower per capita income than China have achieved equal or higher literacy rates—Sri Lanka (84%) and Burma (70%).

The problem in India is clearly rooted more in culture than in poverty—as seen, for example, in Kerala's high literacy rate for both females (65%) and males (almost 70%), although the state has a lower per capita income and a higher proportion of rural population than the Indian (or the Chinese) national average.

CHAPTER 13

Science: Old and New

Traditional Science

Joseph Needham has comprehensively detailed Chinese historical contributions to science.[149] A few of the well-known creations of the Chinese were: (1) explosive chemistry; (2) magnetic physics, including the compass; (3) mechanical clockworks and astronomical instruments; (4) iron and steel technology; (5) the sternpost rudder and fore and aft sailing; and, of course, (6) paper and printing.

Chinese science was in large part inspired by the Taoist search for the alchemists' secret and for formulas of divination. Not surprisingly, the Taoist motives were utilitarian, if fanciful. While the Taoists never found the Midas formula or the Blessed Isle of the West, the inventions that eventually sprang forth as side effects of their labors had a dramatic effect. But as Needham notes, the consequences of Chinese inventions were much more earthshaking in Europe than they were in China,[150] literally blowing up the European feudal system, showing Columbus the way to America, and allowing the Age of Reason and, ultimately, democracy to flourish in the West. Chinese technology, except for paper and printing, did not have a strong cultural impact on Chinese society. Despite the new instruments for improved navigation and sailing and the military potential in explosives, the Chinese did not set off on a period of exploration or conquest. The inventions for which the Chinese are famous are eminently practical. But Chinese science was weak in theory and analysis. It concentrated on observation and the formal ordering of phenomena as reflected in the 64 hexagrams of the I Ching. Acupuncture was developed empirically as a high skill, but Chinese thinking about the "why and the how" of acupuncture never went beyond the fanciful and primitive.

India also made critical contributions, but more in mathematics, astronomy, and medicine than in mechanics, physics or chemistry. The loom was probably the major practical invention of India. Indians were the first to have a clear conception of abstract numbers and, as noted, they contributed the ultimate transcendental invention, the zero, which, together with the decimal system, they passed on to the Arabs and, through them, to the Europeans. (The ancient Chinese simply used empty spaces instead of zeros. Thus, as Needham argues, they first developed the decimal place order of numbers, adopting the zero apparently from the Indians in the Middle Ages.)

While the Greeks concentrated on geometry, the ancient Indians developed a rudimentary algebra which allowed complicated calculations. Medieval Indian mathematicians surpassed their European contemporaries. It was, of course, an Indian who established that infinity, however divided, remains infinite.

In the sixth century A.D., Indian astrologers discovered the correct length of the year, the rotation of the earth around its axis, and the true explanation of an eclipse. Indian fascination with the concept of perpetual motion may have also inspired Europeans in their later development of the laws of mechanical motion.

But having set the stage for modern science, both China and India failed to take the next step. Part of the reason was social and economic. In the West the rise of the bourgeoisie, the Renaissance, and the Reformation created a new intellectual and social environment that encouraged the development of a cumulative, methodical approach to science. The persistence of a highly conservative culture in China and an extremely hierarchical society in India did not permit the blossoming of entreprenurial classes with practical interests in applied science. The right social chemistry just did not come together in either China or India.

Another major catalyst in Europe that was missing in both India and China was a strong sense and tradition of personal autonomy. In Indian and Chinese cultures, social relationships overwhelmed individuality, and there was therefore less inclination to think and act independently. As Needham suggests, there were also important philosophical factors including, in the case of India, the concept of time. Despite a passion like that of the Chinese for classification, the Hindus' cyclical view of life and their belief in the non-sequential nature of time did not encourage an interest either in history or in a minute study of nature. Thus the Indians excelled in theoretical and abstract endeavors such as mathematics. Indians intuitively perceived atomic theory, believing that the single atom was "a mirror point in space without magnitude." Chinese thought, on the other hand, reveals no trace of atomism, but instead suggests an early inkling of wave theory.[151]

But while atomism and other Indian theories reflected brilliant imagination, they were not arrived at by anything resembling the scientific method. Indian belief in the ultimate unreality of the phenomenal world encouraged a speculative, rather than an empirical, approach to the development of knowledge. Since all things existed in limitless time and in the absolute were one, particular phenomena had little value. Change, including the current of time from past to future, was illusory.

Indian language refers to "effect and cause" not as in Chinese or Western languages "cause and effect." Chinese scholars translating Indian texts invariably reversed the word order of "effect and cause."[152] Indian thinkers concentrating on effect rather than cause were further limited in their ability to take an empirical approach to understanding nature and the universe. Focusing on effect required a leap of imagination to devise the cause. The Chinese stressed cause and should have developed a more empirical, inductive approach to science. As Needham notes, the Chinese also had a distinctly sequential view of time. Despite early Taoist speculations and neo-Confucianist metaphysics, neither Chinese peasants nor scholars have ever for a moment doubted the passage of time from a fixed point in the past straight to the present, from whence it will continue on into the future. In addition, the Chinese were materialistic and acquisitive—and they should have had a strong interest in pursuing applied sciences and in following up their discoveries with a more disciplined and experimental development of knowledge about nature. But another catalyst that was essential to the evolution of the scientific method in Europe was absent in China. Needham suggests that the idea of the existence of laws of nature, unvarying rules that determine all natural phenomena, was a key philosophical concept that underlay the development of science in the West. The Taoists were too cynical and skeptical of logic to develop such a theory and the Confucianists were interested only in social and political phenomena. Natural law for the Chinese had to do with the evolution of human relations and general principles of behavior, not with nature itself.

Very likely, however, historical and social factors, not philosophical ones, accounted for China's failure to continue its pre-eminence in science. Again, the main factor was the political and intellectual orthodoxy of the Ming and Manchu periods. If China had maintained the more open and eclectic spirit of pre-Mongol times, the Age of Reason and of Science would have probably flourished in the Middle Kingdom early on.

Technology and Theory Today

> We must . . . take that jump to the front, to the cutting edge of research and technology. . . . In India, traditionally we have concentrated on the development of the soul. . . . Today . . . our task is to end poverty and the challenge to our modern scientists is . . . to achieve this goal . . . through scientific and technological knowledge.
>
> —Rajiv Gandhi,
> Indian Science Congress,
> January 7, 1986

> Economic prosperity must rely on progress in science and technology. This must be taken as the basic guiding ideology for economic construction from now on. Once it is put into use in production, advanced science and technology will become a powerful and dynamic social productive force.
>
> —Zhao Ziyang,
> National Science and Technology Awarding Conference,
> October 24, 1982

From rudimentary beginnings in 1947 and 1949, India and China have achieved some remarkable successes in science and technology. Most impressive in both cases is the duplication of existing technology from the West or the Soviet Union, and creation of self-reliant or near self-reliant production of some very sophisticated equipment and facilities. Nevertheless, both countries face a serious problem in simply keeping up with the pace of technological change. Even more difficult and long-term will be the development of scientific tempers in the two countries, which can lead to sustained progress in pure science and scientific innovation.

India is one of the few nations which has built a full cycle of capabilities in the nuclear power field, including exploration, mining, extraction and conversion of nuclear materials, fuel fabrication, heavy-water production, design and construction of reactors, reprocessing of spent fuels, and nuclear waste management. By 1983 India had four power reactors in operation with a 220-megawatt capacity each. Three of these reactors were U.S.- or Canadian-made, but the fourth was largely built indigenously. Four other Indian-designed reactors are in various stages of construction. Three heavy-water plants are also in operation.

Looking ahead to the second phase of its nuclear power development, India is building a 40-megawatt, plutonium-fueled breeder test reactor near Madras. In May 1974 India joined a select club by setting off a "peaceful" underground nuclear explosion.

China's nuclear development has also been extensive, but primarily in the weapons and defense fields. Since 1964 China has set off at least 26 nuclear explosions, deployed intercontinental and intermediate-range nuclear-armed missiles, and constructed a nuclear-powered missile submarine. China has not yet built a commercial nuclear-power reactor, but is currently negotiating with Western companies for construction of two nuclear plants in China.

China has poured billions of dollars into its strategic missile program and, as a consequence, possesses advanced rockets for launching commercial and scientific space satellites.

In the late 1970s Peking media reported the training of Chinese astronauts for manned space-flights; nothing further has been heard of this program and it may be in a state of suspension. Meanwhile, China has purchased a U.S.-made Landsat ground station which allows it to exploit U.S. Landsat satellites for geological surveys and other purposes.

Without the boost of a strategic missile program, India has also developed the capability to design, build, and launch earth satellites. So far it has launched small Indian-designed and fabricated satellites, using Indian-made launch vehicles. But other scientific and communications satellites, all Indian-designed and manufactured, have been launched by Soviet, U.S. and West European vehicles. Sometime in the 1980s India hopes to test a four-stage rocket with orbital-launch capability, which eventually could carry 600–1,200 kilogram payloads.

India has used about three-quarters of its research and development spending in the nuclear, space, and defense fields; the comparable percentage figure in China is very likely higher. India employs 10,000 technical and scientific personnel in its space program and an equal number at the nuclear research and engineering center outside Bombay. While China does not provide any figures, the development of such enormously complicated weapons systems as inter-continental missiles and nuclear submarines must require a much larger commitment of personnel and workers than the space and nuclear programs in India.

The nuclear and space efforts of India and China have been driven in large part by security and prestige concerns. Having already spent over $5 billion on its nuclear-power program, India has taken on a costly and complex task. It is debatable whether the Indian decision early on to build an indigenous nuclear power capability was wise, either in economic terms or in terms of the long-term development of Indian science and scientific manpower. China is just beginning with the initial stage of contracting for "turn-key" foreign-made nuclear plants. The delay in China's nuclear power efforts may prove to have been fortuitous, whether or not it was made with this in mind or, as is more likely, because of other higher priorities, namely military.

The achievements of both countries in the nuclear and space fields demonstrate the high-tech potential of poor but continental-size countries such as India and China, which have educated elites and sophisticated cultures experienced in large-scale organization. Such countries—and Brazil is perhaps the only other example in the Third World—have very low per capita incomes, but large enough aggregate economies that they can siphon off substantial amounts to develop indigenous capabilities in selected areas of high technology and sophisticated engineering.

It seems virtually inevitable that India and China because of their size and history and the momentum of their scientific and military bureaucracies would, in their early years, seek to build an independent defense and high-technology capability. In development of science and technology, as well as in economic modernization, however, there has recently been a moderation of expectations in both New Delhi and Peking. Both countries seem to recognize more clearly than in the past that catching up will take more than a generation. The problem is, in fact, keeping up—and this can only be done with extensive cooperation, technology transfers, and investments from the

West and also from the Soviet Union. The goal of self-reliance in science and technology, as in economic development, has been modified or replaced by the objective of building indigenous capabilities over the long term in cooperation with technologically advanced countries.

The leaders of both countries genuinely believe that it is only through science and technology that the deep-rooted economic problems of their countries can be solved and modernization achieved. Consequently, while some of their efforts today may seem uneconomic or duplicative, both countries are building the foundations for competitive excellence in science and technology sometime in the next century. Consequently it is perhaps neither surprising nor depressing for either India or China to realize that in highly sophisticated fields such as nuclear energy and electronics they can only hope to copy and adopt foreign technology. As the Japanese have shown, such an approach can be productive and rewarding.

In the field of pure science the Indians and the Chinese are both likely to make limited contributions over the next decade or so. Individual contributors will, however, occasionally make their mark in international science, like the India physicist, C. V. Raman, who won the Nobel Prize in 1928.

The contributions of the Chinese in pure research today, as in the past, have been primarily in the areas of observation and data gathering rather than conceptualization. As Richard Baum points out, in the field of siesmology Chinese scientists have gathered and analyzed more data on the indicators, precursors and concomitant phenomena of earthquakes than scientists of any other nation. They have even had some success in predicting imminent tremors. Yet all this has been done in the absence of viable conceptual models of—or theoretical insights into—the nature and etiology of tectonic-plate movement. Likewise, Chinese medical scientists have made enormous strides in cancer research, but primarily in terms of quantitative data-gathering and deduction based on non-controlled empirical observation, rather than controlled experimentation and systematic hypothesis-testing.[153]

Indian scientists, keeping with tradition, are particularly good at hypotheses and scientific speculations. In theoretical studies, such as nuclear and astro-physics and number theory, Indians are among the best in the world. Like China, however, India has not developed the critical mass of high talent necessary for sustained achievement in hypothesis-testing. Pure research requires a large scientific support community, dedicated to extremely meticulous, long-term laboratory testing, an approach that does not come naturally to either culture.

In both countries laboratory work is often ragged and behind the times. Moreover, while theorizing is one thing, innovation in research and development is another, and it is in this realm that the cultural bias against independent thought restricts scientific development in both India and China.

In 1981 a group of Indian scientists and intellectuals issued a manifesto calling for a science renaissance: "Only in the measure we succeed in installing the scientific temper as the dominant ethos of our collective being can we hope to face the accumulating problems of our national existence," P. N. Haksar, a former advisor to Premier Indira Gandhi, wrote in the document. "We understand," he said, "that it is not going to be easy."[154]

Rajiv Gandhi believes science and technology hold the key to ending poverty in India. But he also stresses that this will require the scientific temper to permeate down to the average village. He told the Indian Science Congress on January 6, 1986, that Indian farmers had shown that they were capable of using front line technologies, but that there had to be a broader base of people who understood science and a correct educational environment before all sectors of society could absorb modern technology. Rajiv also warned that the biggest problem was that of science management, creeping bureaucracy, and mediocrity.

In China the situation is made even worse by the intrusion of politics and bureaucratic control. Baum quotes two of contemporary China's most eminent historians of science as observing:

> Because academic issues are lumped together with political issues, some areas in the scientific domain are arbitrarily designated as "restricted areas" and some research aims are regarded as "taboo." For example, in recent years few people in our scientific circles dare to touch chromaticity, which the Morgan School regarded as the substance of heredity, or the method of bio-statistics. . . . Associated with this problem is the practice of using organizational methods, administrative regulations or other over-simplified and crude ways to handle academic controversies. . . . Taking an over-simplified view of the subject [these] people are always ready to denounce bluntly as idealism and pseudo-science those schools which they oppose . . . quantum chemistry . . . cybernetics . . . and also mathematical logic . . . were all once considered to be "pseudo-science." . . . In the eyes of the dogmatist, the highest criterion of truth is not practice, but certain fixed dogmas and the sayings of authorities.[155]

The prolonged interruption of education over the past 25 years has also seriously handicapped China's development of technical and scientific manpower. According to a State Planning Commission survey in 1982, China had only 9.08 million technicians and specialists, 6.26 million of which were in the natural sciences and 2.82 million in the social sciences. But only a total of 3.55 million of these actually had university degrees. Senior engineers, scientists, and college professors in the natural sciences numbered only 60,000.

Meanwhile, Indian universities and technical and polytechnical institutes have produced 2.4 million scientific and technically qualified graduates. India claims to have the third largest complement of such manpower in the world. Many of these graduates cannot find employment in India and a government study has estimated that each year 25 percent of graduates in the sciences and technologies go abroad, primarily to the U.S., the U.K., Canada, and Australia. But India's investment in these graduates is not lost, as most of those who settle abroad will send sizable sums of money to their families in India each year and frequently travel back to India, occasionally taking up temporary or permanent jobs in the home country after some years abroad. Established Indian scientists have also long been accustomed to taking periods of study and laboratory work abroad in order to bring themselves up-to-date or to test hypotheses in more sophisticated laboratories. In this manner, India has been very much a part of and a contributor to international science. On the other hand, Chinese scientists are only now moving out into the world to make up for lost time. Peking traditionally has been very concerned about its trained scientists or engineers emigrating abroad and has tightly controlled their travel. In early 1985, however, Beijing relaxed rules to allow any student who could arrange private financing to go abroad for study, and it decreed that Ph.D. holders could take a one year sabbatical every four years including foreign travel and research abroad.

Outside of the nuclear, space, and defense fields, industrial research and development in India and China have lagged. Both governments have concentrated their R&D resources in the most sophisticated areas and their economic structures have not rewarded enterprises' investment in technological innovation. In China, introducing new technology was risky and promised no benefit to management. Indian companies, also operating in a protected market, were reluctant to invest in R&D; consequently, 90 percent of R&D expenditures in India have come from the central government, and government-sponsored R&D has tended to be poorly coordinated with the needs of industry or the market. Likewise, Chinese academic institutes perform most of the research in high technology. As in India, a major problem has been transferring this technology from the laboratory to industry.

Both India and China have also accelerated efforts to obtain foreign technology through joint ventures and licensing agreements. Some leftist observers in India have criticized the liberlization of technology imports as undermining native development of such technology, and while in China such debates do not usually surface publicly, it is apparent that some conservative elements are opposed to a broad technological opening to the West.

Both countries have made major advances in repatterning genetic architecture and independently developing hybrid maize, millet, and cotton, as well as dwarf high-yielding rice and wheat. India and China have also each done important research on the conversion of human and animal waste into energy, and both have constructed bio-gas facilities for this purpose. In the medical sciences, China has made important contributions in cancer research, as has India into the nature of leprosy.

CHAPTER 14

Population and Health

Juggernauts

Unlike Europe and North America, India and China—along with the rest of the Third World—happened to enjoy the benefits of immunization and chemical fertilizer long before industrialization, urbanization, and universal education had progressed sufficiently to slow their birth rates through social and economic dynamics. Now, stopping their biological multiplication will require heroic and possibly forceful measures.

In 1986 about 50,000 babies were born in China every day. As stunning as this figure may seem, it is 25,000 less than the daily average in 1970. China's population policy, similar to its policies in other areas, has developed in fits and jerks and the average birth rate has fluctuated accordingly. But since the days of the Cultural Revolution, when family planning efforts broke down for the second time, the birth rate has been steadily dropping. The official population growth rate was 2.9 percent in 1957 but had plummeted to 1.08 by 1984.[156] In 1982, as a result of greater incomes in the countryside and a loosening of government controls, there had been slippage in the program, but a massive sterilization campaign in 1983 sharply made up for lost ground.

Meanwhile, the Indian census of 1981 showed a total of 683.8 million people, reflecting a higher growth rate than expected.[157] The Indian population had increased 24 percent since 1971, but extensive family planning efforts averted 37 million births that would have occurred had the birth rate continued at the 1971 level. Actually, the 2.4 percent average growth in the population between the 1971 and 1981 census was the same as that between 1961 and 1971, but over the last decade the death rate has fallen and this offset a declining birth rate. The population growth rate in 1982 was estimated at 2.24 percent, almost a full point over that of China.

But the young populations of both India and China—65 percent under 30 years old in both countries—are juggernauts that even superhuman efforts will not be able to stop in a short period of time. It will take over 100 years to halt the Indian population wave and at least 80 years in the case of China. According to World Bank estimates, India will have about one billion people in the year 2000 and may level off in the year 2115, with a population of 1.7 billion. This means that sometime early in the next century India will become more populous than China, which according to the World Bank is calculated to level off at 1.5 billion people around the year 2070. At that time the combined populations of these two countries would be greater than the total world population in 1950.

The Chinese, however, are certainly seized with the problem and they could possibly top off well under the bank's estimate. Peking so far has achieved impressive success with its one child per family program. Family planning in China is the responsibility of a special commission of the state council, and family planning offices exist in every street committee, work unit, and village. Work units allocate and approve births for married female employees who wish to have children; those who become pregnant out of turn or, even worse, have a second or third child, are subject to reductions in pay and to social pressures from their comrades at work as well as their neighborhood committees.

Since the unit still controls most aspects of a Chinese worker's life, few are willing to get out of line over an issue like family planning, and to incur the ostracism of their work or office-mates. Other disincentives include the loss of ration coupons for a second child, fewer education and job opportunities for such children, and possibly later even harassment by their school peers. The success of this program again reflects China's disciplined political and social organization and the pervasive influence that the government and party exercise over every citizen. Between September 1982 and the end of 1983, more than 20 million sterilizations were performed in China among couples with two or more children.

Indians are far more resistant than the Chinese to such programs initiated by the authorities, particularly when they conflict with tradition. During the 1975–1977 emergency, Mrs. Gandhi's government also pressed a sterilization program. Seven million were performed in 1976, but the political backlash to this program was one of the principal reasons for her defeat in the 1977 elections. Subsequently, for several years family planning was only gingerly pursued.

Stunned by the 1981 census reports, however, India is now trying to revitalize its birth-control program. One of the goals is to raise the use of contraceptives from 23 percent of married couples to 36 percent. But the program today involves promotion of a broad spectrum of birth control methods and studiously avoids a crash campaign focused on one particular means. One-hundred-and-eighty-thousand village guides, selected by the villagers, are spreading the idea of family planning, and 220,000 additional guides are being enlisted to enlarge the program.[158]

Lacking coercive measures and strong disincentives to promote contraception, abortion, and sterilization, it is clear that the rapid expansion of literacy and public health is essential if there is to be any hope of population control in India. It is not a coincidence that Kerala has India's highest literacy rate, its lowest infant mortality rate, and its lowest birth rate. Kerala's population increases only about 1 percent a year. Replication of this record elsewhere will require more than increasing government efforts to promote family planning through contraception and sterilization.

Kerala vividly demonstrates the impact of female literacy and other broad socioeconomic changes on the birth rate. Studies have shown that 30 percent of the fertility decline in Kerala during 1968–1978 was the result of women marrying at an increasingly later age. This phenomenon is, in turn, a direct result of increasing female literacy and expanding female participation in the workforce over this period.

In China the regime encourages a delay in marriage until 28 or 26 years of age for males and females, respectively; but in 1980 it made the legal marriage age 22 and 20 and there was a sudden burst of weddings. Peking had 40 percent more marriages in 1981 than in the previous year. Nevertheless, among China's 200 million urbanites, one-child families have, in the past ten years, become the norm. In 1984, 90 percent of all births in China were either first or second births compared to 38 percent in 1970.

In the Chinese countryside, however, the traditional desire for larger families is much stronger than in the cities. There is still a deep fear of growing old without a son, and there are economic incentives to have more hands for labor. Despite the establishment of old people's homes in some communes and the promises of pensions for one-child parents, promises are not believed and the "retirement homes" that do exist offer a very basic and, for old Confucians, not very emotionally satisfying existence. Nevertheless, even in the countryside, the Chinese birth rate is about half that for peasant populations in other developing countries. A great deal of the credit must go not only to political control and organizational skills, but also to China's progress in health and education. China's low infant mortality rate has reduced by half the number of babies a couple needs in order to insure a surviving child or children. The literacy rate among Chinese women—which is more than twice that of Indian women in general—is also a primary contributor to China's relatively low birth rate in the countryside. To achieve an average of two children per family, however, not to speak of one, will be very difficult in the rural areas. To provide a legal basis for sanctions, the new state constitution passed by the 1982 National People's Congress included a unique provision making family planning an obligation of each citizen.

Medical Care

The foreign visitor, accompanied by the block development officer, arrives by car at a village near Madras. Pre-schoolers, lining up for their free lunch, break into wails and sobs. The official explains that the children fear the visitors are coming to give innoculations. In Peking's Altar of the Sun Park one Sunday, the same foreigner finds that the local hospital has set up a large outdoor display on cancer, including bottled specimens of diseased organs. Doctors and nurses are on hand to explain it all to the large crowd of attentive on-lookers.

Indians and Chinese today are both keenly health conscious, reflecting the substantial health programs carried out by their respective governments. As far as Western medicine is concerned, Indian and Chinese peasants generally feel it is useful for operations, setting bones, and for injections. If they go to the clinic they are not happy without an injection. Traditional medicine, however, has an ancient history in each society and the herbs and other potions concocted by the old style doctors are still widely used in the cities as well as in the countryside. Although traditional medicines are now manufactured by the state in China, far-fetched therapeutic claims for each concoction are still retained. In India, ayurvedic traditional medicine has been supplemented by homeopathy, of which there are practitioners in any sizable town, and by "sexologists" whose training and expertise are obscure.

China's basic health-care system is outstanding in comparison with that of other low- or even middle-income countries. India has also out-performed most of these same countries in the health field, but it still lags considerably behind China's achievements. There are about 2,500 Chinese for every fully qualified Western-type medical doctor in China.[159] In India the figure is 3,620. Life-expectancy in both China and India has increased from 36 and 32 years, respectively, in 1950 to 68 and 55 years in 1983. China has thus expanded the average life-span of its people by a dazzling 88 percent; but India is not that far behind, having registered a 72 percent improvement.

Still, it is clear that the Chinese have given higher national priority than has India to public health. According to the World Bank, while the total annual cost of China's health program is low because of the very low pay of health workers by international standards, it spent $4 per person in government funds for public health compared with $2 per person in India.

Some Indian states, like Kerala, spend much more per person on medical care and public health than the national average; this, combined with high female literacy, means that Keralans have a much lower infant mortality rate and higher life-span than the average Indian. The death rate in Kerala per 1,000 population (1976–1978) was almost one-half the national average. Kerala's infant mortality rate (1975–1977) of 52 per 1,000 was only slightly lower than the 1980 rate of 56 per 1,000 in China.[160]

India's national rate of infant mortality in 1980 was 123 per 1,000. Even more staggering is the 17 percent death rate of Indian children between the ages of 1 and 4; this is lower than the 22 percent average of other low-income countries, but three times the Chinese death rate (5%) for the same age group. While significant advances have been made in India in controlling communicable diseases like smallpox, and combating malaria, the rate of tuberculosis has not declined in 15 years and only 33 percent of Indian villagers have ready access to safe drinking water.[161]

According to a national sample survey in the 1970s one-third of India's 40 million urban households had no latrines, and 7 million of these used the open ground for defecation. China's lead in the basic areas of hygiene, safe drinking water, and human waste disposal, in large part, account for its higher health standards. Traditionally, the Chinese have drunk tea or boiled rather than cold water and this custom combined with a much smaller tropical area also accounts for a healthier population.

India, like China, runs a comprehensive national health service which involves a network of urban and rural hospitals and dispensaries, as well as 50,000 primary health centers (PHCs), each of which is staffed with at least one or two trained doctors. PHC sub-centers are staffed with mid-wives and other auxiliary medical workers. The ambition is to have one PHC sub-center for every 5,000 people, but achieving this goal is still years away. In many areas, however, caste groups have set up clinics that often provide more health care than the counterpart government center.

There have been suggestions in India that traditional practitioners should, as in China, be brought into the public health system, but so far this has not been done. India's private doctors of Western medicine are concentrated in the cities; two-thirds of India's 177,000 Western-style doctors are, in fact, resident in urban areas and, thus, the number of persons per doctor in the countryside is eight or nine times that in urban areas. Only 30 percent of hospital beds in India are in rural institutions.

There is a great deal of agitation in India to revamp the country's medical education and to concentrate resources on training basic health workers and on community and preventive health programs. India has already launched more than 30 pilot integrated child-development projects in which an *anjawari* (or "courtyard") worker in each village or center is responsible for maternal and child health and educational work. Hopefully these and a number of other experimental schemes to develop para-professional preventive health services at the village level will be expanded throughout the country.

There are, however, strong conservative forces in the Indian health field who wish to continue to emphasize modern training for doctors, specialization, and curative medicine. It is also very difficult in a non-regimented society to order trained doctors into the countryside. The Indian government does require rural service by graduating doctors, but most young physicians find a way to escape this fate.

One secret of China's impressive performance in the health field is the use of local villagers as basic health workers who are familiar with strongly ingrained village customs and attitudes toward illness, childbirth, diet, and hygiene, and who can thus more easily persuade the peasants to adopt modern practices. This basic program, which includes 1.4 million "barefoot doctors" and 2.6 million mid-wives and other health aides, is paid for out of local resources or under the "responsibility system" by levies on households or by fees. Although the "barefoot doctors" receive only rudimentary skills and medicines for curative purposes, their role in preventive medicine, hygiene, and birth control has apparently been successful.

There is, however, a wide range in the quality of health care in the countryside in China; as the World Bank report notes, in the poorest areas of China the quality of health care is unsatisfactory or non-existent. The rural-urban gap in health is also wide in China. Infant mortality rates in Chinese cities are one-half the rural rates. In Tibet the rate is four times the national average. The city resident in China, as in India, can expect to live considerably longer than his country cousin. In Shanghai, the life-span is 8 years longer than the national average.

CHAPTER 15

Internal Divisions: Two Solutions

Communal and Minority Problems

Communalism and regional nationalism threaten the domestic peace of both India and China. India's problems are far worse than those of China in the former instance, but Peking may face an equally or even more serious long-term threat of regional secessionists. The two governments have responded to these two sorts of problems in quite different ways. There have been wild swings in Chinese government minority policies, from forceful assimilation to moderation and reconciliation, but always under full political control and always with the goal of assimilation. In India, while regional, communal and separatist sentiments have flared up and died down over the years, the government has pursued a relatively consistent course, using force to maintain order and the country's integrity, and occasionally pushing linguistic integration and greater central authority, but always compromising in the face of pressure and accepting plurality and diversity as one of the permanent facts, if not joys, of Indian life.

India is still haunted by the memory of the communal butchery of 1947, and each year there are outbursts of violence between Hindus and Moslems. Moslem intellectuals, and in the South, Christians as well, fear that Hindu revivalism is increasing. It is not impossible to find conservative upper-caste Hindus who come close to justifying Ghandhi's assassination on the grounds of the Mahatma's persistent gestures toward the Moslems such as the conciliation trek across the Punjab which he was planning just prior to his death. While they are a small minority, there are some who have not accepted the partition of the sub-continent and who still dream of Greater India recapturing its old Moghul boundaries. The great majority of Hindus, however, have no interest in absorbing millions more Moslems.

Hindus assert that if Hindu fundamentalism is growing, it is in reaction to Moslem revivalism, allegedly fed by the Ayatollah's revolution in Iran and by Middle Eastern funds. While most of India's 70 million Moslems are not members of the Shiite sect, as are the Moslems of Iran, there is a dark strain of reaction in the souls of some Indian mosque leaders. Sectarian organizations, like the Tablighi Jamaat and the Jamaat-e-Islam, have long propounded an Islamic fundamentalism that opposes the community's participation in democratic politics as destroying the cohesion of Moslems and legitimizing an un-Islamic state. A small number of Moslem fundamentalists in India have still not reconciled themselves to living in a secular, non-Moslem nation.

The Moslems, who comprise 12 percent of India's population, fear disintegration and assimilation, and many charge that the constitutional guarantees protecting the cultural rights of the minorities are not being carried out. They demand more state aid to Moslem schools, protection of the Moslem character of Aligarh University, privileged status for the Urdu language, and no state-sponsored changes in the Moslem Personal Law. Even Hindus, who are not religious chauvinists, fear that separate schools, language and civil laws for Moslems will prevent the evolution of a harmonious pluralistic society and, in the end, will foster separatism.

The Hindu-Moslem dichotomy is the biggest communal problem in the world in terms of the numbers involved. India is, in fact, one of the world's largest Moslem countries. In addition to its size, the problem is exacerbated by deep personal grievances going back to the holocaust of 1947, and by the identification of many Indian Moslems with the international Islamic movement. Competition between the lowest economic orders of the Hindu and Moslem communities, however, is probably the main source of tensions. Over 400 cases of Hindu–Moslem violence were reported in 1982, almost all in the cities, and 238 people, mostly Moslems, were killed.

Still the problem has so far been surprisingly contained. This is because most of India's political leaders are committed to a plural society and protection of minority rights. This, in turn, reflects the limited constituency of the Hindu fundamentalists. Most untouchables and tribals are hardly likely to support Hindu extremism politically although on occasions they can be used as instruments of violence by the extremists. Combined with India's Moslems, Christians, and other minorities, there is a strong bloc comprising about 45 percent of the population who are inherently opposed to Hindu chauvinism.

At the same time the majority of Indian Moslems, rejecting the extremists in their community, have recognized the utility of participation in the Indian political process as the way to protect their communal interests while promoting a more stable and harmonious community in which they can live and work. And, with the exception of the Moslems of Kerala and Kashmir, Indian Moslems have engaged in politics primarily through support for national non-sectarian parties, mainly the original Congress Party, and then Mrs. Gandhi's Congress (I). Moslem participation in voting, running for office, election campaigning and party membership is as high as that of Hindus.[162]

By comparison, China's communal or minority problem is miniscule. China officially records 56 "nationality" groups, with a combined population of about 67 million or 6.7 percent of the national population. Of these, over 12 million are Uygers, other Moslem inhabitants of Xinjiang, and Buddhist Tibetans. These two groups, the Tibetans and Xinjiang Moslems, pose a special problem which is more appropriately discussed under "Regional Nationalism" than under "Communalism."

The remainder of China's minorities, 4.6 percent of the population, are in most cases overwhelmed by their Han (ethnic Chinese) neighbors. Of the 9 million residents of the "autonomous" region of Inner Mongolia, only 15 percent are Mongols. In the northeast (Manchuria) 1.8 million Koreans and 4.3 million Manchus reside among more than 100 million Han. In addition to Tibet and Xinjiang, where minorities are a majority, a number of other Chinese provinces contain sizable minority populations which consist primarily of mountain tribes, including the largest single minority in China, the Zhuang, who number about 13.3 million. Another large minority in China, the 7.2 million Hui, are ethnic Chinese Moslems or, in some cases, mixed descendants of Moslem traders. The Hui are scattered over China and, as they are Chinese in everything but religion and diet, they pose less of a political issue or a problem of assimilation than other minorities. Mao, in keeping with Marx, believed that ethnic distinctions would disappear when class distinctions were eliminated. Thus nationality characteristics, including religion, could be tolerated until the true communist state emerged. Assimilation into a homogeneous culture, however, has always been the goal of the CCP—and the KMT—whether the approach was a gradual one, as advocated by Liu Shaoqi and, later, Deng Xiaoping, or a radical one as pursued by Mao and his leftist supporters.[163]

The stated goal of integration clearly envisions a culture that is communist, proletarian, and Han. With a much smaller minority population to contend with, the Chinese communists have seemed committed to a much more assimilative course than Moscow.[164] The CCP radicals who emphasized a class-struggle approach to integration of the minorities actively pushed abolition of minority customs and special privileges, attacked the special autonomous area system, and insisted on "immediate adoption of the Han Chinese communist model of economic and social organization."[165] When in control, the moderates have returned to a long-term approach to integration, respecting both the nationalities' special characteristics as well as the existence of autonomous, but controlled, political areas for the minorities.[166]

During the Cultural Revolution and until the death of Mao, the regime viewed the traditions of the minorities as reactionary, sought to eliminate the "four olds" (including old customs and traditions), and to force the pace of assimilation. The teaching of minority languages was ended or reduced, many religious institutions closed, priests and nuns rusticated, and even fundamental changes in diet and farming were ordained by Peking.

Under Deng's new order, Peking in 1980 shifted back to a "hearts and minds" approach, significantly relaxed political, economic, and cultural controls, provided new liberal tax reliefs and budget support to the autonomous areas, and restored preferential treatment for minority students. The application of responsibility systems to agriculture in minority areas also meant a return to more traditional ways of farming and animal husbandry. Meanwhile, renewed efforts were launched to train minority youth for party and state cadre positions. In 1981, there was some backing away from rapid promotion of minority cadre, apparently because of a lack of qualified candidates, but also partly because of resistance by Han cadre.

As in India, there has also been a backlash in China to some of the concessions given to the minorities, not only in special educational and job opportunities, but also in their exclusion from the country's rigorous birth-control restrictions. "Minorities have more fun," a young Chinese coed complained to her American teacher. Indeed, the average Chinese, who leads an austere life, often looks on with envy at minority groups in colorful costumes carrying on with lavish and boisterous weddings and other festivals, all of which the government sternly discourages among the Han population.

Incidents of violence between Han and Chinese minorities have occurred in various places, although such events are not reported publicly in China. Nevertheless, the communal problem is likely to remain well under control in China proper and in those "autonomous" regions like Inner Mongolia, Guangxi, and Ningxia where the demographic gate to separatism has irreversibly closed. The great Han blanket has descended over the Mongols, Miaos, Manchus, and most other minorities, and these relatively small groups if not eventually assimilated will never pose any serious political problem.

States' Rights

Aside from the sharp Hindu-Moslem religious division that runs throughout much of the country, India faces serious problems of regionalism even among the Hindu states, problems which have no counterpart in China proper.

In the mid–1950s, Selig Harrison wrote a book called *The Dangerous Decades,* in which he highlighted the centrifugal forces at work in India and the possibility of Balkanization. Three of the "deadly decades" have passed and India has not yet flown apart; instead, it has gobbled up two additional, if tiny, pieces of real estate—Goa and Sikkim. Divisive and separatist forces, however, continue to challenge the nation's integrity.

The contest between centralism and states' rights has gone through several stages in India. Under Nehru the state chief ministers were often dynamic leaders in their own right and the Congress Party had a truly federal character. Mrs. Gandhi, however, imposed her own nominees as chief ministers on Congress (I)-controlled states, and during the late 1960s and up through the emergency the center tightened its control over all state governments. A pronounced reaction in the other direction, however, has been underway for some time.

Over the long term, the trend in India has been toward accommodation of regionalism and local parochial interests. As India has come to live with a plurality of religions and cultures, it has also learned to live with a wide variety of state governments, including those controlled by communists and nationalist Moslems.

China, on the other hand, has no provincial leaders with the strength and independence of those in India. In fact, provincial leaders in China are usually not provincials at all. Following an ancient Chinese tradition, the governors and first party secretaries of China's 29 provincial-level units are in most cases not natives of the provinces they lead. Nothing so demonstrates the absence of popular politics in China above the village level as the fact that when, for example, the Shanghai Municipal Council or the Heilungjiang Provincial People's Congress elects a new mayor and a new governor respectively, they usually do not "choose" a native. The same is generally true in the selection of provincial first party secretaries.

Reflecting historical divisions, a number of China's provinces, as in India, follow linguistic lines; but China's centralized system of political control, and its long tradition of unity and strong central authority, deter regional chauvinism at the level of provincial politics. Provincialism, of course, exists in China and provinces like Guangdong tend to carry out central directives in their own way even when the leaders are not natives.

While in India there is a volatile interplay between the center and the states, the center still has a very strong hand constitutionally and economically vis-a-vis the states. Under the constitution the central government appoints the state governors who are normally titular but important in times of political crises or stalemate. In the Chinese pattern, the state governors in India are usually not natives of the state to which they are appointed. Unlike China, in India, police come under the state governments, but senior officers are members of the national police service. New Delhi may also unilaterally deploy the Central Reserve Police Force and the Border Security Force in any part of the country. Under a 1981 bill, the center has authority to declare an area disturbed, and to set up special courts for speedy trial of offenses committed in the disturbed area. Previously, only the states had this authority. President's rule, meaning direct executive administration from New

Delhi—if necessary with assistance of the military—can and has been imposed, displacing a state government for 6 months or a year before new elections must be held. This power has been used on a number of occasions, turning out governments, for example, in West Bengal, Kerala, Punjab, and Assam.

Over the years, New Delhi has backpedaled on efforts to promote Hindi as the national language. Following widespread agitation in the 1950s, state boundaries in the south were redrawn on linguistic non-Hindi lines. Again, in 1965, when Tamil Nadu erupted against renewed efforts to promote Hindi, the requirements were simply shelved in regard to that state. Meanwhile, in China—as in Taiwan—Mandarin has been successfully imposed as the official language and the language of education.

Within the Indian states, language minorities continue to press for new autonomous regions or statehood. Meanwhile, states which have experienced a heavy immigration of out-of-staters have "sons of the soil" movements demanding educational and employment preferences for natives over migrants. Regional parties throughout the country, including the Communist Party Marxist in West Bengal, exploit the feeling of locals that New Delhi is dominating the state's political life and that more and more autonomy is necessary to protect separate cultural and economic interests.

Mrs. Gandhi was thought to be inflexible on federal matters, but she also backed down when she sensed that she had gone too far. This was demonstrated, for example, in August 1984 when the Indira-appointed governor of Andhra Pradesh ousted the popular chief minister and movie idol, N. T. Rama Rau, alleging that the latter had lost a majority in the State Assembly. Rama Rau charged that the Congress(I) had used intimidation and bribes to win over some of his supporters in the assembly, and that anyway he still had a majority. The new chief minister, who promised to cooperate with the central government, explained that "all's fair in love, war, and politics." But the move boomeranged as public opposition swelled and Rama Rau suddenly loomed as a national leader. Mrs. Gandhi quickly named a new governor, who hastily reinstalled the movie actor as head of government.

Rama Rau's victory and other state election results fanned new speculation in the early 1980s about a wave of regionalism. Some Indian observers once again saw the center folding and the states turning to local forms of chauvinism. Mrs. Gandhi issued ominous warnings against the trend. Meanwhile, in China, states' rights was hardly an issue worth mentioning.

In early 1983 India's northeast state of Assam burst into flames of insurrection following prolonged agitation by Assamese Hindus against illegal immigration of Moslem Bengalis from Bangladesh. The steady flow of refugees into Assam, which had continued since the great influx during the 1971 war with Pakistan, had swelled the immigrant population in the state to almost 40 percent of the total. Some of the Assamese agitators spoke openly of secession. In 1985, however, to the surprise of many, Rajiv reached an accord with leaders of the dissident Assamese, accepting most of their demands regarding autonomy and immigration. The Congress (I) lost the subsequent state elections.

Alienated Regions

While provincialism is quite different in India and China, both nations face similar problems in strategic areas where alienated national minorities form a state or region-wide majority. Since its beginning the Union of India has come to terms with regional nationalism through a combination of compromise, stratagem, force, and then yet another effort at compromise. Rajiv Gandhi understands how to employ all three tactics, but he has excelled in conciliation. He showed this talent in Mizoram, whose population of 488,000 was overwhelmingly tribal, Christian, and rebellious. After the 1962 Sino-Indian war and into the 1970s, the Chinese provided training and material support to Mizo guerrillas fighting for secession. In 1986, Rajiv Gandhi negotiated an accord with the leader of the Mizo National Liberation Front, Laldenga. The agreement promised statehood for Mizoram, a coalition interim cabinet of Congress (I) and the MNLF led by Laldenga, supremacy of Mizo customary law over Indian civil and criminal law, and preservation of regulations restricting entry of outsiders to Mizoram. It is difficult to imagine the Chinese ever agreeing to similar autonomy for Tibet.

Tibet is, of course, a much bigger problem of national integration for China than that posed to India by the northeastern tribals. Certainly it is a bigger problem in terms of land and population. The "autonomous region" of Tibet extends over 1.2 million square kilometers, and only half of China's 3.4 million Tibetans live within the present borders of Tibet.

The Chinese are probably confident that, despite the political alienation of most of the Tibetan population, they can retain control so long as there is no major intervention from the outside. They are concerned, however, that—together with Xinjiang—Tibet provides a strategic weak point that the Soviets might someday choose to exploit. In addition, latent instability in Tibet poses a continuing complication in Sino-Indian relations and this is another reason for Peking to try to seek some accommodation with the Tibetans.

Beginning in 1980, the Deng group introduced major reforms in Tibet, seeking to build a more positive and conciliatory relationship between the center and the Tibetan people. The Chinese began negotiating with the Dalai Lama for his return to a titular position and, possibly, as a vice-chairman of the National People's Congress. Tibetans were also promoted into official positions and many of the 120,000 Chinese who had reluctantly served for years in Tibet, usually without ever learning Tibetan, were allowed to transfer back to China proper. In 1986, the governor was Tibetan but the party secretary, Han Chinese.

Between 1980 and 1983, three delegations from the Dalai Lama visited Tibet and were welcomed by wildly enthusiastic crowds. The delegations reportedly asked for inclusion in Tibet of adjacent Tibetan-speaking areas and an autonomous status, equivalent to that which Peking had offered Taipei in 1979. While the outcome of China's negotiations with the Dalai Lama are uncertain, there is no doubt that Peking intends to retain firm control of the region. Moreover, it seems highly unlikely that the Chinese would permit Tibet to be returned to the type of autonomy it enjoyed in the 1950s or to that promised Taiwan.

In India's northeastern tribal areas as well as in China's Tibet, the presence of the national army is essential for retaining control and suppressing secessionist sentiment. Both regions also depend heavily on the center for financial support. The Nagas, Mizos, and other tribals in India's northeast, however, have considerably more control over their own affairs than do the Tibetans. The Nagas and now the Mizos directly elect their own state legislatures and there is no supreme policy body controlled by the center such as the Communist Party represents in Tibet. Politics in Nagaland and the other tribal states and regions in the northeast provide an outlet for dissident sentiment. While organizations supporting independence are banned, tribesmen in these areas of India have the freedom to organize and agitate for greater autonomy and to criticize sharply the central government, rights which are not likely to be given to Tibetans, as they are denied to other Chinese.

The Sikh Problem

While Indian troops in 1983 were battling contending groups in Assam, the army was rushing reinforcements into the Punjab, where Sikhs were fomenting civil disobedience in support of territorial and water claims against neighboring states, political demands for more Punjab autonomy, and religious concessions such as allowing Sikhs to carry their symbolic daggers on-board Indian domestic airline flights. The Sikh religion, which had derived from both Hinduism and Islam, had become more institutionalized over the years and thus more conscious of a distinct identity. One of the Sikh demands was to expunge the constitutional reference to Sikhism as a Hindu religion. At the same time the booming economy of the Punjab had fed a desire among a minority of Sikhs for a Sikh homeland or "Khalistan." Sikhs, however, are only 52 percent of the population of the Punjab and, with many Hindu migrant workers remaining in the state and Sikhs continuing their own pattern of emigrating abroad and to other parts of India, it is quite possible that this figure could rather quickly diminish. Hindu Punjabis are a majority in the main cities and in most towns of the state. Despite the strength of the Sikh party Akali Dal, the Congress (I) up to the mid-1980s had controlled the state government through the support of the

Hindus and many of the untouchable and landless Sikhs, as well as the small percentage of Sikh cultivators who were not members of the Jat caste.

These political and demographic realities suggest that Sikh nationalists, whatever violence they may use, have little prospect of achieving their goal. In any event, with the Punjab supplying most of the country's nationally marketable grain, New Delhi will go to drastic lengths to prevent secession.

Mrs. Gandhi and her allies in the Punjab, seeking to split the Sikhs, for a brief time politically supported a Sikh fundamentalist named Jarnal Singh Bhindranwale. This political maneuver backfired as Bhindranwale turned radical and gained ascendency over the autonomy movement, which increasingly turned to terrorism. After the assassination of a prominent Hindu editor in Amritsar in 1983, Bhindranwale was arrested but released after a violent riot in protest. Bhindranwale grew bolder and he and his supporters set up headquarters in the Golden Temple in Amritsar, the most sacred shrine of the Sikhs. Mrs. Gandhi hesitated to move with force against the temple and it continued to serve as sanctuary for the extremists. By June of 1984 Sikh terrorists had killed over 300 persons in the Punjab, mostly Hindus but also a number of Sikh opponents. A senior Sikh police officer was mowed down by automatic fire from inside the temple as he left after prayers. Finally, the army surrounded the temple and on June 6, 1984, after a group of moderate Sikh leaders had surrendered, Indian troops with the support of tanks and helicopters stormed the complex of buildings that surround the enormous "Pool of Nectar" (Amritsar) with the brilliant gold leaf temple in the center. After two hours, the resistance ended. About 600 terrorists, according to official accounts, and at least 83 soldiers lay dead. Some claimed the total was more than a thousand. In the aftermath, Sikh recruits in at least two units mutinied, in one case killing their Hindu commander before being suppressed. But the overwhelming majority of the more than 100,000 Sikhs in the military forces (who constitute 24% of all officers) remained loyal.

Although there was strong popular support for the government's crack down from the Hindu majority of all India, there was also ample and vivid opposition, charging that Mrs. Gandhi had acted hastily or else not soon enough, and that in any event she had been moved by base political motives. Mrs. Gandhi made conciliatory gestures, calling for a "healing touch" and authorizing compensation even for the deserters who had been killed. On October 31, two Sikh members of her personal security guard riddled her body with 16 bullets as she walked from her residence to her office. Ironically, the prime minister's devotion to Indian unity as well as her political machinations had led to her death. After the army attack on the Golden Temple, she had insisted on retaining Sikhs in her bodyguard.

Whatever the judgment of Mrs. Gandhi, her tolerance of vehement dissent from government action during the crisis with the Sikhs reflected the continuing if still tenuous strength of Indian democracy. In 1959, when Chinese troops in Tibet bombarded the Dalai Lama's summer residence and several monasteries, no Chinese voice of dissent was heard.

A thousand or more Sikhs were killed by Hindu mobs after Mrs. Gandhi's death and communal tensions in the Punjab intensified. In 1985, Rajiv Gandhi conceded most of the demands of the Akali Dal, which won the state elections that year and formed the new government. In 1986 the extremists continued their terrorism. Yet the odds are that Punjab will remain a part of India so long as the Union lasts.

Xinjiang and Kashmir

Demographic changes in China's far northwest region of Xinjiang and India's state of Jammu-Kashmir tell a great deal about differences in the approaches of Peking and New Delhi to dealing with alienated and nationalist minority regions. The Chinese tried and to a large extent have Sinicized Xinjiang. In 1949 the Han population in Xinjiang was only about 5 percent of the total; after liberation, Peking conducted a planned migration program, moving Han Chinese from Shanghai and other areas into the remote desert and semi-desert region. Today about 42 percent of Xinjiang's population of 14 million are Han Chinese. The other 58 percent are various Moslem tribes, the largest group being the Uygers, a Caucasian people who speak a Turkic language.

The Uygers physically resemble the Kashmiri who inhabit the nearby vale of Kashmir. The state of Jammu-Kashmir in India is about 83 percent ethnic Kashmiri and 70 percent Moslem in religion. Most of the Hindus live in Jammu over the mountains to the south, and in the far north of the state on the desolate high plateau of Ladakh reside almost 100,000 Buddhists of Tibetan origin. But the religious and ethnic profile of Jammu and Kashmir has not changed over the past 30 years. Non-natives of Jammu-Kashmir are forbidden to own land in the state or hold jobs without approval of the state government. Kashmiri can migrate to other parts of India, but other Indians cannot migrate to Jammu-Kashmir. Senior central government officers in the state are mostly non-Kashmiri, but in the state service, officials, including senior police and district magistrates, are mostly Kashmir natives.

The capital of Srinagar is distinctly Kashmiri. Houseboats crowd the rivers, canals, and lakes; men in traditional ponchos and women dressed in black wander the crowded lanes. With its unique wood and steepled mosques, its multi-storied houses with high-pitched roofs and balconies, the city has a central-Asian, renaissance-era look about it. In contrast, Urumqi, the capital of Xinjiang, is 70 percent Han Chinese and most of the city is indistinguishable from a hundred other drab industrial cities of China. The streets are dominated by cavernous Soviet-style public buildings, smokestacks, and rows of unattractive housing blocks. In the marketplace and near the mosque and the Western Gate one finds remnants of the old atmosphere.

Uyger men, bearded and black-booted, haggle over prices; bakers slap large discs of "nan" dough into oven barrels; a lively wedding party in several open-bed trucks goes noisily by; old men smoke pipes by the mosque; and Uyger women, in colorful skirts and jewelry, gossip and tend their flocks of children. Still, Urumqi is a city of Han.

Xinjiang is ruled by the Communist Party, which has been headed by a succession of Han Chinese first secretaries. Some district party first secretaries are Moslems, but most are still Han. The chairman of the government of the autonomous region and most of the People's Congresses are Uygers or other locals; 64 percent of the students at Xinjiang University are Uygers and classes are taught in Uyger as well as in Mandarin. After the Cultural Revolution there were only 500 mosques; now there are 13,000 and 16,000 immans. Large-scale immigration of Han into the autonomous region has apparently stopped. Given the higher birth rate of the Moslem population; the Han percentage may begin to diminish, but the death rate is considerbly higher among the natives.

In contrast to Xinjiang, Kashmir politics have been dominated by natives, specifically the National Conference Party, originally headed by folk hero and Kashmir nationalist leader Sheikh Mohammed Abdullah, who died in 1982. In 1947, Abdullah agreed to the accession of Jammu-Kashmir to India with a constitutionally prescribed special status, and he backed India's resistance to Pakistan's armed intervention. Abdullah, however, expounded Kashmir's right to self-determination and resisted Indian efforts to erode the state's special status. Abdullah was jailed twice for long periods. Last released in 1974, he again headed the national conference and the Jammu-Kashmir government until his death.

Kashmir's handful of Moslem intellectuals very likely would favor independence for the state, if given the choice, and most Kashmiri Moslems would probably support them. The Hindu and Buddhist populations, however, would not likely agree. (The ancestors of Indira Gandhi and her father were Kashmiri Hindus.) Even Sheik Abdullah and his colleagues, after the events in East Pakistan in 1971, began to see benefits in continued association with a secular and democratic India. Although many of the symbols of Kashmir's special status in the Indian Union have been lost, such as the title of Prime Minister for the state government leader, now called Chief Minister, the state continues to be a preserve for Kashmiri.

While the central government will not allow autonomy to be carried too far and it can and has manipulated state politics, the people of Kashmir clearly run their own affairs. There is no threat to the cultural, linguistic, or demographic balance of the state, and the Indian government provides more per capita economic aid to the Jammu-Kashmir government than to any other state.

In Kashmir the presence and effectiveness of the Indian army discourages any serious thought of secession. In addition, the defeat of Pakistan in 1971 appeared to end the possibility that international pressures might bring India to accept a plebiscite on the future of the state. The outlet of politics, personal rivalries among the Moslem leaders, the co-option of many National Conference politicians into the system through corruption, and the interest of Kashmiri timber and carpet merchants in stability have tended to dissipate secessionist sentiment and to encourage a general resignation to simply getting the most autonomy possible out of New Delhi.

In July 1984 Mrs. Gandhi exploited divisions within the National Conference to oust Mohammed Abdullah's son, Farouk Abdullah, and his party from power. Farouk's brother-in-law and rival for leadership, Ghulam Mohammed Shah, set up a splinter faction and was joined by 12 members of the National Conference. This deprived Farouk of a majority in the 78-member state assembly, and the governor appointed Ghulam Mohammed Shah to form a new government, a feat which he could accomplish only by allying his group with the local Congress (I)—and Mrs. Gandhi. While this sort of manipulation—and some suspected bribery—may not have been good cricket, it was within the rules of the game of hardball Indian democracy.

In 1986, however, Rajiv Gandhi effectively ousted Shah from office following a period of Hindu-Moslem violence. The prime minister was reportedly unhappy with Shah because of the latter's unpopularity with Kashmiri Moslems and because of charges of corruption. Later in the year Gandhi reached an accord under which Farouk Abdullah would lead a new coalition government in which the Congress (I) would participate. Dramatizing the remarkable ups and downs of center-state relations in India, in a November 7 rally in Srinagar, Abdullah raised Rajiv's hand aloft and proclaimed, "I will strengthen his hands, and he will strengthen mine."

Neither the outlet nor the stimulation of democratic politics exists in Xinjiang or Tibet. Local nationalists in Tibet, as well as in Xinjiang, however, are also very likely increasingly resigned to indefinite Chinese sovereignty. As in the case of Kashmir, local Tibetan nationalists have little hope today that international events will open the way to future independence. The Soviet Union is the only effective force that might some day see it in its interests to support the separation from China of either Tibet or Xinjiang. At present, however, Moscow shows no interest in any such undertaking with its enormous implications.

CHAPTER 16

Dealing with the World

Different Enemies

Indian and Chinese foreign policies share a number of objectives, including maintaining national integrity and seeking regional preeminence. Until the early 1970s, India and China each believed itself under immediate threat. China, and to a lesser extent India, also felt outside powers were maliciously limiting their regional and world influence. These fears dominated their respective foreign policies for over two decades. All along, however, there has been a basic difference in the nature of the two countries' security concerns: China has had more of a global strategic perspective than India. This reflects China's greater power, its more ambitious perception of its world role at this period of history, and, in part, the "super" character of China's enemies over the years.

China's vital national interests, its most sensitive issues of sovereignty, its security, and its regional influence directly involve the super-powers. With such potential adversaries, China has had to think in terms of nuclear deterrents, global strategies, and the international balance of power. Thus, as in other areas, China has shaped its South Asian policies primarily to serve its strategic relations with the superpowers.

Except for Soviet propaganda support for internal communist rebellions in India in the late 1940s and the U.S. show of force in 1971 near the Bay of Bengal, India has never been directly threatened by either of the super-powers, and its foreign policy has been dominated by its concern vis-a-vis Pakistan and, after 1962, China.

Independent India has from the start enjoyed a certain world influence through its hortatory stance and non-aligned diplomacy, but never has it pretended to strategic involvement outside of its region. There is no evidence that Nehru ever gave a thought to Western European security and its consequences for India. In his day, however, the U.S. was indisputably the predominant world power and the Soviet Union a powerful but essentially regional force. Consequently, Nehru's tilting toward the Soviets on issues like Hungary and the Middle East could be seen as an effort to exploit what political influence India had to balance the scales. Nehru's anti-imperialist intellectual proclivities and his neutralist ideals moved him to give the Soviets the benefit of the doubt on issues that did not really involve India.

Nehru's policies worked fairly well. He maintained a clear independence of action for India, and while his pandering to Moscow irritated the West, it did not diminish Western interest in aiding democratic India economically, and may have encouraged it. Nehru ran into trouble when he combined a tough military posture during the border dispute with China with a weak defense establishment to back it up.

The National Consensus

No opposition party has taken over in Peking since 1949, nor are contrary views on foreign policy openly voiced. Backstage domestic politics, however, has played a major part in China's foreign policymaking over the years. On the political skids in 1971, Lin Biao and his military supporters violently opposed the opening to the U.S., and the Gang of Four also had strong differences with Zhou Enlai on the direction of foreign policy in the Cultural Revolution period.[167] The gang was silenced a few months after Mao's death in 1976, and only four years later Deng eclipsed Mao's chosen successor, Hua Guofeng. But conservative neo-Maoists were still powerful, and their influence in foreign policy would be felt again.

The dynamics of China's foreign policymaking today are radically different from those of the Cultural Revolution. For a short period, 1967–1968, the Cultural Revolution group, with Mao's approval, enjoyed unusual scope to make radical foreign policy moves; even the pragmatic Zhou Enlai bent with the wind, although he tried to limit the damage. In 1969, the Sino-Soviet conflict gave Zhou the opportunity to recover his influence but, again, this was primarily because Mao decreed it. Today, Deng and his chosen successors must arrive at a consensus on important foreign-policy questions within a much broader, more collective leadership. Considerable bargaining and give-and-take is involved. Still, the power base in China is relatively narrow, and the leadership has a greater scope for altering the consensus by fiat than in India, where public as well as private debate and pressures are brought to bear on foreign-policy decisions.

The records of the Janata Party, and of Mrs. Gandhi when she returned to control in 1980, indicate the limited range of safe or rational foreign-policy options that are available at any one time. Because of the momentum of the past and the logic of current relationships, opposition groups, once in power, either in India or China—or the U.S., for that matter—usually reach an assessment of national interests not fundamentally different from that of their predecessors. Extreme departures in foreign policy are carried out by charismatic leaders or revolutionary regimes swept away by spiritual, ideological, or nationalistic visions; for example, Mao in the 1960s, and in the 1980s the Ayatollah Khomeini. But the cost of ambitious leaps in foreign as in domestic policy is usually high.

Regional Preeminence

Paradoxically, China today does not seem to harbor the same degree of ambition as does India in regard to establishing "preeminence" over its neighbors. This is the result of geo-political realities and the maxim about the art of the possible. Militarily and economically India overshadows all of its neighbors with the big exception of China. Pakistan is still a major force to be reckoned with, but it is highly dependent on outside support and India can imagine that it will someday be brought to accept the benevolent primacy of India.

All of the sub-continent has historic and cultural links with India, and British rule or protection over virtually the entire region reflected a certain historic logic. Most Indians realize that dreams of a united subcontinent are far-fetched and in any case undesirable. But there is a strong consensus that all the neighboring countries, save of course China, which is viewed as beyond the borders of the region, must by their actions acknowledge the preeminence of Indian interests. The Indians naturally view their attitude toward their neighbors as benign and protective. They have tried to achieve their goal of paramountcy through a combination of substantial economic and in some cases military aid, and occasionally diplomatic and economic pressures. In response, Nepal, Bangladesh, Bhutan, Sri Lanka, and Pakistan all look to China, among others, as a counter-balance. This provides an ongoing conflict of interest between India and China that will never be entirely resolved. Other vital interests, however, encourage the two powers to try to reconcile their competing regional interests or at least to keep their rivalry within manageable limits.

China, of course, harbors the same sort of patriarchal tendencies toward its neighboring regions as does India. These instincts were starkly proclaimed during the Cultural Revolution, when China adopted an openly chauvinist posture toward overseas Chinese in Southeast Asia and unabashedly supported Maoist guerrilla wars against many non-communist governments—including India—by groups who proclaimed unquestioned loyalty to Peking. This hegemonist posture, dressed in the cloak of revolution, was set loose by the domestic upheavals in China during the Cultural Revolution and by anti-imperialist militancy sparked by the Vietnam War and the Sino-Soviet dispute. Essentially, the radical line in foreign policy came from Chairman Mao; but its fervent implementation for several years revealed a self-righteous side to China's inner personality. Despite India's patronizing and occasionally arrogant attitude toward its neighbors, it has not yet revealed the same intense capacity for rationalizing dominance as was reflected during the Chinese Cultural Revolution.

Peking, however, has rejected the extremist policies of the Cultural Revolution and blamed the Gang of Four for diplomatic excesses at that time, such as burning down the British Embassy and openly interfering in the internal affairs of other countries. Interestingly, the Dengists have not blamed Mao for any errors in foreign policy, although they have charged him with responsibility for the domestic debacle. This seems in part related to the Chinese reluctance, shared by the Indians, to admit to errors in their relations with foreigners.

China's neighbors are an even more difficult lot to dominate than are India's. China's largest neighbor, the USSR, is one of six contiguous communist countries, two of which, Mongolia and Afghanistan, are dominated by the Soviets and harbor large Soviet military deployments. The Chinese, incidentally, tend to look upon Mongolia as some Indians view Pakistan—historically, a part of greater China, which was severed, probably for good, by foreign machination, in this case the Soviet Union.

The Soviets also provide extensive military support to two other neighbors, Vietnam and its client, Laos. Of China's six Marxist neighbors, only North Korea has friendly relations with Peking; but Korea also lies adjacent to the Soviet Union, and Pyongyang is not likely to find it either desirable or necessary to recognize China's primacy. Similar to New Delhi's view of the Himalayan states, Peking sees Southeast Asia as an area of special Chinese interest because of security, historic, cultural, and ethnic reasons. But it cannot reasonably entertain the notion of preeminence there for the foreseeable future. Nepal, Bhutan, and Pakistan are also seen in Peking as border-lands in which China has legitimate interests but Peking's emotional and nationalistic identification with these countries is weaker than that of India.

Nationalism

In both countries the fervor of nationalism has died down in comparison with peak years. In India it is generally agreed that Westernization, in terms of customs such as clothing, is greater now than in the past when an Indian congressman would not be seen dead in Western mufti. Chinese chauvinism reached its post–1949 height during the Cultural Revolution. As expectations of rapid growth and the prestige of the political elite have waned in India and China, nationalism has become more important as a unifying cement and a spur to sacrifice and hard work. Nationalism is the one force that can transcend family, self, clan, and caste.

Both New Delhi and Peking in their domestic media continually highlight their international roles and their space and science achievements. Enormous funds were spent to host the 1982 Asian Games in New Delhi, as well as the 1983 Non-Aligned Meeting, for reasons of domestic as much as international prestige. Meanwhile, Chinese television news seems almost daily to highlight the visit to Peking of some illustrious foreign leader. Peking also has an expensive and elaborate organization to train young boys and girls for world-class competition in pursuits ranging from gymnastics to playing the cello. Many sports in which China is aiming for world ranking, such as tennis, have almost infinitesimal participation and spectator interest at home. China's victories in the 1982 women's volleyball championships in Tokyo, for example, set off a series of exuberant unofficial demonstrations in Chinese cities.

The Indians have been less organized in building up their sports competitiveness, but have nevertheless put considerable effort into it. International victories in cricket, soccer, field hockey, or any other sport are esteemed by Indians, as by Chinese, and serve to strengthen the sense of nationhood.

In the 1984 Olympics and the 1986 Asian Games, China overwhelmed Indian sportsmen and women. In the latter event, China won a total of 222 medals of which 94 were gold. India took only five medals altogether. Traditionally, neither India nor China emphasized athletics as did the Mediterranean world. Thus, one suspects that China's superior showing is due to the highly organized approach of the People's Republic to sports and to the higher nutrition and health levels of Northeast Asians as compared to Southeast and South Asians.

The most important element of nationalism in both countries, however, is the perception of economic and military muscle. The strong remain united and the weak are soon divided. This was the lesson of China's century of chaos and foreign rule, and of India in the eighteenth century, when a few Englishmen captured the whole lot. Indian military strength as revealed in the 1971 war with Pakistan probably contributed to Indian unity more than any other phenomenon in the past 30 years. The elaborate military parade and fly-past on Republic Day in New Delhi every January costs a great deal of money, but its clear purpose is to dramatize to the home audience the impressive strength of the country's military establishment.

Except for 1984, the PRC's 35th anniversary, China has not held a mamoth Soviet-style military parade for years. But missile launchings, nuclear tests, and military maneuvers have always been prominently featured in Chinese media. The CCP built the image of a new, powerful Chinese nationalism by defeating the KMT, pushing the U.S. back in Korea, and cavalierly punishing the unprepared Indians in 1962. It was an impressive 13-year performance. Subsequent engagements along the Sino-Soviet border in 1969, and with the Vietnamese ten years later, had more ambiguous outcomes, although victories were claimed nevertheless. China probably would have stayed unified if none of these had occurred, but any Chinese regime, to secure its position and to achieve national discipline and commitment, must demonstrate military strength, national dignity, and global influence.

The CCP's slogans today do not call for the creation of something new under the sun—an egalitarian collective state—but, instead, promise to build China into "a powerful and prosperous nation." Reviving the ancient vision of a refined and cultured society, other slogans call for the creation of a "socialist spiritual civilization." Official discussion of the new "civilization" that is to be built suggests simply a society marked by discipline, hard work, civility, and good health, as well as a vigorous artistic, recreational, and intellectual life. Nothing specifically Chinese is suggested by the image of the "socialist, spiritual civilization." Some of the attitudes called for are rather traditionally non-Chinese: public politeness, concern for the general welfare, not spitting in the streets, etc.

The vision suggests an ideal in which Chinese would work in a modified Marxist economy, internalize Western-style civic virtues, appreciate Mozart and "Swan Lake," and for recreation play basketball or soccer. The ideal could, of course, also include those who like Peking Opera and practice shadow boxing in the parks. But the point is that, except for eating Chinese food, the sought-after good life contains no specific trappings of Chinese culture or tradition as a necessary element. Yet it is treated in the media and perceived by most Chinese as somehow distinctly Chinese and profoundly reflecting Chinese culture. The main reason Chinese—and outsiders—identify this vision of modern life as Chinese is primarily race.

More than any of the other continental powers present and potential, including the U.S., the Soviet Union, Brazil, and India, China embodies the fundamental element of nationalism in its original, tribal, and nation-state form—ethnic homogeneity and historical continuity.

Nationalism and the sense of greatness in China today, as in the past, has more of a racial element than in India, as we suggested previously; and this implies a potentially greater volatility. Racial pride or identity in China is certainly not referred to in these terms, and the sense of ethnic pride has so far been overwhelmingly of a positive rather than a negative nature. But while racism is strongly condemned by both India and China, it does exist in terms of a sense of cultural superiority and socially in terms of color. A fair complexion is valued in both societies. African students studying in China as well as in India report incidents of racism; but some who have left colleges in China to study in India say social discrimination is stronger in the former. India has not experienced the violent racial incidents involving foreigners like those that have occurred in a few Chinese universities. In May 1986, for example, a dispute over a loud party given by African students at Tianjin University turned into a five-hour rock and bottle throwing brawl between Chinese and Africans.

Many Indians are, of course, as ebony as any African, while in China an

African, like a European, is more of an oddity. Color in India has a social and caste correlation; the upper castes are usually fair-skinned, but this is not always the case, and in the east and south there are brahmans who are darker than peasants or untouchables. Thus in India the preference for light color is, to an extent, a matter of perceived cosmetics rather than racial prejudice. An Indian woman might openly express the wish that she were fairer, just as a Swede might wish for an olive complexion or no freckles. The same applies in part to popular attitudes in China about variations of complexions; but these varieties are, with few exceptions, relatively narrow compared to those in India. In any event, Chinese national pride is likely to continue to have a greater element of racial identity, although unstated and perhaps unconscious, than in the case of India.

Defense Structures

China's military structure reflects the superpower status of its potential enemies, as well as Peking's intention to play in the high-stakes game of nuclear deterrence. India's defense budget in the 1985–1986 fiscal year was 76.8 billion rupees, or about $6.1 billion. In 1981 China, for the first time, gave figures on its defense spending, estimating $11.87 billion for 1981 which was later reduced to $10.2 billion. Due to a large decrease in the official value of the yuan, the 1985 budget amounted to only $7.8 billion. Nevertheless, official defense expenditures as a share of the national budget had fallen from more than 15 percent in 1978 to just under 12 percent in 1985. In the seventh Five Year Plan, it was slated to fall below 10 percent. This figure, however, does not include R&D and other costs not reflected in the budget.

The U.S. government estimates that Chinese defense expenditures, if calculated in the same way as in the U.S. (and in India), would be four times as high as the official figure or about $30 billion depending on the exchange rate employed.[168] This is a stab in the dark and some Western sources estimate that the real figures are only twice the official budget numbers. Nevertheless, looking at differences in the aggregate size and nature of the Indian and Chinese military establishments, it seems likely that the cost of the Chinese defense effort could easily be four or five times that of India; that is, about $30 billion.[169] If so, China is spending as much as $30 per capita on its military establishment each year or about 13 percent of its GNP. This compares to about $8 per capita in India or about 3 percent of GNP.

In 1985 China had almost four times the number of military personnel as India. After reducing total strength by about one half million, Peking's armed forces at the end of 1986 still numbered more than three times that of New Delhi. China has twelve times the number of submarines, five times the number of fast attack naval craft, and almost nine times the number of military combat aircraft.

Equipped with MiG 23s and MiG 27s—and with a 1986 agreement for limited purchase and licensed manufacture of the MiG 29—the Indian Air Force probably has a quality edge over the PLA Air Force. India also recently purchased advanced U.S. jet engines for its own indigenous fighter. India's other lead in major war systems is its two aircraft carriers, of which China has none.

The greatest difference, however, is in the two countries' strategic programs. According to the International Institute of Strategic Studies, China has deployed 6 ICBMs, 60 IRBMs, 50 MRBMs, and two nuclear ballistic subs. Reflecting its strategic military program, China has conducted at least 26 nuclear tests and India only one. The cost of this strategic nuclear force has been an enormous burden for China. In 1986, the PRC was hoping to recoup a small portion of its investment by actively seeking foreign contracts to launch commercial satellites.

The chairman of the Indian Space Commission has claimed that his country possesses the ability to produce 1,800 to 2,000 mile range missiles. By mid—1986, India was preparing to launch an augmented satellite launch vehicle—ASLV—that would be capable of putting payloads into low-earth orbits. This was to be followed by the four stage polar satellite launch vehicle—PSLV—which would place 1,000 kg. class satellites in polar sun-synchronous orbit, and which could be modified into an intermediate range ballistic missile. New Delhi continues to deny that it has a program to build nuclear weapons or a delivery system. Nevertheless, it has refused to sign the nuclear non-proliferation treaty and it clearly has the potential in a fairly short time to develop a weapon and means to deliver it. So far, however, it has resisted the temptation to build the *force de frappe* which would put it, together with China, Britain, and France, in the league of secondary world powers, but which could also double or triple its per capita spending on the military.

While China intends to remain a competitor in the second rank of strategic powers, it is clear that Peking has significantly downgraded the priority of military spending and preparation for early nuclear war. In 1985 not only were hundreds of thousands of soldiers in the process of being discharged but some defense industries were switching to the production not of plowshares, but of mopeds and televisions. That year, military factories turned out about $1 billion worth of civilian goods, more than four times the amount in 1984.

Deng and his colleagues seemed determined to have a leaner, more modern and more effective defense establishment. The human wave was to become a modern army. Since 1985, in addition to the severe thinning of the ranks, thousands of older officers have retired, the operational and training commands have been drastically reorganized, the defense doctrine recast to emphasize a conventional forward defense, spiffy, if disappointing, new uniforms issued, and formal ranks set to be resumed in 1987.

Like the PLA, the Indian army, tied down in the Punjab and other areas of unrest, wants to be relieved of internal security matters so that it can concentrate on modernizing its forces to deal with potential foreign enemies, i.e., China and Pakistan. Rajiv Gandhi has promised more paramilitary forces to handle internal chores. Meanwhile, Indian naval strategies not only seek the capability to defend the nation's long coast line but also to establish India as the major power in the Indian Ocean. The navy is pushing for a third carrier to achieve this goal. Overall, like the Chinese, the Indian military hopes to keep expenditures down while increasing firepower, mobility, intelligence, and command and control.

Foreign Aid

The economic and technical assistance programs that India and China have carried out in the Third World also indicate the commitment of both countries to asserting strong leadership abroad. India and China, although ranking among the poorest countries, have each provided aid to certain nations with higher per capita incomes than their own, but India has done this less than China. India's total loans and grants to other countries through 1982–1983 totaled $1.8 billion, over 80 percent of which went to India's immediate neighbors—Bangladesh, Bhutan, Burma, Nepal, and Sri Lanka—all of whom rank even lower than India in per capita income. The next largest recipient has been Vietnam, which, as of March 1983, had been authorized Indian loans and grants totalling $115.5 million.

China, on the other hand, from 1961–1977 extended $7.5 billion in economic and technical assistance to a wide range of countries from Albania to Zaire. In terms of per capita spending on winning friends abroad China has forked out three times as much as India. In 1981 and 1982 China's aid to the Third World sharply diminished, reflecting a pragmatic concentration on China's own development, but over the next three years China averaged over $300 million a year in aid commitments.

The 1962 War and Polarization

A survey of the last two decades of the foreign affairs of the two countries reflects their separate styles in dealing with the world and each other.

China's actions against India in 1962 were part of Peking's rapidly worsening relations with Moscow and the related radicalization of Chinese foreign policy, a radicalization aimed at challenging both superpowers and building a revolutionary world constituency for the PRC.

Whatever India's mistakes, complacency and missed opportunities leading up to the 1962 border war—and there were plenty of each—the scale of the Chinese response was, to say the least, inordinate. Peking had other forceful but more limited options in protecting its strategic road in Ladakh and in reacting to the Indian policy of pushing forward with outposts and patrols in disputed areas. The Chinese decision to launch a major military blow at the Indians and then in most areas to pull back to previously occupied lines appeared intended by Mao to demonstrate to the Soviets the efficacy of a tough posture toward bourgeois adversaries, and to put Moscow in the dilemma of either backing or deserting its Chinese ally. Khrushchev chose not to support Peking, and Sino-Soviet polemics grew increasingly heated.

Sweeping the out-gunned and out-manned Indian army off the Himalayas and then withdrawing pretty much back to where they had begun did not result in any significant tactical or political gain for Peking; likewise, in Ladakh the Chinese had previously occupied the territory that gave access to Tibet and presumably was, and still is, their major strategic concern. Taking over additional parts of the desolate high plateau was of limited military and political utility. The strong Chinese action only served to stir up hostility in India and to make efforts to reach a negotiated settlement of the border problem impossible for more than two decades. More importantly, it provoked New Delhi to turn first to the U.S. for military aid and, eventually, to the USSR.

After the 1962 debacle, India launched a campaign to build up its military forces. Following the 1965 U.S. arms embargo on both India and Pakistan, the Soviets were happy to fill the vacuum with increasingly large-scale military sales to New Delhi and joint production arrangements for the manufacture of defense equipment. In addition, the Soviets, no longer supplying economic aid to China, poured more development assistance into India, primarily in heavy industry. "The great game" in South Asia became primarily a Sino-Soviet affair, with each supporting a surrogate.

Moscow viewed its heavy investment in India in terms of isolating and encircling China, and at the same time out-flanking U.S. moves to block Soviet influence in South and Central Asia. Of course, Moscow, like Washington, also pursued good relations with India because it was an important Third World country occupying almost the whole of a subcontinent. But both super-powers shaped their policies toward India—and Pakistan—largely in response to their own strategic and political rivalry and to changes in their respective relations with China.

After the 1965 war and up to 1971 the U.S. adopted a low posture in the area. Political relations with India were exacerbated by issues like Vietnam, Czechoslovakia, Mrs. Gandhi's ideological attacks on Washington, and U.S. relations with Pakistan. The Soviets and the Americans, however, both kept options open in the area. Moscow mediated the end of the 1965 Indo-Pakistani War, provided some arms to Pakistan, and also failed to endorse Indian claims on the Sino-Indian border. Meanwhile, even through years of strain in bilateral U.S.–Indian relations, Washington continued to be a major aid contributor to India via multilateral organizations such as the World Bank. As of 1981, U.S. total direct economic assistance to India, including development loans and commodity sales for local currency, came to over $12 billion.

The U.S. continued to aid India, directly and indirectly, because it had no basic conflict of interest with New Delhi and it recognized the long-term American stake in democratic Indian development and stability. Moreover, India, despite its economic, military, and treaty relations with Moscow, retained its independence of action and did not provide military facilities or in other ways become directly involved in the Soviet security system. Mrs. Gandhi, for example, rejected the Soviet offer to mediate a settlement with Pakistan after the 1971 conflict, she placed restrictions on the proliferation of Soviet cultural centers in India, and while continuing to rely primarily on Soviet weapons she also purchased arms in Western Europe.

The Tectonic Changes of 1971

In 1971, the strategic scene in Asia took several sharp and unexpected turns. In sudden strokes India and China each achieved a greater degree of regional ascendancy and national security than they had won in more than two decades of diplomatic and military action.

Henry Kissinger's visit to Peking in 1971 meant the end of U.S. efforts to isolate China and contain its regional and world influence. For the first time, the Chinese regime would not perceive the U.S. as a near-term military threat and all the countries of the East Asian region, except Vietnam and its future satellites in Indochina, would put good relations with China as a top priority. While Japan would remain economic king, the world would accept China as the political and military power of East Asia.

Likewise, India's military victory in 1971 and the internationally accepted division of Pakistan accorded India an unchallenged position in South Asia. New Delhi would continue to view truncated Pakistan as a military threat, particularly following the 1981 U.S. agreement to sell F–16 fighters to Islamabad; but, after 1971, Pakistan could only pose a serious military challenge to India in conjunction with an attack by one of the powers or China. And any such attack seemed increasingly unlikely.

In the 1980s, India and China were still enjoying the benefits of these geopolitical movements which, like sudden tectonic shifts, had realigned the political landscape. One result was that the environment of Sino-Indian relations would improve to the point that in 1981 New Delhi and Peking, for the first time in 20 years, would be able to sit down and discuss their border dispute. But the immediate result of the dramatic developments of 1971 was increased, rather than reduced, tension between the two Asian neighbors. Each saw the other's actions at that time as threatening its own vital interests.

Eventually, this perspective would change, but in 1971, the U.S. and China were fulminating helplessly as India, swamped with millions of refugees from then East Pakistan, and clutching a new treaty with the Soviets, proceeded to put the *coup de grace* to greater Pakistan. At the same time, India was quietly sulking over U.S.-China rapprochement, seeing dark implications. Mrs. Gandhi may have been more moved by events in Peking than those in East Pakistan in formalizing the Soviet treaty which had been ready for signing since April. Apparently Mrs. Gandhi did not believe the treaty was necessary to ward off direct military counter-moves by either China or the U.S.[170] Instead, it was the price of a long term Soviet commitment.

The developments of 1971 revealed the inner relationship of U.S., Soviet, Chinese, and Indian foreign policies, but also the essentially peripheral role of India in the maneuverings of the other three. China accepted the U.S. overtures for detente for many reasons: to free itself from the unenviable position of having hostile relations with both super-powers at the same time; to counter continuing Soviet threats on the Sino-Soviet border; to gain long-term leverage over both the Soviet Union and the U.S.; to encourage a stable balance of power in East Asia; to cause the U.S. to abandon its isolation and containment policies in regard to China; and to win U.S. concessions on the Taiwan issue. Peking also expected that rapprochement with the U.S. would facilitate the end of the Vietnam War, end hostilities on China's borders, and allow U.S.-Soviet contention to shift to the Middle East and other areas far removed from China.

India was not an important consideration in either the American or the Chinese approach to U.S.-China detente. New Delhi, however, tended to see the dramatic development to the north in light of its own interests and to exaggerate India's importance in the geopolitics of the great powers and China. Some Indians feared that one of the goals of the new Sino-American entente would be to contain and weaken India. In any event, as Peking and Washington were both friends of Islamabad, their reconciliation could only give Pakistan a psychological boost as a new and critical period of Indo-Pakistani tension was emerging in 1971. This was true even though the U.S. had ended its military and economic aid to Pakistan as tensions increased on the subcontinent. India's acceptance that year of a quasi-alliance relationship with the Soviet Union ran counter to a basic Indian foreign policy objective of non-alignment and balance in its relations with the super-powers, but apparently the winning argument in New Delhi was that the Soviet pact was a necessary geo-political move and secondarily was welcome insurance to cover the forthcoming Indian intervention in the Pakistan civil war.

The 1971 Indo-Pakistani war was the first time China and the Soviet Union were clearly on opposite sides of a conflict within the Third World, and the first such conflict in which China and the U.S. took the same position. While the U.S., and even more strongly China, may have perceived a geopolitical stake in the unity of a strong Pakistan, the Pakistan civil war and the threat of the division of Pakistan was not the real cause of concern in Washington or Peking; rather, it was their perception of a Soviet power play in backing India. Neither the U.S. nor China, however, was willing or able to bail Islamabad out of its predicament. The U.S. did send the carrier *Enterprise* steaming into the Indian Ocean—as it had done in support of India against China nine years before.

Whether or not such a ploy was unnecessary posturing is debatable. But the decision was also shaped, in part, by Washington's desire to make some show of force to divert attention from the Indian and, indirectly, the Soviet victory in East Pakistan. In addition, Nixon and Kissinger believed that to assure success of their initiative with China in 1971 it was important to demonstrate not only that the U.S. did not threaten China, but also that it was a reliable partner, determined to counter Soviet moves.

Shifting Sands of the Seventies

After the events of 1971 geopolitics in Asia continued to evolve in twists and turns. Mrs. Gandhi declared an emergency in 1975 and assumed autocratic powers. Two years later she startled the nation by calling for a free election, which she promptly lost, only to return victorious and vindicated in 1980. Meanwhile, in 1973, Deng Xiaoping returned to the Peking scene but was purged again after the 1975 death of Zhou Enlai. Mao went to his reward the next year; the "Gang of Four" were wrapped up, and Deng enjoyed another political rebirth. By 1980 he had elbowed aside Mao's chosen successor, Hua Guofeng, in favor of Deng proteges, Zhao Ziyang and Hu Yaobang. Nixon visited Peking in 1972 and three years later Hanoi swept to victory in South Vietnam, and the U.S. ambassador and his staff fled the scene in helicopters. The brutal Pol Pot seized Cambodia but soon began to bite the Vietnamese hand that had fed him. In 1978, Vietnam took the opportunity not only to knock down Pol Pot but also to occupy all of Cambodia, and the next year the Chinese People's Liberation Army in response administered a "lesson" to Vietnam, costly to both, and a long anti-Vietnamese resistance in Cambodia began. The Soviets gained the use of base facilities in Vietnam and Soviet military deployments throughout East Asia and the Pacific continued to grow. On the subcontinent, India set off a "peaceful" nuclear explosion in 1974, and at the end of 1979 Soviet troops invaded Afghanistan, three million refugees fled to Pakistan, and the Afghans dug in for a long guerrilla war.

Through it all, India's preoccupations remained regional and its link with the USSR primary, while China's attentions were global and its tilt, despite occasional wobbles, was still decidedly toward the US. At the same time, both New Delhi and Peking continued whenever possible to seek the middle ground between the superpowers in order to maximize their leverage and independence as well as their non-aligned images.

Even under the conservative Janata government, India viewed the Soviet Union as its most reliable supporter, and likewise, after the advent of the

Reagan Administration, China still saw the United States as a de facto ally against the USSR. Moscow was a more reliable friend of India because close relations with New Delhi served Soviet geopolitical interests vis-a-vis China and the U.S. Washington, likewise concentrating on its superpower rival, gave priority to its relations with Pakistan and China, both of whom felt threatened by Moscow, over concern for Indian interests. Thus the Chinese Marxist, Deng Xiaoping, viewed informal strategic cooperation with the U.S. as vital to China's interests, while the Indian social democrat, Indira Gandhi, saw Soviet support for India's security and regional preeminence as critical for the indefinite future.

Mrs. Ghandhi, however, recognized the need to maintain a balance where possible in the security field and to assure some alternative sources of military equipment. For this she looked to Western Europe. Her son restored even more balance to the equation, visiting Washington and Moscow within a year of taking office and in 1986 entertaining in Delhi U.S. Defense Secretary Weinberger and then Gorbachev. The young Indian leader refused to endorse Moscow's Asian collective security idea, but because the Soviets offered unbeatable prices signed up to purchase and produce under license the MiG 29.

Nevertheless, under Rajiv, the Soviet Union's share of India's total military purchases abroad declined significantly. The new prime minister believed that Western not Soviet technology held the secret to Indian development. By the end of 1986 the way seemed clear for India's purchase of a U.S. super computer and an advanced jet engine. But still, like his mother, Rajiv could not consider America to be a reliable long-term supplier because of Washington's ties to Pakistan and China and the idiosyncracies of the U.S. Congress.

Deng Xiaoping and Indira Gandhi

Deng is a peculiar figure in China. He does not have the mien of an emperor or a Mao and he can hardly be said to be charismatic. He is the anti-Mao, no more than five feet tall, French educated and upper class, skilled at the spittoon and bridge, and capable of downing eight or more glasses of high octane mai tai at lunch and carrying on with business in the afternoon. He is not revered in China as was Mao nor held in great affection as was Zhou Enlai. But he is no doubt the most admired man in China today, respected for his vigor, tenacity, integrity, and candor. Above all, however, it is his no nonsense practicality that has made him a popular leader among the Chinese, who are still recovering from their ideological binge with Mao.

While Deng could easily be taken for a Sichuan peasant, Indira Gandhi was a handsome even classically beautiful woman. Only a few generations back the roots of Deng's family tree disappear into the "good earth" of China. Mrs. Gandhi's family, however, has been upper caste since time immemorial. The Kashmir brahmans, including the Nehrus, consider themselves the most urbane and clever of all the brahmans, and thus it is no surprise that Mrs. Gandhi shared with Deng a certain authoritarian nature. She was extremely charming but always aloof. Deng, on the other hand, is highly convivial and spontaneous. Mrs. Gandhi liked music and sculpture and followed developments in all the arts. She also remained sincerely religious and consulted astrologers and gurus. Aside from an occasional Peking opera and a hand of cards, Deng is not known to have any great cultural or spiritual proclivities or for that matter any major interests other than politics and his family. The latter affection was portrayed in a 1984 article by Deng's daughter, who described the family's exile in the early 1970s in an unheated house in Jiangxi province.

Like Deng, Nehru's daughter and only child studied abroad but did not complete her university studies. Both Deng and Indira Gandhi returned to work in their respective national movements. Each eventually bore a badge of honor: Deng went on the "Long March" with Mao, and Mrs. Gandhi was imprisoned by the British.

Indira's leader and mentor was also her father. Jawaharlal, however, had little time for familial affection and he remained for Indira a Mao-like, remote father figure. She inherited her father's political acumen but not his charisma, and she assumed a different relationship with her people. Like Deng, she was admired or held in awe, but not adored, at least not until her last years.

Both Deng and Mrs. Gandhi knew the political wilderness and family tragedy. Deng was purged twice and most of his friends were sacked in disgrace and humiliated or killed during the Cultural Revolution. Deng's son was thrown from a fourth floor window and remains a quadriplegic today. Thus Deng understands better than most the tragedy of utopian visions relentlessly pursued. Mrs. Gandhi also made a remarkable comeback from political oblivion, but the same year her son and heir-apparent, Sanjay, was killed in a stunt plane he was piloting. Determined to continue the Nehru dynasty, Mrs. Gandhi groomed her eldest son, Rajiv, a former airline pilot, to succeed her. Paradoxically even if Deng wished to have a relative assume the future leadership of China, such a grand stroke of nepotism would not be possible in the People's Republic today. Like Mao, Mrs. Gandhi in her later years came to identify herself intimately with the fate of the nation. Having no particular ideology to bequeath, she turned to familial succession. Deng, on the other hand, seems satisfied to leave behind a rational political and economic basis for a modern and prosperous socialist China.

Mao was the heir of the ancient Legalists like Qin Shi Huang. Deng, to some extent, is, like Hu Yaobang, a descendant of the Confucian innovators of the Sung Dynasty. But while Hu, per force, rode the wave of bold liberalization, Deng has been a dynamic but essentially pragmatic reformer who continued to give high priority to control and order and thus to rationalization of the Party's power through formal adherence to the old moral order—Marxism.

Thus Deng can also be compared to Zhang Zhitong (Chang Chih-tung), a moderate reformer statesman in the last days of the Manchu Dynasty who advocated retaining Chinese and Confucian "substance" and values while adopting Western "functions"—practical methods, science, etc.

After the ouster of Hu Yaobang in early 1987, three secret Party documents revealed that Deng's liberal attitudes on economic matters and on China's opening to the world for technology and investment did not extend to the cultural much less the political realm. The documents, which in an unprecedented and puzzling move were read to foreign reporters, may in part have been intended to counter pressure from the neo-Maoists. But they also reflected Deng's strong belief that pragmatism for China over the next several decades meant not only drastic reform of the economic system but also knocking serious political dissidents in the head.

In one of the documents, Deng reportedly praised the leaders of Poland for adopting a firm attitude in the face of opposition from the Solidarity movement and the Roman Catholic Church. "They adopted martial law and controlled the situation," Deng said. "That shows that if we don't use dictatorial methods it won't do. We must not only talk about dictatorial methods but also practice them."

Historical parallels are not so evident in India where models of political leadership or philosophy were not, as in China, subjects of scholarship and fascination. While Mahatma Ghandi was in the tradition of the holy man, Nehru, the strong but idealistic unifier of India, was perhaps the modern equivalent of the first emperor and Buddhist convert, Asoka. Nehru's faith was Fabian Socialism and parliamentary democracy. Some say he was the last Englishman to rule India.

Indira Ghandi, however, brings to mind Kautiliya, the wily and pragmatic fourth century minister who wrote the famous *Arthastra*, the Machiavellian Indian tome of statecraft as an artful game.

Mrs. Gandhi was well practiced at socialist rhetoric just as Deng can ardently praise Marxism and "Chinese socialism." But she and Deng both ruled at a time when slogans had been worn out and panaceas had little credibility. Indira was accused by domestic critics of lacking a systematic ideological or philosophical framework for either internal or foreign policy. Likewise, Deng's preference for cats, whatever their color, that catch mice, as well as his pursuit of good relations with the U.S., evoked mutterings of ideological heresy. Deng attacked "bourgeois liberalism" not because he was philosophically opposed to it, but because he was convinced Western democracy would not work in China but result in chaos.

The efficacy of Mrs. Gandhi's domestic posture, leftist in image but pragmatic in practice, led her to development of a similar approach in foreign affairs. It was the instinctive stance of a skilled and experienced politician. Henry Kissinger described Mrs. Gandhi as a "cold-blooded practitioner of power politics." Her interests and her values, despite occasional errors of judging the point of maximum leverage, he said, were inseparable.

India's neutral and independent policy at times seemed threatened by Mrs. Gandhi's latent and sometimes active hostility toward the West and capitalism. This attitude manifested itself in seemingly gratuitous slaps at the U.S. and unnecessary endorsements of Soviet actions. But Mrs. Gandhi's friendship for Moscow was essentially non-ideological. She would not have sent her children or grandchildren to school in the USSR. Nevertheless, she saw the Soviets backing India's regional policies, supporting its defense, and providing economic aid while asking little in return. On the other hand, she regarded the U.S. as at best an unpredictable and inconstant friend and at worse a consistent backer of India's principal foes.

Deng's assessment of the superpowers is also a hard-headed one, but it is shaped by a broader *Weltanschauung*. Deng perceives that the central reality of world politics is the Soviet drive to dominate Eurasia while laying down markers of Soviet power in the Third World margins of the board. He recognizes that for the indefinite future global equilibrium will depend in large part on U.S. power and will and the viability of U.S. alliances in Asia and Europe. While Deng has rhetorically distanced China from the U.S. since the advent of the Reagan administration, his basic strategic assumptions have changed little. Deng, however, does not see China's security now or in the future as dependent on U.S. cooperation or assistance. While interested in the possibility of obtaining U.S. military technology to assist in modernization of the PLA, he is determined to retain China's basic self-sufficiency in defense. He believes that for such an enormous country as China there is no realistic security alternative to self reliance. Mrs. Gandhi also was determined that India stand independent of any power, and as Deng has tried to reduce tensions with Moscow, she sought where possible to improve relations with Washington.

CHAPTER 17

Stereotypes and Images

Looking at Each Other

Today the interests of China and India in each other are reversed from that of the Tang Dynasty. Indians view China as their strongest potential enemy, but they are also fascinated by this even more populous country than their own, which usually maintains such order and which seems to move ahead in so many fields. As Chinese pilgrims were drawn to India 1,300 years ago, some Indian leftists have been pulled to the Chinese communist model. The revolutionary Indian Naxalites still worship Mao as the font of all wisdom. In Peking there are two or three relatively moribund centers for the study of South Asian or Indian affairs. Chinese studies in India are hardly prominent but there certainly is much more study of China in India than vice versa. Many Indian scholars, but to my knowledge no Chinese, have made comparative economic studies of the two nations; if the Chinese should do so, the results would not likely be favorable to India. Many of the Indian studies on China, on the other hand, are quite favorable to China.[171]

We have seen that in the cosmopolitan Tang Period, Chinese were interested not only in Indian religion, but in its culture, including its food. Today, every major Indian city has one or more Chinese restaurants. In China there is only one known South Asian restaurant, in Peking, and this is in a hotel for foreigners. Many Indian commercial films are shown in China, but this is because they are inexpensive and their stereotyped stories meet Chinese moral standards.

There are several thousand overseas Chinese living in Calcutta and other big Indian cities, but unlike the old days when large groups of Indian Buddhist missionaries resided in China, today there is no Indian community on the mainland.

In short, Chinese today are intellectually not very interested in India. They are much more keen on figuring out Japan, the United States, and European countries, somewhat in that order. When Indians think of China they think of monolithic power and great numbers. When the Chinese think of India they conjure up visions of religious fervor and frequent disorder, conditions of little interest to Chinese, traditionally or today.

American Views of India and China

Americans for their part remain much more fascinated with China than with India. In China, where most news comes out of government releases or in the *People's Daily*, foreign correspondents beat the bushes to find something off-beat or unusual to report. In India, politics and society present a circus of news. The bizarre is commonplace. Yet there are many more American news media with a bureau in Peking than in New Delhi. The majority of American correspondents in China are also handicapped by a lack of any usable level of Chinese language. Communication and reporting in India is facilitated by the wide knowledge of English among the educated population; still, the *New York Times* carries more articles on China than on India, and the Harvard bookstore in Cambridge, Massachusetts, has several times the number of books on China as it does on India. Likewise more Americans trod the tourist trails of China than go to India.

Part of the explanation for America's fascination with China lies in its deep involvement with that country over the past 200 years and its rather peripheral role in India. U.S. traders, missionaries, sailors, and diplomats imprinted strong images of China on the American consciousness. India was in the sphere of the British, who made sure there was as little commerce as possible between the sub-continent and the U.S. In the early 1800s an American merchant ship venturing up to Calcutta was chased out of the Hooghly River and back to sea by the English. Later, American merchantmen did take part in the opium trade from India.

There were large numbers of American missionaries in India (about 2,500 at their maximum in the 1920s), but somehow they did not make as much impact on the folks back home. Indians also did not emigrate to the United States in any numbers in the nineteenth and early twentieth century, and, while Chinatowns were exotic outposts in American cities, Americans were much more familiar with Chinese than with Indians.

Americans have also seen China as looming much larger on the political stage of the world; even in the nineteenth century China was viewed as the sleeping giant of Asia who eventually would shake the world. And, in the twentieth century, the American hope was that China, "the sick man of Asia," would be able to regain his health and vigor and thereby balance Japan. With the communist takeover, the awakened dragon suddenly turned threatening and more powerful than anticipated. India, on the other hand, was generally viewed as permanently moribund and after its emergence on the world stage was not seen as threatening but as irritatingly evangelical and self-righteous.

In 1958 Harold Issacs' classic book, *Scratches on Our Mind*, described nineteenth and twentieth century American images of China and India up to and including the first postwar decade.[172] When Americans in the 1950s thought of India it was as an ambivalent but essentially monstrous stereotype that conjured up images of maharajas, bejeweled elephants, the Taj Mahal, fakirs, and Mahatma Gandhi on the one hand; and on the other a concurrent vision of cobras, beggars, and a torpid listless mass. China occupied a much more "special place" in a great many American minds. The American image of China has altered over the years and also at any one time differed among individuals and groups. Nevertheless, positive associations like China clippers, "the open door," the returned indemnity, *The Good Earth*, and *The Burma Road* dominated the American image of China. Even when China was "lost" and quite unexpectedly our relations with the Chinese government had become bitter and hostile, Americans in 1958 still regarded the Chinese people as "most attractive . . . down to earth . . . practical, good, vigorous, industrious . . . dynamic . . . cheerful" and so on.[173]

As Isaacs recounts, there were numerous dark sides to the American view of China and of Chinese, as well as periods of contempt by a large portion of the American public when their expectations were unfulfilled. Nevertheless, there is a remarkable continuity in the American habit of thinking fondly of China or at least of the Chinese, while they have usually been shocked or bedazzled by India.

In his 1958 study Isaacs found 70 percent of his panel of 181 successful and educated Americans expressed predominantly positive or admiring views of Chinese, and only 18 percent "disliked" Chinese. Fifty-four percent of the same group, however, expressed strongly negative views about Indians and only 30 percent admired or liked Indians. Even more interesting, 12 of 16 China specialists on the panel were strongly positive about the Chinese, 4 were "mixed," and none was negative. Of the 25 India specialists, only 9 were positive about Indians, 9 negative, and 7 mixed.[174]

Isaacs suggests that Confucian-bred skills in human relations, including a high degree of courtesy and sensitivity, have made the Chinese attractive and charming to foreigners, particularly Americans. The system of "face" and showing deference was intended to keep relations formal and harmonious while avoiding deep commitment or revealing one's inner self, but it often led disillusioned Americans to charge insincerity and deviousness.[175] Over the long term, however, Chinese charm hardly ever fails to work on the emotionally more open and relatively idealistic Americans. In addition, some of the most positive traits that Americans see in Chinese are virtues that Americans also recognize in themselves: hard working, pragmatic, materialistic, and honest.

In contrast, as Isaacs suggests, some of the negative traits Americans see in Indians are ones that others, such as Europeans, often find in Americans, such as: intellectual aggressiveness, unmannerly brashness, a know-it-all arrogance, and moral self-righteousness. Moreover, we have observed that Indians, like Americans, self-consciously seek approval from others and, while each society engages in sharp self-criticism, each resents criticism from outsiders. Thus Indians, sensitive about the existence of caste and other social evils in their country, lash out at "vulgar" America and its racial problems.[176]

Hierarchical Indian culture did not emphasize surface civility and matters of face except with one's own family, clan, and caste. Toward caste superiors one is of course dutifully respectful but those lower in the pecking order could be treated with little regard for their self-esteem or for the need to retain interpersonal harmony. Indians can thus be frank to the point of gaucheness.

The upper caste Indian with his British education also tended to inherit high brow English prejudices about Americans. The first generation of political leaders like Nehru were not only infected with a bit of British snobbery but as Fabian socialists also shared a leftist disdain for the fountainhead of capitalism.

Chinese intellectuals of the same period, on the other hand, were very much influenced by American education and American democracy. Although China and the U.S. fought a war in the early 1950s and Chinese propaganda for 20 years virulently denounced "American imperialists" and virtually everything Americans had ever done in China, most educated Chinese still retained a favorable impression of Americans. The American involvement in education in pre-revolutionary China, the U.S. help for China in the war against Japan, the substantial emigration of Chinese to the U.S., and the widespread view in China of the United States as the land of milk and honey kept the Sino-American romance a two-way affair that persisted even through tough years of official hostility. Chinese today still seem basically to like Americans, including their informality, practicality, and straight-forwardness. At the same time, there is a growing rapport between Indians and Americans. The new generation of Indian intellectuals are less influenced by the secondhand British view of the Yanks. Some new Indian political leaders are themselves more like Americans than Englishmen. The two movie star chief ministers and Mrs. Gandhi's sons, Sanjay and Rajiv, are good examples. Most of the elite now have relatives in the United States.

While in general having a greater personal affinity for Chinese, or for what they think Chinese are like, the average American likes India as a nation better than China. According to a 1983 Gallup Poll, on a scale of 1 to 7 with 1 representing most disliked foreign country and 7 most liked, Americans rated India 4.3 over China's 4.0. The preference for India presumably reflects an appreciation of its democratic system compared to China's communist society. In the 1950s and 1960s, India would probably have ranked even higher over China.

The perception of strength is a major element in a nation's image that influences foreign views of its people. In this sense, India's image has grown in the U.S. since the 1950s; but Americans have been more deeply impressed with China's expanding power. The coverage of the two countries in the U.S. press suggests this is true. With the vanishing of the maharajas and even their privy purses, the opulent aspect of India's image has faded, but the remarkable resilience of Indian democracy has made an impact among informed Americans. India's defeat of Pakistan, its nuclear explosion, its attainment of basic self-sufficiency in food, and its space satellites and nuclear power plants have revealed an India much stronger than imagined. This has sunk in to some extent, but the great majority of Americans still associate India primarily with poverty and a rip-roaring flood of population. The 1982 film *Gandhi* heightened the popular image in the U.S. of Indians as highly civilized, intelligent, and religious, but it also etched deeper the picture of poor, teeming masses.

In 1985, tens of millions of Americans lined up to see David Lean's beautiful rendition of *Passage to India.* At the same time, even more were tuning in their TVs every Sunday night to the 15 part Grenada production "Jewel in the Crown," a compression of Paul Scott's magnificent *Raj Quartet.* In both dramas Indians are portrayed as noble and cultivated, although curiously forbearing of imperial idiocy. Both productions were essentially British drawing room soap operas. In "Jewel in the Crown" the mean spirited English were all middle-class—either upper or lower case—while the really upstairs characters were treated with due reverence. Oddly enough, the two stories used the same type of event—an Indian unjustly accused of raping a British woman—as their center piece, presumably symbolic of England's passionate love-hate affair with India. In any event, the two films suggested we had come a long way since "Gunga Din."

The Indian image today is also shaped by the practice of Hindu sects in the U.S. such as Hare Krishna and Transcendental Meditation. These groups wax and wane, some appealing to hedonist as well as spiritual needs. There is something in the human soul that longs for a sense of religious or political mission. It is a pursuit that often transcends content. The utopian has a special appeal to the idealism of Americans who believe in progress and often thirst for the panacea. Thus the attraction of Maharishi, who through meditation can levitate, raise the stock market, or prevent war; and alternatively of Mao, the political yogi.

In different ways India and China have appealed to the American demand for solutions. Usually Americans seek to engineer their way out of problems. (Only the U.S. could have found a mechanical answer to impotency—the goose-neck appliance.) But a few years ago a good number of Americans eagerly accepted that Nirvana could be achieved—at least in China—through the politics and violence of Maoism, while today the trend is to embrace the cult of some Rolls Royce-conveyed guru as the way to enlightenment.

Our opinion of foreign governments can alter the popular view we have of the people concerned; but the status of U.S. relations with India and China and their respective ideologies seems to have even less influence today than in the past on our ethnic stereotypes. Isaacs' study was made at a time of deep animosity in Sino-American relations, but this did not affect the favorable view of Chinese which he reported. Perhaps in part this was because there were "good Chinese" in Taiwan, Hong Kong, and Singapore, not to speak of the United States.

Meanwhile, the American affair with China, as with any great romance, continues to be mercurial. China "lost" has been regained. As in the past, the reconciliation has led to exaggerated expectations and, in some quarters, disillusionment once again. Isaacs recounts the backlash, particularly among liberal Americans, during the Second World War when it was discovered that the noble Chinese ally was corrupt and unreliable, and that the country was full of squalor, filth, and ignorance. A notable example was Leland Stowe, a correspondent of "liberal and crusading impulses," who confessed to having had romantic notions about China before he discovered its "dark blotches and its darker side."[177]

Similarly, after a long period in the 1970s of favorable books and reporting on China by Americans who often bent over backward to excuse or ignore shortcomings, a new disillusionment was encountered in 1982 when U.S. correspondents and writers, again mostly of liberal persuasion, discovered the dark side of communist China. News of the existence of corruption, deprivation, and political authoritarianism in the new China was hardly a revelation, but books like Fox Butterfield's *China: Alive in the Bitter Sea* and Richard Bernstein's *China: A Message from the Center of the Earth*, provoked a great deal of breast-beating about how Americans had been misled and beguiled.

The Cambridge, Massachusetts–based Ross Terrill wrote several popular books on China in the 1970s, including the best selling *800,000,000: The Real China*. Terrill was originally optimistic that China could "push through the straitjacket of a communist political system." By 1983, however, he had sadly concluded that China is "first and foremost a repressive regime" and that "the dead hand of Leninism was not likely ever to be removed."[178]

Typical of "The God That Failed" school of American Sinophiles is Orville Schell. Schell spent several months in China in 1975 and even at that late date came away impressed with Mao's discovery of the secrets of a non-materialistic society. In his book *In the People's Republic of China*, Schell exhibited the articulate gullibility of many contemporaries, noting only some "ominious tendencies" beneath the surface. Ten years later, it became clear to Schell that the Chinese who had seemed happy enough at the time had actually been frozen into "a combination of fear and socialist rectitude."

But Schell is not pleased with what he sees in China today—materialism. Thus, he has ventured forth once again to instruct Americans and others about what is happening in the real China. His latest book, *To Get Rich Is Glorious: China in the Eighties*, posits that the move away from collectivism and the opening to the West represents a loss of China's "national essence." Schell seems in effect to prefer that China remain poor, backward, and isolated rather than see it deal with the inevitable corruption, abuses, and social illness that come with a more open society and dynamic economy.

The current dismay of some Western liberals with China is ironic, as it has come at a time when the human rights situation in the People's Republic is much improved over that of the 1960s and early 1970s. China in fact appears tenatively to be on the path of transition from a totalitarian to an authoritarian and more pluralistic society. But that may be just the point. Liberal intellectuals in the West often hate authoritarian regimes, even of the left, more than they do totalitarian ones.

The recent crisis of disillusionment, however, seems much more limited than that of the 1940s. One reason is that, in the earlier period, the perception of weakness and ineptness was a large part of the American sense of frustration with China. But by the late 1950s this image had changed and by the 1980s the perception of China's growing national strength had moved ahead markedly. China's intercontinental ballistic missile test, its nuclear explosions and space shots, as well as the sense of a billion well-ordered, mostly well-fed and disciplined people, engenders considerable respect. There is also a healthy recognition among most Americans of the vital importance to peace in Asia and in the world of stable and cooperative relations between the U.S. and China. The danger to this new relationship lies in the possibility, hopefully remote, of another radicalization of Chinese politics or of a U.S. failure to continue to deal subtly and flexibly with issues that touch on Chinese sovereignty—most particularly, the question of Taiwan.

With India the danger is America's underestimation of the country's long-term importance globally as well as regionally and its inevitable strength. When India becomes the most populous country in the world sometime in the twenty-first century, historians will view the fate of Indian democracy—whatever it may have been—as one of the truly great milestones in the movement of world culture. They will also note the irony of the ill-will that existed between the two greatest democracies in the latter part of the twentieth century. Presumably they will see this paradox as yet another proof that democracies can have clashing national interests just as communist countries can become bitter enemies.

But cause and effect are often illogical in history. Those who pursue the paradox of U.S.–India relations may conclude that the result was beneficial. India's quasi-alliance with the Soviet Union insulates its moderate democratic government in some ways from internal radicalism. The Soviet Union may be a quasi-ally of India, but the U.S. and the West continue to provide most of India's economic assistance, investment capital, and markets. This is probably a more viable and productive arrangement for India than if it were diplomatically and militarily closer to the U.S.

The latter alignment would also tend to polarize the four most populous countries of the world on an ideological axis. If the U.S. had sided strongly with India in its disputes with Pakistan, one wonders how Sino-U.S. and Sino-Soviet relations would have developed. Over the long term, India and China, who share the most densely populated corner of the world, will always tend toward a rival relationship and thus each will seek a security link with a different superpower. Because events have led India to seek association with the USSR, this has contributed in some degree to China's link with the U.S.—a link that fosters moderate and pragmatic policies in Peking, provides the foundation of stability in East Asia, and contributes significantly to a world balance of forces unfavorable to Moscow.

In addition, Indians, like Americans, are idealists and want to be loved; Chinese, like the Soviets, are materialists and want to be held in awe. Perhaps that is why neither Indians and Americans on the one hand, nor Chinese and Soviets on the other have made good matches.

CHAPTER 18

Prospects for the Future

Pluralism and Pragmatism

China is the supreme political society, but its contributions to political development since 1949 have not been great successes. Perhaps in the long Chinese sense of history this has only been a teething period and the new order will eventually evolve a more creative political synthesis of Marxism and Chinese tradition. So far, however, the PRC's experimental departures have, by the account of the Chinese themselves, mostly been debacles. The hundred flowers, the continuing revolution in the superstructure, rural communes as both political and economic organizations, revolutionary committees, big character posters, worker-soldier-peasant-students, cadre labor, rustification of youth, struggle campaigns, and other Mao inventions have been discarded on to the garbage barge of history.

India also has had its debacles, and structural reforms in India have only partially succeeded, like land reform and the Community Development Program; or they are dormant, like the village panchayats; or they have not worked, like the legislative elimination of discrimination against untouchables and of dowries; or to some extent they have even had the opposite effect of that intended, like some programs to help the landless poor. Still, India in the midst of its ordeal has given birth to a remarkable political achievement. It has proved that freedom of expression, populist politics, the right of dissent, and representative government are not the monopoly of rich nations. Indian democracy is still evolving and, if it survives, will be doing so for generations to come, but it already has distinct qualities. Its achievements cannot be a precise model to others because they have grown out of the peculiarities and necessities of Indian life. Nevertheless, the Indian experience has a clear philosophical relevance to other poor countries: democracy is possible in such societies; it can work.

China on the other hand has shown that non-democratic governments can also work, but that absolutist regimes, aside from their general unpleasantness, in the long term do not. The Chinese experience conveys the lesson that "pluralism is pragmatism." Whether corrupt democratic as in India or modified authoritarian as in China, the tolerance of autonomous individuals and sectors in society is vital to creativity and growth.

India and Political Change

Through trial and error the Indians are evolving a flexible structure to accommodate a dizzying array of communal, linguistic, and political differences. There is no other developing country, and few of any sort, which under a strong democratic center have managed to accommodate such a diversity of state governments, including several run by Communist or regionalist and linguistically based local parties.

This has not come easily and has been accompanied by a lot of head-bashing as well as endless palaver, maneuvering, co-opting, and compromising. The Indian army and police rush hither and yon to put down violence; and government leaders deal with the political spokesmen of partisan movements by alternately jailing them and negotiating with them. While tragic mistakes are made, for example in pressing ahead with elections in Assam in 1983, Indian political leaders have become experienced in dealing with regionalism, separatism, provincialism, and all sorts of intergroup violence.

It is doubtful that an authoritarian political system of the right or the left would have managed the past three "dangerous decades" in India so well. Unity and democracy in India are closely related, perhaps symbiotic. Flexibility, compromise, and tolerance, inherent in the democratic system, have been essential in holding the union together. Indians have a talent for diversity and a high tolerance for chaos. The Chinese have a penchant for uniformity and a longing for order and authority.

Leftists and rightists in India clamor for the early death of democracy. There is no question, however, but that the Indian people, at least today, still prefer democracy, with all its infirmities, to the promises of regimented ideologies. The common man in India, despite his support of democracy, however, would not create much commotion if it disappeared; Indians, like Chinese, are survivors, and, if necessary, they would passively accept authoritarian rule. Consequently, India's democracy is a fragile creature. Whether or not it survives will depend on numerous factors, including not only the maintenance of national unity, but also the rate of progress in economic and social development.

There is speculation in India that the government could someday seek a constitutional change to adopt a presidential system in order to strengthen the power of the center. A presidential system might work as well or better than the present one, but in any event the dilemma will remain that efforts to tighten central control excite regionalism, while the exercise of too little authority by New Delhi accelerates centrifugal forces.

A violent revolution in India, led by either Marxists or rightists, seems unlikely over the next decade and probably for much longer because it is not the Indian character and because democratic politics provides an outlet and an option to radical solutions. The landless and poverty-stricken half of the population at certain places and times might be sympathetic to calls for violent revolutionary change; but, barring a national disaster, such sentiments are likely to be isolated. At any one time and place the better-off half of the Indian population will most probably see revolutionary change as threatening. Even when violent groups like the Naxalites make headway in some areas, they can, if necessary, be suppressed by the national army and special police forces. The states of the Indian union indicate the lines of possible separation, but they also provide a tensile strength to the nation. China is solid oak, India laminated plywood; each has its own strength.

In the foreseeable future, the communists are unlikely to come to power in India through revolution, but it is remotely conceivable they could do so through elections. If so, it would be due to superior organization and their record in running relatively, although far from totally, honest governments at the state level and in carrying out more effectively than others the reforms promised by the non-communist parties. Such an eventuality would, of course, depend on a complex of factors, in particular, the success or failure of other parties to offer credible alternatives. Today non-communist observers generally dismiss the CPI as lacking a base of popular support and the CPM as a regional Bengali party. Events could prove them wrong. An important step toward national power for the communists would be a united front government with Congress (I). Soviet academics have touted this possibility. Again, the common wisdom is that Mrs. Gandhi would never have agreed to such an arrangement, nor would Rajiv now, seeing themselves as inevitably losing control and power through any such union. If the Congress (I) lost its parliamentary majority, however, and a united front was the only way to retain power, it might well seize upon this option, as in 1969 Mrs. Gandhi relied on the votes of the communists (and several other parties), although they did not join her government. The opposition parties, for that matter, could also at some point offer a united front with the communists in order to displace a Congress (I), which in a general election had won only a plurality. All this is of course academic at the moment as Rajiv Gandhi, boosted by a large sympathy vote for his slain mother, led the Congress (I) to a sweeping victory in the December 1984 elections, winning more than three quarters of the parliamentary seats.

Economic stagnation at or below the "Hindu growth-rate" could further increase support for the communists. Also, as the poorer and uneducated half of the population slowly grows more literate, the communist parties might be able to recruit even more effectively among this group. The growth of the urban labor force will also provide opportunities. It is possible, therefore, that instead of developing its unique brand of democracy, India could develop a unique brand of communism which might be more quasi-democratic and pluralistic than the one in Peking. The CPM in West Bengal has succeeded because it must act as a social democratic rather than a Leninist party. It must compete for votes. Thus it has dampened down the notion of class struggle, pursued pragmatic policies, and tried to moderate labor relations and entice business investments. More than one Calcutta capitalist prefers a CPM state government to a Congress-dominated administration.

Nevertheless, without some combination of unusual circumstances involving internal and external upheavals, the odds are heavily against the Indian communists coming to power in the next two decades. Indian society is resistant to radical change and there is a cultural bias against atheistic communism. Nevertheless, most intellectuals agree that if the communists could in one way or another seize power, the Indian masses, like the Chinese, would bend with the wind.

While a turn to the left, in the form of a united front, is possible, a shift in the other direction is equally, and perhaps more, likely. This would probably take the form of a democratically elected conservative government representing the interests primarily of the economic cultivators, both middle and large size. Recent representation in the Lok Sabha and in most state assemblies reflect this trend. The cultivator-landowners are still by far the most active and influential force in village politics. The Janata coalition that ruled from 1977–1979 represented this class in part, and the return to power of a similar alliance, perhaps backed by regional parties, is a real possibility.

On the other hand, the Congress (I) appeal to the poor, the minorities, the urban middle class, and the bureaucracies remains strong. Mrs. Gandhi's charisma was a special factor which Rajiv despite his unprecedented election victory does not yet possess. Back in 1967, however, Mrs. Gandhi herself did not appear to have much charisma, but it magically materialized, and the same phenomenon will probably work for Rajiv.

Democracy in Pakistan and Bangladesh has fallen victim to military coups, but such a denouement seems less likely in India. The Indian army has been highly professional and apolitical and everything possible is done to encourage this tradition. As in the U.S. military, senior officers have relatively short tenure. The size and communal diversity of the military is perhaps the greatest deterrent to a military takeover. An Indian general, rationally contemplating such a move, would have to be assured that the major army and air force commands throughout the country were on board. Taking a brigade or division into New Delhi would not do the job. Lining up regional commanders would be made more difficult because they include a mixed bag of Sikhs, Christians, and Moslems, as well as Bengalis, Tamils, and other Hindus. The Indian army also has many linguistically based units. A military coup attempt cannot be ruled out, but unless there was some plausible national emergency any such effort could well spark a civil war—a prospect which is itself the strongest deterrent.

An effective and united national military force is critical to putting down succession movements when all else fails. The simultaneous outbreak of several rebellions at once could, of course, overwhelm the military's capabilities; but other cohesive factors are at work and even increasing in strength. National marketing of goods, the expansion of power grids, rail and air networks, the sharing of more and more irrigated water, and the growth of other economic ties across the nation are steadily building a national economic entity. The large public sector, which has absorbed so much savings, is widely viewed as a national asset. The interest of the elite in the revival of Indian traditional culture, and national pride in India's science and technological accomplishments, also suggest that a strengthening of the Indian identity is occurring simultaneously with the continuing assertion of regional loyalties. Moreover, while more attention is being paid to fostering regional languages and literature, the knowledge and use of English as a lingua franca also continues to spread. The circulation of the English language press is increasing, although Indian language papers are growing at an even faster rate.

In the future, the quality of English spoken in India could diminish, as populist pressures increase for the substitution of Indian languages as the medium of instruction in public schools and even universities. There is already a noticeable difference in the English spoken by younger Indians. At the same time, English words are sprinkled throughout conversation in Hindi and other Indian languages. Within another hundred years a new Anglo-Indian patois may emerge, much as Urdu developed during the Moghul period from a combination of Persian and Hindi. The Bombay films have produced their own "Hindi film English" or HFE which incorporates so many Indian words that it is incomprehensible to the non-initiated. The process of cross-fertilization has been going on for more than a hundred years, and some "Indo-Anglican" writers such as novelist Raj Anand have deliberately sought to Indianize English. Whatever its nature, the emerging Anglo-Indian language will increasingly serve to bind the nation together.

The rate of economic growth and improvement in nutrition, health, and education will of course influence political stability; but, assuming a muddling-through scenario in which the "Hindu rate of growth" of about 3.5 percent per year continues, important changes in Indian policies and leadership are likely to take place within the framework of the present democratic structure.

China and Political Change

There is even less prospect for basic political change in China than in India. For the foreseeable future, internal dynamics seem highly unlikely to threaten the unity of China. Only powerful intervention by the Soviets could endanger Xinjiang's or Tibet's place in the People's Republic of China—intervention which could only occur in the context of a Sino-Soviet war.

Although the Communist party in Peking has lost much of its elan and prestige, there is hardly any doubt but that it will continue to rule for the indefinite future and that no significant opposition—which, given the nature of things, would have to be a violent one—is likely to arise outside the party or if so last for very long.

The Chinese army is not apolitical in the same way as the Indian army. Military commanders have always had an important political role. The 56 military representatives in the 1985 Central Committee of 343 constitute the largest single bloc, but this is the smallest military percentage (16%) in several decades. The military is, of course, tightly organized as a subservient wing of the party. This orientation and an even more unwieldy size than the Indian army diminishes the possibility of a military coup succeeding. A military coup was apparently attempted in 1971, when the Defense Minister Marshal Lin Biao, together with the most prominent military commanders, allegedly tried to assassinate Mao. Apparently no regional military commanders sided with Lin and the bizarre plot collapsed with Lin crashing to his death in a plane while trying to flee into the lap of the Soviets. Five years later, after the death of Mao, an alleged non-military coup was also reportedly nipped in the bud by the arrest of the Gang of Four.

These and other political upheavals in China, except for the Cultural Revolution, have been generated within the confines of the leadership hierarchy. That was a big exception, but Mao in the mid–1960s could have easily dismissed his enemies by fiat. He employed mob violence because he wanted a violent upheaval not simply the riddance of certain people. Conceivably, a future faction could generate popular or mob action to attack its enemies. Some observers, for example, speculate that Hu Yaobang may have encouraged the December 1986 student demonstrations that in fact precipitated his fall.

But all the factions in Peking now seem united in their commitment to avoiding a recurrence of the politics of struggle. Future twists and turns in the leadership will very likely be determined by backstage maneuvering of power groups and personal factions, as in Deng's ouster of Hua Guofeng in 1981 and Hu Yaobang in 1987.

Having gone through a period of violent politics and draconian change equivalent to that carried out by Qin Shi Huang, China may now be settling down once again into the long reign of a highly ordered society in which the succession of power is determined by a small elite operating under an undefined but clearly understood set of ground rules. In this traditional dynastic system the elite tempers its intramural rivalries because of a common interest in maintaining the image of strength and single-minded purpose. If this is so, and a new long era of domestic peace and progress is beginning in China, then the 1980s and the last decade of this century will set the pattern for the future.

It will in any event be a time of historic transition for China. The forces of rebellion and cathartic change are passing away. The revolutionaries who "swung the golden cudgel" to destroy the old order are one-by-one passing away. They were both mandarins and peasants, the sort that are drawn to war and revolution—idealists, patriots, adventurers, and opportunists. At the very top were rebel mandarins or intellectuals like Mao, Liu, Zhou, and Deng, but there were other leaders who came from less exalted classes, like Zhu De, Peng Dehuai, and He Long.

The peasant nature of the movement, however, was reflected, not in the highest ranking leadership, but in the tens of thousands and eventually the hundreds of thousands of junior and middle-level military and party officials who came from peasant and worker backgrounds. After liberation they would take over the running of enterprises, communes, and party and government offices throughout the country. Today they are the several hundred-thousand aging factory managers and local officials with only a primary or a junior middle-school education who are rapidly being replaced.

The emergence of a new intellectual elite in place of the Old Guard is reflected in the increased education and younger age of new ministers and vice ministers in the state council, members of the Central Committee, the National People's Congress, and the party's Secretariat. The same process is quite visible at the lower levels in enterprises and local government and also within the PLA. While the educational level of India's political elite, as seen in the Lok Sabha membership, is diminishing, in China the level is increasing. This suggests the growing populism of democratic politics in India and the concurrent professionalization of directed elite politics in China.

Well before the end of this century, the new post-revolutionary China elite will be firmly in place. Like the literati system of old, it will be a meritocracy and fresh blood from the culturally poorer orders of society will trickle into the system. But, as with intellectual elites in all societies, it will also in large part be a self-perpetuating one, as family environment will continue to be the most important factor in educational achievement. Despite increasing income disparities, continuing limits on the accumulation of wealth will be greater than in India and will diminish somewhat the ability to inherit one's social position. The job assignment system, assuming it continues, will also encourage to a limited degree a downward recirculation of non-achieving children of the Chinese elite. But many if not most of this group will find a "back door" to success.

While this new elite is being formed, an historic contest is underway for the soul of China. The struggle between reformers/innovators and neo-Maoists in China, as between liberals and conservatives in any society, will continue indefinitely in one form or another. The course of this struggle over the next decade of transition, during which time the old guard will completely fade out, will, however, determine whether China will continue as it has since the Sung Dynasty to allow its obsession with intellectual and doctrinal uniformity and social order to smother creativity. Will China become an oriental version of a Soviet bureaucratic state? Or will it develop a more plural Sino-communism, a unique mixture drawing on the models of Hungary, Yugoslavia, Singapore, and Confucian China?

The homogeneous quality of the Chinese people and their tradition of orthodoxy for 700 years and even back to the beginning of the siege society, strengthen the forces of conservatism. While Westerners were fascinated with the "democratic spring" in Peking in 1978–1979 and the student demonstrations of December 1986, they tend to overlook the conservatism of the popular masses and their fear of disorder. Only 2 percent of university students were involved in the December 1986 protests. And a similarly small fraction of the Chinese people would opt for the unpredictable consequences of an upheaval over continuation of the political status quo. The majority of Chinese today are well fed and adequately clothed and sheltered and their lives are reasonably stable and harmonious. The "social contract" or the "mantle of heaven" seems fairly secure. If given a ballot-box choice, they might choose a different government, but this is not a real option and it excites the imaginations of only a handful of young intellectuals. What the Chinese people want is a strong, effective, and benevolent government. If they could, and did, vote out the CCP it would be because it had not measured up in these areas, not because it was undemocratic.

The exclusive, universalist ideology of communism reinforces the Chinese craving for orthodoxy, and the enormous bureaucratic structures which have been built up over the past 35 years have created powerful vested interests in inertia. Leaders of internal security organs and the powerful military establishment also tend to oppose any weakening of control or permissiveness toward autonomous activity. This desire for order was reinforced by the experience of the Cultural Revolution, and it has made it difficult to gain acceptance for more liberal outlooks that intrinsically tolerate, if not condone, a certain amount of social discord and, from a Chinese perspective, even chaos. As a younger and more educated generation of Chinese take over, will the system continue to evolve toward greater pluralism? As with all important matters in China, the answer will come from the top. The reformers around Deng believe some fundamental political reform is necessary and possible. They rationalized the 1981–1983 fallback from political reforms as a necessary tactical retreat. Time was needed, they argued, to consolidate the political strength of the reform group, to ease out the Old

Guard, and to revamp the bureaucracy. Between 1984 and 1986, liberals around Hu were on the offensive, downgrading Marxist shibboleths, loosening social controls, encouraging artistic creativity, advocating human rights, launching new incentive reforms in the economy, and promising a more participatory political system. Hu's ouster in 1987, however, put a big question mark on political reform. Whether the less liberal reformers will be able or willing to loosen significantly the rigidity of the political system at the cost of some substantial loss of social control is still uncertain.

Stability in China's relations with the super-powers and the absence of perceived near-term threats will also increase their chances.

Ideological Revision

India does not need—in fact it probably could not tolerate—a monolithic orthodoxy. Rajiv Gandhi need not worry about rationalizing his policies with some over-reaching political dogma. On the other hand, he must be constantly alert not to violate cultural norms or tread on the feet of some religion or other sensitive group or caste. India has no ideology save the new humanism of the late Mahatma, a vague socialism, and a nationalism based on unity amid diversity.

Chinese society, however, tends to be uncomfortable without an all-embracing doctrine on the political order. The national ethos requires a political creed and something of a universal mission.

The amalgam of watered down Marxism, pragmatism and nationalism that the reformers have concocted since 1978 and labeled "Chinese style socialism" seems a weak brew indeed to the neo-Maoists. Gone are the hoary ideas of class struggle, the continuing revolution, and the goal of an egalitarian society. Improving one's ideological outlook today means essentially to work hard, be honest and unselfish.

The mundane tone of current ideology is reflected in the proclamation of the month of March as "socialist ethics month" during which time the Chinese people are urged to foster good public manners, environmental sanitation, and good services. The on-going campaign to promote a "socialist spiritual civilization" likewise underscores civility and traditional values. "Bourgeois liberalism" and ultra-individualism are denounced, but as it was with Confucianism for two thousand years, acceptance of Marxist orthodoxy today is pro forma and largely detached from actual behavior.

In ideology as in religion, faith is more important than content. Thus the cruelest cut of all for the conservatives is the knowledge that the revolutionary mission has lost most of its heart.

But some moral imperatives are necessary to maintain the cohesiveness of human societies, and China like India, as a very poor and enormous country, needs such imperatives more than most. Deng and his moderate reformers know that the consumer approach in China will always be plagued by a large gap between reality and rising expectations. Thus the Dengists in January 1987 sided with the neo-Maoists, probably in large part because it was politically expedient to do so, but also in part because they feared that Hu Yaobang and his intellectual associates had in fact gone too far and too fast in shedding the ideological rationale of the Party's rule.

The strength of India lies in its traditions which provide stability amid seeming chaos. In China, the old moral order has been cast aside and the family, while still strong, is losing its centrality. The problem for the Chinese rulers is how to supplement consumerism with some sort of system or creed that is inspiring without being given to extremes.

Hu Yaobang appeared to have a bold but only vaguely perceived answer. He seemed to believe that pluralism could provide a creative and popular dynamism that somehow could coexist with a wise but authoritarian government. He and many others saw emerging a new, more benevolent, more Confucian communism that accepted the frailty of humankind and the fallibility of all doctrines save that of moderation. Perhaps he saw China becoming an enormous Singapore. Deng and some of the other moderates probably share a bit of the same vision. But above all they are practical men.

As long as the reformers show that they can improve living standards and steadily build China into a modern power while maintaining social control, they will probably be able to further liberalize the economy in the post-Deng decade. This was promised in the 1986 party plenum resolution that called for an ethic of competition to expand the "socialist commodity economy," and which declared that "on no account should egalitarianism be regarded as an ethical principle in our society."

If all the objective realities are favorable, the reformers might return to Hu Yaobang's agenda of a more plural cultural, intellectual and political life in China. On the other hand, economic, social, or international setbacks will make some major backsliding likely. At this writing, as the neo-Maoists are taking their pound of flesh from the fallen innovators, perhaps the most the Dengists can hope for is a holding of the line and no serious erosion of the major transformations they have wrought in China's political economy.

The Economic Potential

A favorable rate of economic growth more than any other factor will provide flexibility for political reform in China. The question is whether economic and bureaucratic changes, which are essential to an efficient fast developing economy, can be carried out while the political system remains rigid. Under any conceivable circumstance, can a command society significantly modify its command economy and allow market forces to operate to any degree of autonomy and effectiveness? Will the system, as in the past in the Soviet Union, absorb and nullify liberal reforms thus compelling such market forces as remain to flow into the informal economy?

Is it possible to reform and decentralize such an enormous and complicated state-run economy without creating major dislocations, including high inflation and large scale unemployment, which in turn might spark a powerful backlash? The overheated and probably wasteful industrial expansion at the end of 1984 and throughout 1985, along with the ballooning of corruption, suggest the dangers that loom ahead.

For India, the question is whether populist politics in a poor and overcrowded country with a large public sector will allow market forces to operate sufficiently to achieve greater efficiency and a much higher return on the country's hard-earned savings.

Both India and China are groping for a new balance that will restore dynamic growth within the broad parameters of their distinct political economies—mixed and command. For Peking, past experience—both China and communist—with structural reform is not encouraging, whether one looks at nineteenth-century China or the Soviet Union in the last 20 years. Just as orthodoxy stifled China's efforts at modernization in the late 1800s, so in the Soviet Union ambitious campaigns in the 1950s and 1960s against inefficiency, bureaucratization, and irrationality in production were largely swallowed up by the system. Gorbachev has promised major reforms and has made a number of dramatic symbolic changes that would have impressed Hu Yaobang, but he has not yet carried out a fundamental attack on the organizational and managerial problems of the USSR.

But despite the impressive, even dazzling, production figures of the past few years, the future rate and direction of economic growth in China are by no means clear. Nor are the possibilities limited to either replication of the Soviet state or creation of a dynamic new market-socialism. Likewise, India is not simply caught between vigorous, self-sustaining growth on the one hand or prolonged stagnation on the other. Political and social constraints in both countries, the weight of an enormous section of abject poverty, and the impossibility of developing export-fueled growth to the same degree as much smaller states will probably preclude in either case a supernova performance of growth such as Japan enjoyed in the post-World War II years. But the alternative in either country is not necessarily a shrinking white dwarf of an economy, much less a collapsing black hole.

In both countries it may not be possible to maintain the high levels of savings and investment of the past. The Indians, however, with a much larger private sector, absence of a shadow bureaucracy in the form of a mass party, and its less dogmatic adherence to orthodoxy, should have more flexibility in carrying out reforms aimed at getting more out of invested capital and in making better use of market forces. It is simpler, for example, in India to adjust government controlled prices to reflect more closely demand and production costs. Price reform in China, however, is immensely complicated.

On the other hand, Peking can more easily make controversial non-systemic decisions. In both countries, for example, there is opposition to the liberalization of foreign investment and trade policies. Conservatives in China and liberals in India are fearful that such policies will result in importation of world recessions, sacrifice of independence, abandonment of self-reliance, and a sellout to multinationals. By winning a consensus in the core leadership, however, Deng and New Party chairman Zhao can carry through with their "open door" policy as seen for instance in their agreements with foreign oil firms. Rajiv Gandhi finds opposition to a similar policy in India much more diffuse, with numerous politicians, academics, journalists, and vested interest groups continually openly attacking it.

In agriculture, India also should theoretically have an advantage in that each unit of increased yield in the future should come more easily and with less cost than in China, where fertilizer input is at much higher levels. Although India already has more irrigated land than China, it also has much more potential for further expansion of irrigation. If India can quadruple its use of fertilizer as China did over the past decade, its agricultural productivity per hectare could catch up with that of China and, with 40 percent more cropland, eventually surpass China's total production.

At present, however, it is China, rather than India, that is reaping the productivity advantages provided by small-scale household farming. Indian cultivators generally are as hard-working as Chinese, but a sizable portion of the landless in India, as we have seen, come from a culturally unique and deprived group which for a long period, possibly generations, might not be as efficient small-scale farmers as are the poorest Chinese peasants. Thus an Indian version of the household responsibility system, in which farm land was divided among families in a village, while creating a much more equitable society might decrease rather than increase production, at least in the short term.

The danger in China's agricultural scene is a political one. A future conservative leadership fearing the social and political consequences of the household responsibility system in farming might suddenly reverse the policy and, as a result, agricultural production could plummet—as happened in the Soviet Union when Stalin cracked down on the Kulaks (rich peasants) in the 1920s.

Energy is a major constraint on growth in both countries; but the Chinese, despite their enormous waste of energy, are likely to remain in a better position than India over the next 20 years. Due to increased domestic demand (in addition to price factors), China's energy export earnings could diminish, and although coal exports could boom to 40 million tons per year, China might conceivably become an oil importer once again. Higher production than now expected and effective implementation of strict conservation measures could, however, change the picture.

India, meanwhile, is edging toward energy self-sufficiency and, with more luck in the Bombay High as well as continuing progress in opening new coal mines and increasing productivity in present ones, it might attain this goal in the 1990s. China at that time, even under a low-growth scenario and with some oil imports, would very likely still be an energy exporter, primarily in terms of coal exports. China's energy surplus over the next ten, and possibly twenty, years will allow it to maintain its current relatively high level of nutrition through grain imports whenever necessary. It will also allow China to foot a much larger bill than India for the purchase of Western technology.

Because of India's expanding consumption, to achieve energy self sufficiency will require a major conservation program including extensive conversion from oil to coal. Success, however, will probably require giving more scope to the private sector not only for electricity generation but also for oil exploration and production.

In trade, the competitive advantages of the two countries in low wages, a skilled and disciplined work force, and the ability to produce quality products are comparable. China, however, will continue to have a major advantage in the Japanese market, where geographic proximity, economic complementarity, and cultural affinity make for a unique and mutually profitable trade partnership.

The awesome size of India and China precludes the possibility of their receiving international concessionary capital in proportion to the rest of the developing world. India's and China's conservative financial policies are in a sense being penalized, as "soft" loans go increasingly to less frugal but usually no poorer Third World countries. In 1986, for example, India received from the World Bank's soft loan window less than half the amount it obtained five years before. One reason was that China was now in the line.

The alternatives to concessionary loans are foreign investments and commercial borrowings. To maintain moderate growth rates during their current five year plans India and China, according to World Bank estimates, will each need to borrow at least $4.5 billion a year overseas. Both New Delhi and Peking, however, are likely to continue to be very cautious about tapping long term commercial loans. In 1986 India's external debt was about $30 billion and China's approximately $20 billion. These are relatively small figures compared to Third World debt generally, which is expected to rise to around $1,400 billion by 1990.

To obtain the technology and other imports necessary for modernization, India and China will probably increase their respective foreign debt significantly during the rest of the century. But each will probably accept a lower rate of growth rather than assume enormous and costly loans of the sort that now burden Mexico, Brazil, and other developing countries.

India's current advantage in trained manpower for science and technology should begin to narrow as China's ambitious program to expand higher education and technology training moves ahead. Assuming there are no new political attacks on intellectuals or radical experiments with education, the Chinese science and technology manpower pool should, within ten or fifteen years, be proportionately equal to or greater than that of India.

The channeling of the best Chinese science and technology students into graduate work, at home and abroad, and also into research, could give China a lead over India in applied science and engineering by the end of the century. India's advantage in science and technology, however, will continue to lie in its more creative intellectual environment and the absence of political interference. Indian society will also continue to provide greater rewards to outstanding scientists who will probaably enjoy freer interchange with the West, including the right to emigrate. India will continue to suffer a brain-drain, but the return in the long run will be to its advantage.

Over the next 20 years the most important difference affecting China and India's economic growth will be China's lower population expansion. Already there are more Indians being born every day than Chinese. The Chinese plan to reduce their fertility rate within 12 years to 1.6, which will be significantly less than the replacement level; if this goal is achieved even in 20 years it will be one of the world's most remarkable feats of social engineering. India, if it is reasonably successful in its family-planning program may achieve a replacement fertility level by the year 2020. But its population by that time will have doubled and, as observed earlier, by the year 2100 will very likely have surpassed that of China.

China will have to feed, house, clothe, educate and find jobs for at least 200 and probably 500 million additional people; but with its present low fertility rates, the number of persons coming into the labor market will begin to decline in the late 1980s. The number of children entering primary schools has already begun to diminish. For China, the population light is at the end of the tunnel. It can only be reached, however, by continuation of the present command society as well as further advances in literacy and standards of living. Given the past ups and downs on population policy, it is uncertain whether China will prove willing and able to continue to enforce tough measures of population control. Assuming this can be done, a moderate rate of agricultural and industrial growth should allow a healthy improvement in standards of living, as well as accumulation of capital stock. It would, however, also likely mean that the division between the two Chinese worlds, urban and rural, will continue, as much of the additional population will be kept in the countryside and provincial towns and employed in small-scale enterprises and "side line occupations."

With steady if undramatic industrial development, a great deal more fertilizer, and continued expansion of irrigation possibilities, India also has the potential to feed and clothe its projected 1.7 billion people. The numbers seem staggering, but even then India's population density per acre of cropland will be less than that of Germany today and about one-third of that of Japan. And, as John Mellor points out, India's climate, soil, and water resources are conducive to much higher levels of crop intensity than Germany's. Nevertheless, with a slower overall economic growth rate and a birth rate almost double that of China, India's average standard of living, while slowly advancing, is likely to fall further behind that of China. Urbanization in India will also continue to grow faster as India follows the traditional pattern of development and population movement. This will further heighten the contrast between the haves and the have-nots and will increase the possibilities of political and social turmoil. The better-off half of the population, including "organized" factory workers, the middle class, and land-owning cultivators, will gradually grow more prosperous, more healthy, and better educated. Despite a continuing succession of government efforts to assist the poor, the lower half of the Indian population—the landless farm laborers and slum dwellers—will advance at a slower pace, and the disparity between the two worlds of India wil probably grow.

In China the gap in the countryside between poor and well-off peasants will also likely expand over the next decade or two. In both countries, however, as long as the poor are also going forward and not backward, the political tensions created by heightened disparities will be moderated. In China the very poor, in addition, will remain geographically concentrated and isolated, whereas in India they will be found throughout the country while also funneling into the cities.

Events beyond the control of India and China will, of course, greatly influence their future growth. These include the weather, international economic conditions, the price of oil, the availability of foreign capital, and the outbreak of regional or broader international conflicts. Both governments have protected themselves to varying degrees from the full force of international developments. Neither country was caught out like Mexico, Nigeria, or Brazil with huge outstanding debts in the world recession of the early 1980s; both have achieved a high degree of the self-sufficiency that they sought; China much more so, but in comparison with the rest of the developing world, India as well. Each has practiced fiscal conservatism and managed complex economies, including enormous grain procurement and distribution programs. The prospects, overall, are fairly good that India and China, with all of their inefficiencies and irrational economic practices, will achieve at least moderately good economic growth over the rest of the century. Their enormous economies, together with the highly productive ones of Japan, South Korea, and other capitalist show-pieces in the region, should make the twenty-first century the Asian era.

With a modest real growth rate for India of 3.5 to 5 percent and 4–6 percent for China, both countries by the end of the century will be significantly stronger and more influential powers than they are today. Both, but especially China, will be able to siphon off even larger funds than in the past for military, space, and science and technology developments.

China has tended to move in fits and jerks, while India has muddled through. Another seizure of irrationality in China like the Cultural Revolution seems improbable for the foreseeable future, but as we have concluded before, not impossible. More conceivable is a backlash to the current liberalization and open-door policies and a return to a quasi-Stalinist regime in China. In India the main threat to long-term development is the explosive social potential created by communal and regional tensions, as well as those between the haves and the have-nots.

The reaction to such threats in India could, as in China, also be a conservative one. In other words, in both India and China, the vested interests of the respective establishments could assert their dominance. In China, this would mean entrenchment of a bureaucratic state doggedly pursuing a high investment policy focused on heavy industry, and a tightening up of the closed society. The ascendancy of a conservative regime in India would not necessarily mean more irrational economic policies, but rather, a marked slowing of the social transformation of Indian society.

Economic and political realities drive the innovators in China ever forward. They cannot afford to stand still. The alarming drop in irrigated land and the erosion of grasslands, for example, is laid by some Chinese economists to the continued separation of land ownership from management rights, despite the return of household farming. The deterioration of infrastructure in the countryside is seen as a form of natural economic neglect. Fifteen or even 30 year leases may not be sufficient to provide the necessary incentive for full scale maintenance. In 1986, the idea of full private ownership indirectly surfaced. The new Land Administration Law passed by the NPC that year reaffirmed that all land belonged to the state or to collectives, but stipulated that private ownership and sale of land could take place "in accordance with the law."

Whatever the decision on the private ownership of land, ten years after the death of Mao, despite the ouster of Hu, the reformers had seized the initiative and were pushing ahead with remarkable determination to create a dynamic economy driven by incentives, competition, and pragmatism, but still reflective of socialist egalitarian ideals and Confucian humanism. Whether or not this philosophy continues to dominate the scene after the death of Deng will depend primarily upon its material success. As long as the innovators show that they can improve living standards and steadily build China into a modern power, they will prevail.

Meanwhile, Rajiv Gandhi pledges to lead India into the twenty-first century as a modern progressive state in the ranks of the world powers. He and his young associates seek to leap over the last half of the industrial revolution and put India into the middle of the electronic age. This means tempering the goals of nationalism and self sufficiency and attracting as much foreign technology through investment and trade as possible. Meanwhile, social goals, such as reducing poverty, are to be achieved not through political movements and administrative measures, but by increased production.

The Rajiv modernizers see India as a vast market with an enormous reservoir of trained scientific and technological manpower—a growth machine waiting to be activated. Whether or not their approach continues over the long term will depend not only upon its demonstrated success—and this in turn will be tied in good measure to the world economy—but also to their ability to deal with the political and social divisiveness and turmoil that are endemic to India.

The two countries, however, are now operating on similar assumptions, including their belief that: an interdependent world economy is emerging and they must either join it or be left behind; economic growth will depend in good part upon technology transfers and investment from the West; and export-led growth rather than import substitution must be the focus of industrialization.

Both governments are still searching for a pragmatic mix of central planning, incentives, market forces, and private and public sectors that will produce an effective balance between an efficient economy, social goals, and political stability. In each case the planners take as key goals increased productivity and the creation of employment in the rural areas. They agree that these goals require the commercialization of agriculture and the expansion of rural industries and service trades.

According to China's Seventh Five Year Plan, private business is to provide a large number of the 140 million new jobs that are to be created by 1990. The target is 50 million private businesses by the end of the decade. At the end of 1986, there were 11.34 million registered private enterprises (some estimate that there were an additional 4–6 million unregistered). This represented a rapid rise from the 2.6 million registered in 1982, the year the new constitution made such ventures legal, or the estimated 180,000 private units—mostly self-employed individuals—that existed in 1978 throughout all of China!

On the other hand, the 1986 figure represented a small decline from the previous year. Harassment by local officials, endless red tape, inability to obtain buildings or sites, survival outside the state's social security network, and uncertainty about future policies seemed to have slowed if not halted the trend toward entrepreneurship. Thus if the private sector is to play its planned role in absorbing labor, the administration will have to improve the conditions and incentives for such business.

Future Goliaths

Amid the achievements and failures of the revolution, Chinese national character remains unchanged. They are a sober, frugal, optimistic, and confident race, not naturally given to self-criticism or arrogance, although not incapable of either. Xenophobia lies dormant in the shadows, but the basic Chinese instinct in dealing with the world is a practical and hard-headed one. The Chinese do believe that things move ahead and while occasionally seized with spasms they are usually patient about progress and forbearing with their governments.

The Indians have paradoxically remained more distinctly Indian than the Chinese have Chinese. They have held on tenaciously to the trappings of their culture and they are sensitively, often irritatingly, proud. Yet Indians are too divided among themselves to be bully nationalists.

Both India and China want to avoid war and concentrate on development. Yet the volatile agents of nationalism and history produce a mysterious chemistry. Since independence and liberation, each of these poor yet highly sophisticated goliaths has been torn by bloody internal strife and each has fought three major wars in its first three decades. As in the past, future Indian and Chinese foreign policies will be shaped by a combination of internal and external developments; by political and economic dynamics at home interacting with the perception of threats and opportunities abroad. Despite their genuine desire for peace and progress, the odds are that over the next several decades, India and China will each be engaged in one or more quite major conflicts, quite possibly including one with each other. Expansionist policies by either, however, seem unlikely. *Leibenschraum* is not really an option when a country is over or pushing a billion. But strength and size carry with them their own rationale for status and influence, and both India and China may well find themselves drawn into future regional conflicts or possibly intervening in neighboring countries because of some instability or action that is perceived as threatening. If conservatives in India and neo-Maoists in China should come to power, official perceptions of threats and opportunities in both countries would alter perhaps only marginally, but in periods of crises, sometimes decisively. Under left, right, or centrist governments, India in another generation will probably become more concerned with the distribution of world power and the strategic balance between the superpowers. About the time India reaches a billion people early in the next century, the Hindu nation will possibly increasingly be seen as one of the secondary arbiters of world affairs, although still far from being a superpower, and still less globally oriented than the PRC.

The Chinese already perceive themselves as one of the big players on the world stage, although not yet in the major leagues. The PRC, of course, insists it will never be a superpower. But in the Chinese definition, intentions alone, not power, determine whether a nation is a hegemonic superpower or not. Naturally, like other governments, the PRC assumes it will always be benevolent and thus never hegemonist. While remote, conceivably some national trauma in China might again lead to the emergence of a charismatic leader who is prepared to follow utopian visions. China, however, has already had its Ayatollah, and this phenomenon does not seem likely to repeat itself in Peking in the near future. Nevertheless, there are two factors that make a volatile and assertive foreign policy theoretically more likely in China than in India. First, because one basis of Chinese nationalism is race, it is potentially a more powerful force than Indian nationalism. If Hu Yaobang had managed to succeed Deng, China could have become more nationalistic. Having shed the moral imperatives of Marxism, Hu probably would have leaned more heavily on traditional nationalism as the binding non-material essence that would have given legitimacy and dynamism to his rule.

Second, China's national creed is a universalist one, and despite China's current non-interventionist stance and its denial that there is in fact a communist or socialist camp as distinct from an informal world Marxist movement, Peking could conceivably again come to see itself as the true center of an ideological camp. India's national ideology—Nehru socialism and Gandhian ethics—is too India-specific to have any credibility as the fountainhead of a universalist movement. China's political economy also raises the question of how it will apportion increased production between popular consumption and national power. All states must make a division of wealth between the two, but for authoritarian regimes it is both more possible and often more desirable to channel growth into military power.

These unpredictable possibilities aside, the current pattern of proto-alliances between each of the super powers and each of the Third World goliaths appears likely to continue for some indefinite period. Dramatic and unexpected shifts in political alignments are always possible, but China's conflicts with the Soviet Union are much more intractable than Sino-American differences because the former involve on both sides profound questions of security and sovereignty. Thus, the odds are that the security interests of China and the U.S. for the foreseeable future will be relatively compatible, and East Asia will for some period be dominated by an informal entente composed of the U.S., the PRC, Japan, and the ASEAN and the ANZUS alliances. While Soviet military power in the Pacific area will grow, Moscow's political influence will be restricted unless some regional conflict or a local upheaval should provide it an unexpected opportunity to win a new ally. Consequently, the Indian connection will remain critically important to the Soviets and the loose if incongruous collegium of the USSR, Vietnam, and India will likely continue. It is conceivable that sometime in the future, the Soviets could seek to align themselves with Pakistan against India in order to protect their position in Afghanistan, outmaneuver China in a bordering area, and advance the Soviet sphere to the Indian Ocean. "The Great Game" would certainly be reordered in this eventuality, and it is perhaps the only circumstance in the foreseeable future in which India and China might find themselves linked in a quasi-united front with the U.S. The odds are, however, that over the long term there will be more rivalry than cooperation between Hindu and Han.

CHAPTER 19

A Philosophical Choice

The experiences of India and China confirm that cultural values and political systems are more important than methods of economic organization or material factors in economic and social development. Culture and politics, however, have ambivalent consequences for modernization. China's cultural homogeneity and its authoritarian political structure have provided discipline and order, and such concrete benefits as a high rate of savings and a low birth rate. Yet these same attributes also constrain creativity and individuality and encourage closed minds and a closed society.

India's mixed bag of color, language, faith, and ideology and the open political system that accommodates them all provide creativity and vigor, which in turn have produced a large pool of scientists and intellectuals, a dynamic cultural scene, and unity amidst diversity. But the unique Indian political culture also brings chaos, corruption, and inequity.

Our study suggests a "poverty principle"; that is, massive poverty cannot be easily eliminated under any political or economic system—for in most countries, poverty has a cultural dynamic as well as material and social causes. Thus 40 percent of indigenous native Americans still remain on welfare, and the "untouchables" of Japan, the Bukaru, continue to exist on the lowest economic rungs of society. The hundreds of thousands of gypsies in Spain, low caste migrants from India centuries ago, are still today outcasts—partly by choice, partly not. In India, the cultural element of poverty is relatively high and its scale large by any standard. Thus, its substantial reduction and eventual elmination may take one or more generations longer than in China.

Limited command politics in India might possibly have improved its rate of literacy and public health. But we have seen in Kerala and the Punjab sustained economic growth and social development can take place in a populist democracy in the Third World, provided it has a sophisticated culture, the tradition of an educated elite, and provides material incentives to its farmers. The last is probably the most important lesson that India and China have for the Third World—the key to growth in poor overpopulated countries is individual or family farming with generous monetary rewards to the peasants for increased production and the concurrent encouragement of small scale rural industry.

The Dengists are trying to move away from the absolutism of China's recent and distant past for practical not philosophical reasons. Certainly, absolutism in India even more than in China would have been a disaster of staggering proportions. Aside from wars of separation that a communist regime in New Delhi might have sparked, utopian schemes similar to the Great Leap Forward or the Cultural Revolution would probably have resulted in millions of deaths in India. Even a limited type of authoritarian rule might have been at the expense of Indian unity.

India's traditions, even and especially including caste, have evolved to meet the needs of modern progress as well as or better than did social revolution and upheaval in China. While we will never know for sure, China would probably have progressed faster in most fields under either a democratic or a pluralistic and limited authoritarian government.

In any event, both India and China demonstrate Hannah Arendt's premise that nothing could be more obsolete than to try to solve deep social-economic problems by political means. It is technology and rational administration, "not the rise of modern political ideas that have refuted the old truth that only violence and rule over others could make some men free." China has shown that absolutism not only cripples the human spirit, but it is also not the most effective way to enhance the collective welfare. Indeed it can multiply mistakes into calamities.

On the other hand, a number of Sinic-societies—Hong Kong, Singapore, Taiwan, and South Korea—have also demonstrated that limited command or authoritarian politics if practiced within a relatively pluralistic socio-economic and cultural framework, including extensive material incentives and intellectual freedom can produce dynamic growth along with tight political control. This is the general direction in which the Deng reformers are trying to coerce and cajole the Chinese Communist Party. If they succeed, China could dazzle the twenty-first Century.

Politics, culture, economics, and foreign relations are all inter-related. There are costs and benefits in any system. So long as there is effective and rational government which rewards economic behavior, modernization can be achieved by democratic politics with a mixed, controlled economy as in India, or by command politics with a modified command economy as now exists in China. Both methods of political governance can be effective; but both are subject to break-down by human factors. As we have seen, the threat to Indian development is corruption, inefficiency, and insensitivity; and in China it is orthodoxy, waste, and latent irrationality.

Despite their convergence along many tracks and the very important liberalization that has occurred in the PRC, India and China still pose a choice between a political society based on voluntary cooperation, individuality, and mutual advantage, versus a system which stresses mutual obligations, group responsibility, and group loyalty. The danger of the former is its relative inability to act in concert and with effect in dealing with deep social problems. The untamed pursuit of individual interests, especially in a society of scracity, leads to rampant corruption and gross disparities. Individuals, however, pursue ego-interests under any social and political system. To pretend they do not is to create a charade that masks the power-wielders' perpetual struggle for advantage. A system of political governance that claims to work only for the collective interest must necessarily operate within a regimented framework in which non-individualistic behavior becomes stylistic and rote.

Civilization began with the emergence of community, the restriction of individual actions and common acceptance of collective obligations and responsibilities. Civilizations, however, can also become oppressive—whether Confucian, capitalist, or communist—when collective interests overwhelm individual liberty. The leaders of highly collective-oriented and thus regimented societies are subject to the most tempting of all corruptions—absolute power. It is not surprising that deification has been the fate of the leaders of the most egalitarian societies we have seen in recent decades: North Korea's Kim I1-song, Albania's Hoxa, Kampuchea's Pol Pot, and China's Mao Zedong.

The pursuit of a just society is a never-ending search for a balance between collective and individual interests. The Maoists carried collective interests to the extreme of denying the legitimacy of self-interest as the main spur to human conduct. The obvious attachment of Mao, his wife, and the other Cultural Revolution radicals to the trappings of power reflected the hyprocrisy of this thesis and the inevitable difference between utopian theory and practice.

The Dengists have moved sharply away from these extremes and restored a measure of individual freedom to the Chinese people in realms outside those of politics and political orthodoxy. As in Confucian days, there is now room for a fairly lively cultural and family life in China independent of the collective will; but there is still little room for real individuality whether in art or politics, much less for any challenge to the doctrine of the power-holders.

The Indian balance between the common good and individual liberty is heavily flawed, but more susceptible to creative change than is the system in China. The socialist element in India's industry and commerce is very powerful but balanced with a huge private sector which, in turn, is tightly controlled and regulated. Political freedom and individual liberty, including the right to move where one wishes as well as to say what one wants, have generally been at a high level, although occasionally abused, violated, or temporarily curtailed. In the Indian countryside, however, individual prerogatives exist too much at the expense of the wider community. This is not an easy problem to solve, given its cultural aspects and the deep social divisions in Indian society; but in the long term this injustice will be corrected more equitably by the persistent assertion of political rights by the majority, rather than through social upheaval or dictate.

Was John Stuart Mill correct? Without individuality, is stagnation inevitable? Mill suggested that the nations of the East, which had once been the greatest and the most powerful in the world, had failed to progress for a thousand years because of the "depotism of custom." The Chinese, he said, had "succeeded in making people all alike, all governing their thoughts and conduct by the same maxims and rules." Liberal reformers around Deng Xiaoping agree that too much regimentation and leveling will destroy the chances for dynamic growth; yet the limits which they put on individuality and non-conformity would still appall Mill as worse than the "despotism of custom" in the old empire.

Mill suggested that eccentricity in a society is generally proportional to the amount of genius, mental vigor, and moral courage it contains. Eccentricity is pretty much a stranger in China; but in India it is the national custom, practiced even by the intolerant. If diversity of character and culture, liberty and the rule of the majority are the key to human progress, as Mill believed, India should have a large advantage over China. India and China, however, are not developing in isolation, but in a new world community where science and technology have become universal. Thus an authoritarian society may not be as creative in pure science and research as are open and plural societies; but it can obtain the benefits through technology, open scientific communications and, if necessary, espionage. India, therefore, may continue to make greater contributions to scientific theory, while China may excel in its practical application.

In the countryside, China today presents a new balance of individual and collective interests through a system of household farming on publicly owned lands combined with both state procurement and free markets. In the cities, private economic activity, although limited to services and small scale production, is growing rapidly. If these trends continue, this flexible system could offer to much of the world a unique Chinese answer to the problem of resolving the dichotomy between collective and individual needs in a poor rural society and balancing the contradiction between the goals of productivity and social justice.

Despite the converging trends, populist democracy—more rather than less corrupt—and command politics—more rather than less authoritarian—are likely to distinguish India and China respectively for the foreseeable future.

In some galactic age when we are all speaking the same language (perhaps largely a combination of Chinese, Hindi, and English), Indian and Chinese society will merge with others into a world culture. But until that time, the interaction of politics and culture, not economics, will, as in the past, constitute the fundamental difference between India and China.

* * *

Finally, we return to the question raised that autumn day sailing down the Yangtse gorges. Would it be better to be the poorest person in China or in India?

We have seen that the very poor lead very poor lives in both countries. There are simply many more such people proportionately in India—but this has very likely always been so. The choice, therefore, depends on one's view of what constitutes the good life. Many Westerners would choose the theoretical freedom of the poor Indian peasant or worker and the greater color and intensity of Indian life to the relative immobility and regimentation of the Chinese and—to us—the dullness of their lives, even if there was more security in the latter case. Creative individuals and societies do not usually seek physical security at all cost.

Life in China today is less drab than it has been in more than three decades, and probably more enjoyable for most Chinese than for 150 years. The great majority of Chinese do not miss the political freedoms that they have never had. Consequently, some outsiders might opt for the order and stability of life in China and perhaps also for the hope that the reformers and perhaps eventually even the liberal innovators will prevail and that some new, more vigorous balance of individual and collective interests may be in store. They may also sense that in a hundred years China will again be the "central kingdom."

Indians and the Chinese, however, have for the present made their own choices—and that is what matters. Perhaps they will want to make a different choice in the future; if so, it will be easier for the Indians than the Chinese to change their minds and that is a major attraction of the Indian model. Liberal democracy, however, is not inevitable in India, nor totalitarianism, no matter how benevolent, in China. Unique proclivities and instincts, as well as the vagaries of history, have shaped the modern societies of the two countries, but the future is likely to bring dramatic events and changes that neither we nor they can anticipate.

In the end, one cannot choose between them. For although they live together in the greater world, they have different natures and they travel in different elements—one by surface and one by air. Thus the question is "would one rather be a dragon or a wild goose?" The answer, if there is one, lies in the heart and not the mind.

Notes

1. E. T. C. Werner, *Dictionary of Chinese Mythology* (Shanghai, 1932).

2. Heinrich Zimmer, quoted by Joseph Campbell in *Myths and Symbols in Indian Art and Civilizations* (Princeton, N.J., 1972), p. 48.

3. These different approaches are reviewed succinctly by Erik Barrak in "Asian Cultures and Societies: Theories of Divergent Development," in *Technological Change and Cultural Impact in Asia and Europe* (Stockholm, 1980).

4. The expression is V. S. Naipaul's, *India, a Wounded Civilization* (New York, 1978).

5. Sant Elzingar, "Models in the Theory of Science: A Critique of the Convergence Thesis," in *Technological Change and Cultural Impact in Europe and Asia*, op. cit.

6. Ibid.

7. Daniel Bell, *Survey*, 17, no. 2, 1971, cited in Barrak, op. cit.

8. William Buck, trans., *Mahabharata* (New York, 1973).

9. Richard Lannoy, *The Speaking Tree* (New York, 1939), p. 116.

10. David R. Kingsley, *Hinduism: A Cultural Perspective* (Englewood Cliffs, N.J., 1982).

11. Jacques Gernet argues that hunting and gathering were major economic activities in ancient China and it was not until the sixth century B.C. that intensive grain cultivation dominated Chinese village life (*Ancient China*, Berkeley, 1968). Even if we accept Gernet's thesis, which most scholars do not, it is still correct to describe Xiang culture as a sedentary and basically agricultural society similar to Harappan culture.

12. Fredrick Hegel, *The Philosophy of History* (New York, 1956).

13. Myron Weiner, "Struggle Against Power: Notes on Indian Political Behavior," in *Political Change in South Asia* (Calcutta, 1963), p. 156.

14. Bashiruddin Ahmed, "The Crisis of Change," *Seminar*, no. 242 (New Delhi, October 1979).

15. Lucian Pye, *The Spirit of Chinese Politics* (Cambridge, Mass. 1968), p. 25.

16. Diana L. Eck, *Banaras, City of Light* (New York, 1982), pp. 3–15.
17. N. C. Chaudhuri, *The Autobiography of an Unknown Indian* (London, 1951).
18. Akhileswar Jha, *Sexual Designs in Indian Culture* (New Delhi, 1979), p. 121.
19. Ibid.
20. Sigmund Freud, *Civilization and Its Discontents* (New York, 1961).
21. Holmes Welch, *Taoism: The Parting of the Way* (Boston, 1966), p. 52.
22. Ibid., p. 22.
23. Ibid.
24. Marvin Harris, *Cannibals and Kings* (New York, 1977).
25. Wendy Doniger O'Flaherty, *Women, Adrogynes, and Other Mythical Beasts* (Chicago, 1980), pp. 249–51.
26. P. C. Bagchi, *India and China* (Calcutta, 1981), p. 213.
27. Ibid., p. 96.
28. Ibid., p. 281.
29. Ibid., p. 250.
30. Ssu-yu Teng and John K. Fairbank, *China's Response to the West* (Cambridge, Mass., 1954).
31. Christopher Hibbert, *The Great Mutiny, India 1857* (Middlesex, Eng., 1978).
32. Jen Yu-wen, *The Taiping Revolutionary Movement* (New Haven, 1973).
33. Joseph Levinson, *Confucian China and Its Modern Fate* (Los Angeles, 1958), p. 123.
34. Alexander Eckstein, *China's Economic Development* (Ann Arbor, 1975), p. 214.
35. Karl A. Wittfogel, *Oriental Despotism* (New Haven, 1975).
36. N. C. Chaudhuri, *The Biography of an Unknown Indian* (London, 1951), pp. 502–3.
37. Rhoades Murphey, *The Outsiders, the Western Experience in India and China* (Ann Arbor, 1977), pp. 177–86.
38. Ibid.
39. Ibid.
40. Dwight Perkins, *China's Modern Economy in Historical Perspective* (Stanford, Calif., 1975).
41. Murphey, op. cit.
42. Barbara Ward, "Modernization But Not Completed," in Lewis, ed., *The British in India* (Boston, 1962), p. 61.
43. Eckstein, op. cit.
44. Ibid.
45. Edgar Snow, *Red Star Over China* (New York, 1939), p. 132.
46. Richard Lannoy, *The Speaking Tree* (New York, 1971), p. 374.
47. See, for example: J. Bandyopadhyaya, *Mao Tse-tung and Gandhi* (New Delhi, 1973); R. Vaitheswaran, "Gandhi and Mao: A Comparison in Terms of Relevance for the Politics of National Liberation and Reconstruction," *China Report* 12, nos. 5–6 (1976); J. D. Sethi, "Mao and Gandhi: Convergence and Divergence—A Preliminary Note," *China Report* 13, no. 1 (1977); Bjorn Hettne, "Self-Reliance versus Modernization: The Dialectics of Indian and Chinese Development

Strategies," in Barrak and Sigurdson, eds., *India and China Comparative Research* (Copenhagen, 1981).

48. Swami Vivekananda, who lived in nineteenth century India, was the philosophical forefather of Gandhi. Vivekananda was a traditional yogi and guru but he also required of his followers the unprecedented pledge of service to Indian society, a pledge which included the running of schools, clinics, and orphanages.

49. An axiom coined by Lucian Pye.

50. World Bank, *China's Socialist Economic Development*, June 1, 1981, unpublished, but reviewed in various journals such as the *Economic and Political Review* (New Delhi, May 29, 1982), reviewed by Nigel Harris.

51. Li Zhengrui (Li Cheng-jui) and Zheng Zhongli (Cheng Chung-li), "Remarkable Improvement in Living Standards," *Beijing Review* (April 26, 1982).

52. Reported in the Hong Kong journal *Zheng Ming* (February 1982): 11, quoted by Hong Yung Lee, "Deng Ziaoping's Reform of the Chinese Bureaucracy," paper given at May 3, 1982, conference at the Wilson Center, Smithsonian Institution, Washington, D.C.

53. Ibid.

54. Ibid.

55. See World Bank, *World Bank Development Report, 1982* (Washington, D.C., 1982); also article by Tarlok Singh, "A Decade for Ending Poverty," *Seminar*, no. 282 (New Delhi, February 1983): 32–33.

56. Office of Registrar General, *Statistical Outline of India, 1982* (New Delhi, 1982); *World Bank Development Report, 1982*, op. cit.

57. Shigaru Ishikawa, *China Quarterly* 94 (June 1983): 242–81.

58. U.N. Department of International Economic and Social Affairs, *Report on the World Situation* (New York, 1982).

59. Ibid.

60. Ishikawa, op. cit.

61. Myron Weiner, *The Politics of Scarcity* (Chicago, 1967).

62. Myron Weiner, "Political Evolution," in John W. Mellor, ed., *India: A Rising Middle Power* (Boulder, Colo., 1979).

63. See Department of State, *Report to Congress on Human Rights* (Washington, D.C., 1982), p. 969.

64. Martin Wolf, World Bank occasional paper, "Capital and Growth in India, 1950–71," in *Foreign Economic Trends, India* (U.S. Department of Commerce, Washington, D.C., March 1984).

65. Wilfred Malenbaum, "Modern Economic Growth in India and China: The Compassion Revisited, 1950–1980," *Economic Development and Cultural Change* 31, no. 1 (October 1982): 69–71.

66. FY 1984, "India Country Development Strategy Statement," US AID, Washington, D.C., 1982, *Economist*, March 28, 1981, p. 8.

67. Malenbaum, op. cit.

68. Malcolm S. Adiseshiah, "Of Plans and Promises," *Seminar*, no. 285 (New Delhi, April 1983).

69. Wolf, op. cit.

70. World Bank, *World Bank Development Report, 1978* (Washington, D.C., 1978); Arthur G. Ashbrook, Jr., "China: Shift of Economic Gears in the mid–1970s," in Joint Economic Committee, *Chinese Economy Post-Mao* 95th

Congress, 2nd. sess., November 1978; Alexander Eckstein, ed., *Quantitative Measures of China's Economic Output* (Ann Arbor, 1980); CIA, NFAC, *China: A Preliminary Reconciliation of Official and CIA National Product Data*, ER M 79–10690 (Washington, D.C., December 1979); CIA, NFAC, *China*: *Major Economic Indicators*, ER 78–10750 (Washington, D.C., December 1978).

71. *Xinhua*, December 13, 1982.

72. A. Doak Barnett, *China's Economy in Global Perspective* (Washington, D.C., 1981), p. 91.

73. *World Bank Development Report, 1982*, op. cit.; *Statistical Outline of India, 1982*, op. cit.

74. Ibid.; *Xinhua*, April 29, 1983; *Statistical Outline of India, 1982*, op. cit.

75. Subramanian Swamy, "The Economic Distance Between China and India, 1955–73," *China Quarterly*, no. 70 (June 1977): 372–81.

76. *Statistical Outline of India, 1982*, op. cit., claims a larger possession rate of radios for India.

77. John Westley and M. C. Gupta, *Agricultural Growth in India* (US AID/India, New Delhi, 1982).

78. Ibid.; *Economic Survey, 1982–1983*, Government of India, New Delhi, 1983; *Economic Survey, 1983–1984*, Government of India, New Delhi, 1984.

79. *Economic Survey, 1982–1983*, Government of India, New Delhi, 1983.

80. John Aird, "Population Studies and Population Policy in China," *Population and Development Review* 8, no. 2 (June 1982). See also *China Statistical Yearbook, 1983* (Peking, 1983), and an article by Eric Hall in Reuter file, December 28, 1983, Peking.

81. Xue Muqiao, *China's Socialist Economy* (Peking, 1981).

82. *Statistical Outline of India, 1982*, op. cit.

83. State Statistical Bureau, "Economic Plan Communique," Peking, 1983 and 1984.

84. Robert Hardgrave, Jr., *India: Government and Politics in a Developing Nation* (New York, 1980).

85. In mid–1983 the Soviet Union began experimenting with contract systems in its rural collectives, but not on a household basis. After Gorbachev became leader of the Soviet Union in 1985, differences in the USSR over the merits of China's reforms seemed to reflect a dispute between Soviet conservatives and reformers over economic policy. One view in this debate continued to predict that Deng's recasting of China's economy would mean eventually the death of socialism in the PRC. Some Soviet officials, however, argued that the reforms were positive and dynamic.

86. S. S. Grewel and D. S. Sidhu, *Prosperity of Punjab Farmer—Reality or Myth?* (Dept. of Economics and Sociology, Punjab Agricultural University, Ludhiana, 1980).

87. Daip Singh, *Dynamics of Punjab Politics* (New Delhi, 1981).

88. Birha Institute of Scientific Research, *Agricultural Growth and Employment Shifts in Punjab* (New Delhi, 1984), p. 22.

89. Ibid., pp. 20–24.

90. Malcolm S. Adiseshiah, "Of Plains and Promises," *Seminar*, no. 285 (May 1983), p. 23.

91. Birha Institute, op. cit., pp. 42–43.

92. Montek Ahluwalia, World Bank Staff Working Paper No. 279, November 1978, p. 3.

93. Weiner, "Political Evolution," p. 65.

94. *World Bank Development Report, 1982*, op. cit.; *Report on World Situation*, op. cit.; *Statistical Outline of India, 1982*, op. cit.

95. Westley and Gupta, op. cit.

96. Kravis' report is published as an appendix to "The Report of the Committee on Scholarly Communication with the PRC Economic Delegation to China," National Academy of Sciences, Washington, D.C., 1980.

97. Malenbaum, op. cit., p. 71.

98. Jha, op. cit., p. 121.

99. O'Flaherty, op. cit., p. 84.

100. Jha, op. cit., p. 7.

101. Sudhir Kakar, *The Inner World* (New York, 1981), pp. 93–94.

102. O'Flaherty, op. cit.

103. Kakar, op. cit., p. 74.

104. Hajime Nakamura, *Ways of Thinking of Eastern Peoples: India, China, Tibet, Japan.* (Honolulu, 1964), p. 261.

105. Jha, op. cit., p. 58.

106. Ibid.

107. Kakar, op. cit., p. 74.

108. Ibid., pp. 90–91.

109. Sudhir Kakar's *The Inner World*, which I have frequently quoted, is the best available psychological interpretation of the Indian personality. Lucian Pye's *The Spirit of Chinese Politics* is an excellent psychocultural study of Chinese society and political behavior.

110. Kakar, op. cit.

111. Jha, op. cit., pp. 75–76.

112. Ibid., pp. 145–55.

113. Ibid.

114. Kakar, op. cit.

115. Fox Butterfield, *Alive in the Bitter Sea* (New York, 1982), p. 165.

116. Devaki Jain, *Indian Women* (New Delhi, 1975), p. 138.

117. Butterfield, op. cit., p. 166.

118. Many of the thoughts in this paragraph were drawn from a lecture by Simon Leys at Harvard University in April 1983.

119. Kakar, op. cit., p. 30.

120. Ibid., p. 55.

121. Quoted by Partha Mitter, *Much Maligned Monsters* (Oxford, 1977).

122. Hegel, op. cit.

123. Jha, op. cit., p. 121.

124. Ibid., pp. 112–13.

125. Ibid.

126. Fitzgerald, op. cit., p. 358.

127. Kingsley, op. cit., p. 65. See also Stella Kramisch, *The Hindu Temple*, vol. 1, (Delhi, 1976).

128. George Mitchell, "Introduction to Indian Sculpture," in Hayward Gallery, London, eds., *The Image of Man* (New York, 1982), p. 24.

129. Mary Tregear, *Chinese Art* (New York), p. 94.
130. Benjamin Rowland, *The Art and Architecture of India* (Baltimore, 1953).
131. Ibid.
132. Jha, op. cit., p. 112.
133. Merle Goldman, *Literary Dissent in Modern China* (Cambridge, 1967).
134. A. L. Bashram, *The Wonder That Was India* (London, 1967), p. 502.
135. Nakamura op. cit., p. 53.
136. Edward C. Dimock, Jr., et al., *The Literature of India* (Chicago, 1978), p. 11.
137. Ibid., p. 64.
138. Nakamura, op. cit., p. 245.
139. Nakamura, op. cit., p. 54.
140. Dimock, op. cit., p. 63.
141. Evelyn Sakakido Rawski, *Education and Popular Literacy in Ching China* (Ann Arbor, 1979), pp. 5–6.
142. Ibid., p. 184.
143. Raj Bali Pandey, *Hindu Samskaras* (New Delhi, 1969), p. 123.
144. Ibid.
145. *World Bank Development Report, 1982*, op. cit.: *Economic Summary, 1982–1983.*
146. Donna Suri, "Rural and Urban Divide," *Seminar*, no. 272 (April 1982).
147. Ibid.
148. Indian Economic Survey, 1982–1983, op. cit.
149. Joseph Needham, *Science and Civilization in China*, 8 vols. (Cambridge, 1954–1969).
150. Joseph Needham, *The Grand Titration* (London, 1969).
151. Joseph Needham, *Clerks and Craftsmen in China and the West* (Cambridge, 1970), pp. 14–20.
152. Nakamura, op. cit., p. 82.
153. Richard Baum, *Cultural Constraints on the Modernization of Chinese Science and Technology*, paper delivered at conference on China's science and technological modernization, held at the Wilson Center, Smithsonian Institute, Washington, D.C., May 24, 1982.
154. William Stevens, *New York Times*, November 9, 1982.
155. Xu Liang Ying and Fan Dainian, *Science and Socialist Construction in China*, pp. 180–84, quoted by Baum, op. cit., p. 38.
156. Economic Information Agency, *The 1982 Population Census of China* (Hong Kong, 1982).
157. *Statistical Outline of India, 1982*, op. cit.
158. Office of the Registrar General, *Vital Statistics of India* (New Delhi).
159. This is the figure given in the 1981 special World Bank Report on China. The bank's *World Development Report, 1982* provides a figure of 1100, which presumably includes doctors of traditional medicine.
160. *World Development Report, 1982*, op. cit.
161. Ministry of Health and Family Planning, *Pocket Book of Health Statistics* (New Delhi, 1975).
162. Bashiraddin Ahmed, "Process of Integration," *Seminar*, no. 240 (August 1979).
163. June Teufel Dreyer, *China's Forty Millions* (Cambridge, 1976), pp. 261–65.

164. Ibid.
165. Ibid.
166. Ibid.
167. Jay Taylor, *China and Southeast Asia* (New York, 1976).
168. *World Military Expenditure and Arms Transfers, 1979–80*, U.S. Arms Control and Disarmament Agency, Washington, D.C., 1982. One American peace group estimates total military spending by China at $32 billion and by India at $3.8 billion. See Ruth Leger Sivard, *World Military and Social Expenditures 1982*, Leesburg, Va., 1982.
169. See International Institute of Strategic Studies, *The Military Balance 1985* (London, 1982).
170. Tharoor, *Reasons of State: Political Development and India's Foreign Policy under Indira Gandhi, 1966–1977* (New Delhi, 1982).
171. Following a visit to India in January 1984 by a group from the Chinese Academy of Social Sciences, a member of the delegation wrote an article in the Peking journal *Outlook* in which he stated that "There is a lot for China to learn from India's achievements and experience in its economic development." The author referred specifically to India's maintenance of its cultural identity as its economy developed, the importance attached to economic results and a flourishing market economy. Noting the problems of caste and wealth disparity, the writer suggested these could be overcome "step by step"—hardly a revolutionary prescription. *Xinhua*, April 1, 1984.
172. Harold R. Isaacs, *Scratches on Our Mind* (Armonk, N.Y., 1980).
173. Ibid., p. 72.
174. Ibid., p. 383.
175. Ibid., p. 385.
176. Ibid., pp. 386–89.
177. Ibid., pp. 182–84.
178. Ross Terrill, "Trying to Make China Work," *Atlantic Monthly*, July 1983.

Bibliography

India

Adiseshiah, Malcolm S. "Of Plans and Promises," *Seminar*, no. 285, New Delhi, April 1983.

Ahmed, Bashiruddin. "The Crisis of Change," *Seminar*, no. 242, New Delhi, October 1979.

Barrak, Erik. "Asian Cultures and Societies: Theories of Divergent Development," in *Technological Change and Cultural Impact in Asia and Europe*. Committee for Future Oriental Research, Stockholm, 1980.

Bashram, A. L. *The Wonder That Was India*, London, 1967.

Boss, Medard. *A Psychiatrist Discovers India*, London, 1965.

Buck, William, trans. *Mahabharata*, New York, 1973.

Chaudhrui, N. C. *The Autobiography of an Unknown Indian*, London, 1951.

Coomaraswamy, Ananda K. *The Transformation of Nature in Art*, New York, 1956.

de Bary, Theodore W. *Sources of Indian Tradition*, New York, 1958.

Dimock, Edward D., Jr., ed. *The Literature of India*, Chicago, 1978.

Dumont, Louis. *Homo Hierarchicus*, Chicago, 1981.

Eck, Diana L. *Banaras, City of Light*, New York, 1982.

Elzingar, Sant. "Models in the Theory of Science: A Critique of the Convergence Thesis," in *Technological Change and Cultural Impact in Asia and Europe*, Committee for Future Oriental Research, Stockholm, 1980.

Gandhi, M. K. *An Autobiography or The Story of My Experiments with Truth*, New York, 1957.

Grewel, S. S., and D. S. Sidhu. *Prosperity of the Punjab Farmer—Reality or Myth?* Punjab Agricultural University, Ludhiana, 1980.

Hardgrave, Robert, Jr. *India: Government and Politics in a Developing Nation*, New York, 1980.

Harrison, Selig S. *India, the Most Dangerous Decades*, Princeton, N.J., 1960.

Hibbert, Christopher. *The Great Mutiny, India 1857*, Middlesex, Eng., 1978.

Hiro, Dilip. *Inside India Today*, New York, 1979.

Jain, Devaki. *Indian Women*, Ministry of Information and Broadcasting, New Delhi, 1976.

Jha, Akhileshwar. *Sexual Design in Indian Culture*, New Delhi, 1979.

Kakar, Sudhir. *The Inner World*, New York, 1981.

Kingsley, David R. *Hinduism: A Cultural Perspective*. Englewood Cliffs, N.J., 1982.

Kinsley, David R. *The Sword and the Flute*, Berkeley, Calif., 1977.

Kothari, Rajni. *Caste in Indian Politics*, New Delhi, 1973.

Lannoy, Richard. *The Speaking Tree*, New York, 1939.

Mandelbaum, David G. *Society in India, Volume Two, Change and Continuity*, Berkeley, Calif., 1970.

Naipaul, V. S. *India, A Wounded Civilization*, New York, 1978.

O'Flaherty, Wendy Doniger. *Women, Adrogynes, and Other Mythical Beasts*, Chicago, 1980.

Pandey, B. N. *A Book of India*, Calcutta, 1977.

Pandey, Dr. Raj Bali. *Hindu Samskaras*, New Delhi, 1969.

Rosen, George. *Democracy and Economic Change in India*. Berkeley, Calif., 1967.

Rowland, Benjamin. *The Art and Architecture of India*, Baltimore, Md., 1953.

Shrier, William L. *Gandhi, a Memoir*, New York, 1979.

Singh, Daip. *Dynamics of Punjab Politics*. New Delhi, 1981.

Singh, Tarlok. "A Decade for Ending Poverty" *Seminar*, no. 282, February 1983.

Spear, Percival. *India, a Modern History*, Ann Arbor, Mich., 1961.

Srinivas, M. N. *Social Change in Modern India*, Berkeley, Calif., 1967.

Suri, Donna. "Rural and Urban Divide," *Seminar*, no. 272, April 1982.

Ward, Barbara. "Modernization But Not Completed," in Lewis, ed., *The British in India*, Boston, 1962.

Weber, Max. *The Religion of India: The Sociology of Hinduism and Buddhism*, Glencoe, Ill., 1958.

Weiner, Myron. "Struggle Against Power: Notes on Indian Political Behavior," in *Political Change in South Asia*, Calcutta, 1963.

Weiner, Myron. *The Politics of Scarcity*, Chicago, 1967.

Weiner, Myron. "Political Evolution," in John W. Mellor, ed., *India: A Rising Middle Power*, Boulder, Colo., 1979.

Zimmer, Heinrich. *Myths and Symbols in Indian Art and Civilization*, Princeton, N.J., 1974.

China

Ashbrook, Arthur G., Jr. "China: Shift of Economic Gears in Mid–1970s," in *Joint Economic Committee Report, Chinese Economy Post Mao*, 95th Congress, 2nd sess., U.S. Government Printing Office, November 1978.

Barnett, A. Doak. *China's Economy in Global Perspective*, Washington, D.C., 1981.

Bauer, Wolfgang. *China and the Search for Happiness, Recurring Themes in Four Thousand Years of Chinese Cultural History*, New York, 1976.

Baum, Richard. "Cultural Constraints on the Modernization of Chinese Science and Technology," paper delivered at conference on China's Science and Technological Modernization, Wilson Center, Smithsonian Institute, Washington, D.C., May 24, 1982.

Butterfield, Fox. *China, Alive in the Bitter Sea*, New York, 1982.

de Bary, Theodore W. *Sources of Chinese Tradition*, New York, 1960.

Dreyer, June Teufel. *China's Forty Million*, Cambridge, 1976.

Eckstein, Alexander. *China's Economic Development*, Ann Arbor, Mich., 1975.

Eckstein, Alexander, ed., *Quantitative Measures of China's Economic Output,* Ann Arbor, 1980.

Gernet, Jacques. *Ancient China*, Berkeley, Calif. 1968.

Goldman, Merle. *Literary Dissent in Modern China*, Cambridge, Mass., 1967.

Hummana, Charles, and Wang Wu. *The Ying-Yang, the Chinese Way of Love*, London, 1971.

Jen Yu-ren. *The Taiping Revolutionary Movement*. New Haven, 1973.

Lee, Hong Yung. "Deng Xiaoping's Reform of the Chinese Bureaucracy," paper given at May 3, 1982, conference at the Wilson Center, Smithsonian Institution, Washington, D.C.

Levinson, Joseph. *Confucian China and Its Modern Fate*, Los Angeles, 1985.

Maspero, Henri. *Taoism and Chinese Religion*, Amherst, Mass., 1981.

Needham, Joseph. *Science and Civilization in China*, 8 vols., Cambridge, Mass., 1954–1969.

Needham, Joseph. *The Grand Titration*, London, 1969.

Needham, Joseph. *Clerks and Craftsmen in China and the West*, Cambridge, 1970.

Perkins, Dwight. *China's Modern Economy in Historical Perspective*, Stanford, Calif., 1975.

Pye, Lucian. *The Spirit of Chinese Politics*. Cambridge, Mass., 1968.

Rawski, Evelyn Sakakido. *Education and Popular Literacy in Ching China*, Ann Arbor, Mich., 1979.

Schram, Stuart. *Mao Tse-tung*. Baltimore, Md., 1967.

Snow, Edgar. *Red Star over China*. New York, 1939.

Teng, Ssu-yu, and John K. Fairbank. *China's Response to the West*, Cambridge, 1954.

Tregear, Mary. *Chinese Art*, New York, 1980.

Xue Muqiao. *China's Socialist Economy*, Peking, 1981.

China and India

Apter, David E. *The Politics of Modernization*, Chicago, 1965.

Bagchi, P. C. *India and China*, Calcutta, 1981.

Bandyopadhyaya, J. *Mao Tse-tung and Gandhi*, New Delhi, 1973.

Bandyopadhyaya, Kalyani. "Agricultural Situation in Mainland China and India in the 1930s," *China Report* 9, no. 1, 1973.

Barrak, Erik. *Technological Change and Cultural Impact in Asia and Europe*. Committee for Future Oriental Research, Stockholm, 1980.

Barrak, Erik. *India and China Comparative Research*, Copenhagen, 1981.

Beri, G. C. "The Developing of Educational and Professional Manpower in China and India: A Comparative Study," *China Report* 5, 1969.

Bhalla, A. S. "Technological Choice in Construction in Two Asian Countries: China and India," *World Development* 2, no. 3, 1974.

Gupta, Khrisna Prakash. "Traditions of Modernity, a Comparative Study of Asian and Western Systems," *China Report* 9, no. 4, 1974.

Harris, Marvin. *Cannibals and Kings*. New York, 1977.

Harris, Nigel. *India-China. Underdevelopment and Revolution*, New Delhi, 1974.

Hegel, Fredrick. *The Philosophy of History*. New York, 1956.

Hettne, Bjorn. "Self-Reliance Versus Modernization: The Dialectics of Indian and Chinese Development Strategies" in Barrak and Sigurdson, eds., *India and China Comparative Research*, Copenhagen, 1981.

Isaacs, Harold. *Scratches on Our Mind*, Armonk, N.Y., 1980.

Malenbaum, Wilfred. "Modern Economic Growth in India and China: The Comparison Revisited, 1950–1980" in *Economic Development and Cultural Change* 31, no. 1, October 1982.

Marcuse, Herbert. *Eros and Civilization*, Boston, 1955.

Mitter, Partha. *Much Maligned Monsters*, Oxford, 1977.

Murphey, Rhoades. *The Outsiders, the Western Experience in India and China*, Ann Arbor, Mich., 1977.

Myrdal, Gunnar. *Asia Drama*, 3 vols., Harmondsworth, Eng., 1968.

Nakamura, Hajime. *Ways of Thinking of Eastern Peoples: India, China, Tibet, Japan*, Honolulu, 1964.

Richman, Barry. "Chinese and Indian Development: An Interdisciplinary Environmental Analysis," *American Economic Review* 65, no. 2, 1975.

Sethi, J. D. "Mao and Gandhi: Convergence and Divergence—A Preliminary Note," *China Report* 13, no. 1, 1977.

Swamy, Subramanian. "The Economic Distance between India and China, 1955–73," *The China Quarterly*, no. 70, June 1977.

Swamy, Subramanian. "The Response to Economic Challenge: A Comparative Economic History of China and India, 1870–1952," *Quarterly Journal of Economics* 903, no. 1, 1979.

Tannahill, Reay. *Sex in History*, London, 1981.

Vaitheswaran, R. "Gandhi and Mao: A Comparison in Terms of Relevance for the Politics of National Liberation and Reconstruction," in *China Report* 12, nos. 5 and 6, 1976.

Weisskopf, Thomas E. "China and India: A Comparative Survey of Economic Development Performance," *American Economic Review* 65, 1975.

Wittfogel, Karl A. *Oriental Despotism*. New Haven, 1975.

Index

About the Author

JAY TAYLOR is a U. S. Foreign Service Officer. Among other positions, he has served as Deputy Assistant Secretary of State, Bureau of Intelligence and Research, and as Political Counselor at the American Embassy in Beijing. He is also the author of *China and Southeast Asia*, and a contributor to *China Policy and National Security*.